A Diplomatic Meeting

A Diplomatic Meeting

Reagan, Thatcher, and the Art of Summitry

James Cooper

UNIVERSITY PRESS OF KENTUCKY

Scholarly publisher for the Commonwealth,
serving Bellarmine University, Berea College, Centre
College of Kentucky, Eastern Kentucky University,
The Filson Historical Society, Georgetown College,
Kentucky Historical Society, Kentucky State University,
Morehead State University, Murray State University,
Northern Kentucky University, Spalding University,
Transylvania University, University of Kentucky,
University of Louisville, and Western
Kentucky University.

Editorial and Sales Offices: The University Press of Kentucky
663 South Limestone Street, Lexington, Kentucky 40508-4008
www.kentuckypress.com

Some material in Chapter 1 has been adapted from its initial use in the author's article: "The Foreign Politics of Opposition: Margaret Thatcher and the Transatlantic Relationship before Power," *Contemporary British History,* 24:1 (March 2010), 23–42. The article can be accessed via: https://www.tandfonline.com/.

Some material in Chapter 2 has been adapted from its initial use in the author's article: "'I must brief you on the mistakes': When Ronald Reagan met Margaret Thatcher, 25–28 February 1981," *Journal of Policy History,* 26:3 (2014), 275–97. Reproduced with permission from Cambridge University Press.

Cataloging-in-Publication data available from the Library of Congress

ISBN 978-0-8131-5430-5 (hardcover : alk. paper)
ISBN 978-0-8131-5457-2 (pdf)
ISBN 978-0-8131-5459-6 (epub)

This book is printed on acid-free paper meeting
the requirements of the American National Standard
for Permanence in Paper for Printed Library Materials.

Manufactured in the United States of America.

Member of the Association of
University Presses

For Danielle, Macaulay, and Fox

Contents

Introduction 1

1. Before Power, 1969–1981 11

2. A Political "Special Relationship," 1981 44

3. Conflicts at Home and Abroad, 1982 71

4. Reelections, 1983–1984 106

Conclusion 147

Acknowledgments 153

Notes 155

Selected Bibliography 191

Index 193

Photos follow page 94

Introduction

On the day of Ronald Reagan's inauguration as president of the United States (1981–1989), the new president spoke with Margaret Thatcher, the British prime minister (1979–1990), about her upcoming visit to Washington, DC, the following month. Reagan commented: "I look forward to talking to you on international issues . . . as well as the economic problems we face."[1] Thatcher wryly observed, "The newspapers are saying mostly that President Reagan must avoid Mrs Thatcher's mistakes so I must brief you on the mistakes."[2] That both leaders prioritized talks about foreign affairs and economic issues at their first bilateral summit reflected the sense of urgency in Anglo-American relations in dealing with malaise at home and crises abroad. Reagan and Thatcher were both elected in the context of difficult economic circumstances—notably, high inflation and international challenges, such as the 1979–1980 Iranian Hostage Crisis and 1979 Soviet invasion of Afghanistan—which both, of course, dealt a fatal blow to President Jimmy Carter's hopes of being sworn in for a second term on January 21, 1981. When Reagan and Thatcher met before their partnership in power in London in 1975 and 1978, their conversations suggested that they shared political philosophies with regard to economic policy and outlook in the Cold War. Bilateral summits between the two leaders—and multilateral summitry at, for instance, the G7 meetings—were opportunities to test whether a shared philosophy would lead to a commonality in policy. Instead, they showed that political allies and friends were as much of a concern as a country's adversaries, as friends and allies could undermine domestic interests through economic and political decisions. Aspiring for the lofty heights of a Churchillian style Anglo-American relationship would prove complicated.

Indeed, just as Winston Churchill arguably laid down the gauntlet for Anglo-American relations in his speech at Westminster College in Fulton, Missouri, in 1946, he coined, if not popularized, the term "summit" in a speech in 1950.[3] Churchill advocated a conference of the world's most powerful leaders in the mold of the wartime meetings between himself, President Franklin D. Roosevelt (and later President Harry Truman), and General Secretary Joseph Stalin as a means to settle and manage the international scene amid the early Cold War.[4] Summits are typically viewed as opportunities for world leaders to participate at the highest level of politics, surpassing domestic politics and engaging with the historical processes of international diplomacy. There is an existing body of literature that details the history, protocols, and mechanics of summitry.[5] However, Alan S. Alexandroff and Donald Brean offered a recent definition of the term when they introduced their new journal *Global Summitry*. They argued: "Global summitry involves the architecture, institutions, and, most critically, the political and policy behavior of the actors engaged in the influence of outcomes of common concern in the international system. Global summitry includes all actors—international organizations, trans-government networks, states and non-state entities whether individuals, corporations, or associations—that influence the agenda, the organization, and the execution of global politics and policy."[6]

The study of summitry encapsulates a broad array of actors in international relations in an interconnected economic and political system.[7] Nonetheless, for the purposes of this book, summitry is concerned with meetings between executives—meaning heads of governments—particularly the American president and British prime minister.[8] Summits occur in a variety of ways, each of which is touched on throughout this study. They can be bilateral, multilateral, ad hoc, serial or institutionalized, working funerals, or briefer exchanges of views when one leader is visiting multiple countries. Since the First World War, meetings between heads of governments have supplanted centuries-old diplomatic practice in which the careful and nuanced negotiations of diplomacy have been wrestled away by presidents and prime ministers, much to the chagrin and frustrations of professional diplomats. However, in an era of air travel and the need to have "wins" in foreign affairs, government leaders have happily risked the failings of ego, vanity, and incomplete understandings in order to achieve foreign policy objectives themselves.[9] In his memoir, Sir Geoffrey Howe, British foreign secretary (1983–1989), recalled that he came to dislike traveling with Thatcher "because of her unquenchable tendency to play second fiddle as well as first."[10] For her part, Thatcher was reluctant to leave Anglo-American relations to "laid-back generalists" in the Foreign and Commonwealth Office or to "ministerial muddlers."[11] In contrast to Thatcher's increasing desire to be her own foreign secretary, James Baker, the White House chief of staff (1981–1985) was flummoxed by Reagan's failure to prepare for the 1983 G7 Summit in Williamsburg, Virginia, because he preferred to watch *The Sound of Music* the night before.[12]

The broader context of this book is the debate about the "specialness" of Anglo-American relations. Scholars have explored the development and influence of Anglo-American relations with regard to security cooperation, personal connections, overlapping national interests, common values, shared history, and broader Cold War concerns.[13] In general terms, the history of Anglo-American relations since 1945 saw a continuation of the wartime partnership into the 1950s, albeit with the United Kingdom as the junior partner, followed by a waning in the closeness of the relationship during the 1960s and 1970s, partly explained by Britain's entry into the European Economic Community (EEC) and the difficulties of the British economy. Anglo-American relations were reinvigorated during the 1980s and 1990s, but as leaders became ever closer during the early 2000s, anti-Americanism increased among the British public. Despite almost daily consultations between the UK Foreign and Commonwealth Office and the US State Department, British interests were often downgraded in favor of those of priority to the US government.[14] Anglo-American summits often saw disagreements, particularly during the 1960s and 1970s, partly explained by President Lyndon B. Johnson's (1963–1969) indifference toward the British, the withdrawal of British interests east of the Suez Canal, and Prime Minister Edward Heath's (1970–1974) focus on British admittance to the EEC. Yet Anglo-American summits sought to continue and cultivate the impression of close bilateral relations.[15] Thus, as Kathleen Burk suggests, "there is a true love-hate Anglo-American special relationship."[16] Such a description suits that of Reagan and Thatcher. Celebrated, almost in caricature, as an unblemished example of the "special relationship," the Reagan and Thatcher years were far more problematic than suggested in works of higher journalism.[17] Sally-Anne Treharne argues that the two overcame divisive issues in Latin America—namely, the Falklands War, the American invasion of Grenada, the Anglo-Guatemalan Dispute, and Reagan's obsession with the Nicaraguan Contras—to forge a "true" example of the special relationship.[18] Richard Aldous credits institutional connections, rather than the personal relationship between Reagan and Thatcher, dating back long before 1981, to Thatcher's ability to maintain close relations with the Reagan administration.[19] In the context of this debate, this book is both a case study in summitry and uses summitry as a means to further understand the relationship between Reagan and Thatcher. It does so by exploring three central issues—and, thus, making three claims—about (1) economic differences between Reaganism and Thatcherism, (2) the importance of domestic policies and politics at summits notionally focused on international affairs, and (3) the tensions between domestic economic policies and the globalized economy, particularly the global reach of the problem caused by the US budgetary deficit. These issues should be viewed within the context of general principles shared by Reagan and Thatcher, such as reducing the role of government in economic and social policy, coupled with liberating individuals as economic actors.

Reagan's presidency was arguably defined by two key policies—federal tax cuts at marginal rates and a dramatic military buildup (in conjunction with hardened rhetoric toward the Soviet Union, especially during his first term). Reagan wanted to restore America's fortunes at home and abroad, therefore "making America great again."[20] The chosen remedy for this was supply-side economics. Reagan campaigned and signed into law cuts to marginal income taxation from 70 percent to 50 percent over three years in the 1981 Economic Recovery Tax Act. The economist Arthur Laffer and his "Laffer Curve" most famously advocated supply-side economics—or "Reaganomics" as it was termed in the 1980s. In short, supply-siders argued that by lowering taxation, there would be an increase in incentives and productivity, which would ensure sufficient economic growth for the cuts to be self-financing. Reagan's tax reforms were consolidated by the 1986 Tax Reform Act, which reduced four tax brackets to just two tax codes of 15 percent and 28 percent.[21] Unfortunately for the federal budget, Reagan's tax cuts, coupled with a dramatic increase in military spending, saw severe budgetary problems. Neither Reagan nor Congress was willing to make the necessary spending cuts necessitated by the false promise of supply-side economics. Entitlements—such as Social Security and Medicare—accounted for 48 percent of the federal budget in 1982. The defense budget accounted for 25 percent of federal spending in 1982, while servicing the national debt accounted for 10 percent. Therefore, around 85 percent of the federal budget was virtually untouchable for Washington's politicians. Given the public support for Reagan's tax cuts, unsurprisingly, the national debt almost tripled during Reagan's presidency to $2.7 trillion.[22] (Reagan and Congress agreed to attempt to tackle the budgetary deficit through increased corporate taxation in the 1982 Tax Equity and Fiscal Responsibility Act and the 1984 Deficit Reduction Act.) Reagan's tax cuts were coupled with continuing support for Paul Volcker's monetary policy at the Federal Reserve Board. As chairman of the Federal Reserve (1979–1987), Volcker initiated a monetarist policy of "monetary based control," which controlled the availability and quantity of bank reserves, and resulted in high interest rates. However, after 1982, and as the American economy recovered from recession, monetarism was abandoned in favor of a more pragmatic approach based on national interest rates.[23]

Thatcherism should be located in a specific time and was the result of problems in the British economy and industrial relations in the 1970s, which contributed to debates about the extent of national decline. However, as a set of ideas, it was pragmatic and adjusted to changing circumstances; the only constant was that it was about winning and maintaining political power. While Thatcher is often accused of attempting to roll back a postwar consensus in British public policy, she was essentially a defender of that consensus as it was expressed during the 1950s but did represent a desire to reverse the progressive consensus, which emerged during the late 1960s and early 1970s.[24] In sum, Thatcher was arguably more pragmatist than ideologue. She undoubtedly—like Reagan—sought a revival in national pride and Britain's presence on the world stage, as seen in the 1982 Falklands War and her 1980 demand for her "money back" from the EEC after citing British overpayment to the EEC's budget (which happened after 1984 through a regular rebate payment). Yet she was willing to concede to the demands of the National Union of Miners in 1981 before gathering sufficient energy reserves, which meant she could refuse to do so again during the 1984–1985 Miners' Strike. Despite advocating lower taxation, upon taking power in 1979, Thatcher raised indirect taxation, such as sales taxes (value-added tax), to compensate for the reduction of income tax (the basic rate was reduced from 33 percent to 30 percent and the top rate reduced from 83 percent to 60 percent). This decision was criticized by Thatcher's previous right-wing supporters in the United States. For instance, Laffer wrote in the *Wall Street Journal* that this budget dashed hopes that Thatcher's government represented a revival in "classical incentive economics," and instead the budget was one of tax increases and continued high public spending.[25] Her commitment to the "sound money" of monetarism and tightened public spending saw her raise income tax and national insurance contributions while cutting public spending in 1981—at the height of a recession—despite the condemnation of 364 economists in *The Times*.[26]

Thatcher's determination to control inflation through a monetarist policy using high interest rates arguably induced the recession that the 1981 budget sought to address. For instance, in 1979 interest rates were increased to 15 percent, yet inflation still doubled to almost 22 percent during Thatcher's first year in Downing Street. The decision to also abolish exchange controls in 1979 meant that the British economy became subject to the movement of global capital for the first time since 1939. Milton Friedman was critical of what both the British government and US Federal Reserve had actually implemented in the name of his monetarism theory.[27] Yet monetarism, which had shaped Thatcher's economic worldview during her first term, was essentially abandoned after that term closed. After causing a peak level of unemployment of over three million people in 1983, monetary targets were overtaken in priority by, at first, exchange rates after 1982 and suspension of monetary targets after 1985.[28] In fact, Thatcher's reputation as an intransigent ideologue was more worthy of her later years in power, particularly her fixation on the politics of European integration and commitment to the Community Charge (lambasted as the "poll tax")—issues that ultimately proved to be her undoing. For the purposes of this study, Thatcher's first five years in Downing Street were a period of economic turbulence. Nonetheless, they were also the beginning of the privatization program, which was a lasting economic legacy of Thatcher's agenda. The sale of nationalized industries, by offering shares on the stock exchange, began with the sale of British Telecom in 1982 and, during the rest of the decade, the sale of Britoil, British Aerospace, British Petroleum, British Steel, Rolls Royce, British Airways, and major utilities, such as water and gas. The privatization of British Airways was subject to much tension at Anglo-American summits. Therefore, it is unsurprising that any decisions taken in Washington, DC, that may have complicated Thatcher's economic policy and, in turn, political fortunes captured her attention.

It is clear that there were similarities between Thatcherism and Reaganism in regard to policies designed to reduce inflation and restore economic growth. Obviously, there are caveats to such statements. American monetary policy was the responsibility of Paul Volcker's Federal Reserve Board, while the Reagan administration had to work with a Democrat-controlled Congress on policies for taxation and public spending, in contrast to the British government, which controlled both monetary and fiscal policy. Nevertheless, the major reason Reagan and Thatcher could cite a specialness in their relationship was because of the similar rhetoric and, at least on first glance, similar approaches in domestic economic affairs. Thatcher wanted to control inflation, privatize nationalized industries, and confront the power of trade unions in favor of a more flexible market economy. If Thatcher was the Baptist, Reagan was therefore very much the Messiah.[29] Consequently, after a period of divergence since the late 1960s in Anglo-American relations, there was a renewed convergence in outlook in domestic and foreign affairs.[30] The economic policy differences were therefore more pronounced and caused tension at bilateral summits between Reagan and Thatcher.

The second argument of this work revolves around the importance attached to domestic issues before and during summits that were notionally about foreign affairs. While discussions about economic policy were the purpose of G7 meetings, Anglo-American bilateral summits in this period typically included some focus on the transatlantic impact of both Reagan and Thatcher's domestic agendas. However, in addition to economic tensions between allies, a key aspect of domestic politics in this study is that of political cover and support. After all, both the United States and United Kingdom embarked on a monetarist experiment to curb inflation after 1979, and both governments subsequently faced fallout from high unemployment and the worst recessions since the Great Depression. Therefore, unsurprisingly, both Reagan and Thatcher welcomed public displays of solidarity as they sought to implement controversial domestic policies and pursue a tougher strategy in the Cold War. In 1981, Reagan publicly lauded Thatcher as the western leader who was closest to him in foreign affairs and political philosophy, with the Reagans even hosting the Thatchers for coffee at the White House residence before their departure. Thatcher's support for America was not necessarily shared by her fellow citizens, which represented a political challenge in pursuing a close relationship with the United States. For instance, a Gallup poll suggested that between March 1982 and August 1984, the British people believed that there was a divergence in Anglo-American relations.[31] Thatcher was determined to address this, and it was a stated priority for the British government when working with the White House on Reagan's visit to London in 1982. Indeed, the first chapter underscores the significance that both Reagan and Thatcher attached to successful transatlantic expeditions as a means to strengthen their domestic political position.

The third contention of this study is that the Reagan-Thatcher relationship was problematized by the impact of globalization on the development and, crucially, implementation of domestic economic policy. The interconnectedness of the global economy—namely, international trade, capital flows, interest rates—and its broader international political implications and ramifications was a source of tension between the Reagan administration and its allies, with Thatcher caught between loyalty to her ally and sharing the concerns of other leaders of major industrialized countries. Western domestic economies were impacted by the decisions of the Reagan administrations and this, in turn, impacted international relations. As detailed in this book, Thatcher was concerned by the American budgetary deficit and Reagan's anti-Soviet trade embargoes that harmed British companies. The powerful influence of globalization represented an inheritance that was passed on to Reagan and Thatcher by their predecessors in the 1970s. As Daniel J. Sargent observes in his seminal study about American foreign relations in the 1970s, during this decade, globalization was clear in the integration of economic markets and the enlargement of economic and social processes. The 1970s saw policy makers and commentators in awe of the reciprocity of decisions across national boundaries as economic interdependence boomed. For instance, in 1964 offshore financial holdings totalled 1.2 percent of global gross domestic product, but this increased to 16.2 percent in 1980. While some economists warned that globalization undermined the ability of individual nations to preserve their economic stability, others noted that governments should no longer pretend to claim economic sovereignty.[32] Moreover, the United States' transition from a creditor to a debtor nation in the mid-1980s meant that while globalization provided the import of capital and goods to sustain its international military role and its citizens' levels of consumption, indebtedness did usher in a reality of economic vulnerability.[33] Thus, it was a political and economic necessity for Reagan to attend economic summits with other heads of government—such issues were too important to be delegated to professional and institutional diplomats. Similarly, it was the globalized world of integrated and interdependent financial markets that was prioritized by Thatcher for the economic revolution. This was personified by her government's agenda of privatization of nationalized industries and deregulation of financial services, as seen in the 1986 Big Bang on the London Stock Exchange. Moreover, both Reagan and Thatcher grappled with the tensions between high inflation and high interest rates and the impact of external economic actions on those policies. As such, due to the effects of globalization, money was a source of tension even in what proponents and opponents claimed to be the most "special of relationships."[34]

In chapter 1, by way of a prologue to this study, it is demonstrated that Reagan furthered his credentials as a presidential candidate with his four visits to Britain between 1969 and 1978. Likewise, Thatcher's visits to the United States in 1975 and 1977, and meetings with US presidents Gerald Ford (1974–1977) and Jimmy Carter (1977–1981), afforded her the opportunity to downplay her inexperience in foreign affairs and claim American support for her policies that legitimized her leadership of the Conservative Party and, ultimately, the United Kingdom. Given that neither was in power during these meetings, both Reagan and Thatcher were therefore engaged in a "shadow summitry" designed to prepare them for national office. The remainder of this book focuses on Reagan's first term in the White House. These years represented the implementation of Reagan and Thatcher's ostensibly common economic agenda before Reagan's second term became dominated by his diplomatic endeavors with Mikhail Gorbachev and the Iran-Contra scandal.

Chapter 2 reveals that the politics of these transatlantic expeditions persisted after Thatcher and Reagan secured national office in 1979 and 1981, respectively. Their summitry meetings—both one-on-one and in the context of the G7—were contextualized by debates about their economic policies at home and in each other's respective country. This chapter observes that the fortunes of Thatcherism were viewed in American political discourse as a harbinger of Reaganism. Similarly, high US interest rates were a threat to the economic recovery of major European countries following the economic shocks of the recessions of the 1970s and of 1981–1982.

Taken together, chapters 3 and 4 reveal how Thatcher used her meetings with Reagan from 1982 to 1984 to continue to pressure the president on the American budgetary deficit and high interest rates, the grand jury investigation of British Airways' colluding role in the collapse of Laker Airways, and unitary taxation. This all represented a roadblock to the Thatcherite revolution in Britain. Major international events were also the cause of disagreement between the administrations. Chapters 3 and 4 thus include ongoing domestic and international hostility to Thatcherism and Reaganomics; the legacy of the 1981 Siberian gas pipelines crisis; American trepidation about the 1982 Falklands War; the 1983 US invasion of Grenada (which caused much embarrassment to Thatcher); and Irish American reactions to Thatcher's rejection of the New

Ireland Forum that attempted to offer constitutional options to address the Northern Ireland question. These issues proved to be ongoing concerns for Thatcher, much to the chagrin of Reagan's aides. These chapters also reveal that for Reagan, visits to the United Kingdom were an invaluable opportunity to be seen at home as cultivating support for his security policies with key Western allies. The footage also provided invaluable material for Republican campaigns in 1982 and 1984. Throughout the chapters, other meetings between the Reagan administration and Thatcher government are included. Although not strictly "summits," they do emphasize the ongoing politics of Anglo-American relations and contextualize Reagan and Thatcher's summitry.

This book yields the results of archival research from both sides of the Atlantic. The author owes debts of gratitude to, for instance, archivists at the Ronald Reagan Presidential Library in Simi Valley, California, the British National Archives at Kew in London, and Chris Collins's *Margaret Thatcher Foundation* website. Interviews with key protagonists have supplemented this archival research, with most of their comments a key contribution to the conclusion. The new and ongoing release of the relevant volumes in the *Foreign Relations of the United States* has been a welcome development, particularly in regard to Anglo-American relations and the Falklands War. This work is, in many respects, traditional diplomatic history, focusing on the interaction between two heads of government. This approach remains valuable to the study of global affairs. After all, heads of government bring agendas and interests to interactions with each other. Summits without purposes are not summits; instead they would be merely social events.[35] In summary, this book offers an innovative basis to understanding the development and nature of the fêted "special relationship" between Reagan and Thatcher as a case study in Anglo-American summitry. It reveals Reagan and Thatcher's efforts to use summitry to gain power and, in turn, act on their domestic priorities through Anglo-American agreements. Thus, it is an examination of their period as candidates for high office and then the formative years of their ostensible special relationship in power. This period alone demands exhaustive and exclusive attention. In essence, this book offers a unique and significant study about the making of the Reagan-Thatcher relationship and inimitably uses their key meetings as avenues of exploration into the priorities of summitry. Summits that were often ostensibly about international relations and security concerns frequently masked attempts by Reagan and Thatcher to bolster their respective domestic positions.

1

Before Power, 1969–1980

Margaret Thatcher and Ronald Reagan were determined to cultivate their transatlantic relationship and set out to do so before their respective election wins in 1979 and 1980. Given his previous career in Hollywood, Reagan sought to be viewed as a serious statesman, which had been a prerequisite in his efforts to secure the American presidency. Thatcher was determined to establish her credentials as a potential British prime minister, and a favorable reception in the United States was important. Both Reagan and Thatcher were outsiders even in their own parties. Reagan was seemingly too extreme to secure the Republican presidential nomination, particularly given his support for Senator Barry Goldwater's (R-AZ) presidential campaign in 1964. Thatcher was viewed as a temporary political accident; her position was based on backbench support and was not really secure until her second general election victory in 1983. It was within this context that Reagan and Thatcher crossed the Atlantic Ocean before winning their respective positions in national office, and it was also the backdrop for their first meetings in 1975 and 1978. By achieving approval abroad, both Reagan and Thatcher hoped to enhance their own political standing at home. For instance, in his memoir, Reagan recalled that international relations were a key component of his time as governor of California, given that the state's economy would be ranked as seventh in the world if California were an independent country. He remarked that he was able to gain experience in working with foreign leaders, which prepared him for the presidency.[1] Similarly, on returning from the United States in 1975—her first foreign expedition as Conservative Party leader—Thatcher told *The Times* that she had proven her credentials in foreign affairs.[2]

The 1970s marked a period of both British economic decline and a culmination in the decline of Anglo-American relations in global importance. Britain was preoccupied with domestic issues and had a relatively diminished role in international affairs. British relative decline was, in some respects, complemented by the self-doubt that gripped American political discourse following the Vietnam War, Watergate, rising energy prices, and the economic challenges posed by Japan and Germany.[3] Regardless of Britain's post-imperial search for a global role, bilateral relations with the United States remained relatively close due to common interests, such as well-established security cooperation, as in intelligence and nuclear weapons. American and British politicians and officials sought a settlement in Rhodesia, and President Jimmy Carter (1977–1981) agreed to provide Britain with its next generation of nuclear weapons. Furthermore, James Callaghan (as prime minister, 1976–1979) prioritized Anglo-American relations over relations with European allies.[4] Anglo-American relations were therefore still close, to some extent, before and regardless of Thatcher and Reagan's friendship. The importance that both Reagan and Thatcher attached to Anglo-American summitry when in government was foreshadowed in their use of visits across the Atlantic as a means to solidify their political credibility. Thus, Reagan and Thatcher engaged with "shadow summitry" as a means to gain experience for future summits and as a means to solidify their political support and ambitions. While Thatcher was doing this under the guise of leader of the Opposition, Reagan mostly did so while representing California and the Nixon administration.

Reagan's Rationale for Visiting Britain

Before 1980, Reagan was known in Britain as a former Hollywood actor who became a right-wing Republican governor of California (1967–1975) with unfulfilled presidential ambitions. Reagan was not taken seriously in Britain for either of his chosen professions. Yet Lou Cannon, a journalist who covered Reagan from the beginnings of his political career, has argued that after watching as a boy in Dixon, Illinois, *Journey's End,* a British antiwar play, featuring the character Captain Stanhope, Reagan developed a long held and deep affinity for Britain.[5] The play, set in the trenches, followed the experiences of a British army infantry company before the major German military offensive that commenced with Operation Michael and then the Spring Offensive in March 1918. In 1949 Reagan starred in *The Hasty Heart,* an Oscar-nominated Second World War drama, which was filmed in Britain. Twenty years later he returned to London in 1969 as governor. In the time between these visits Reagan underwent a political journey from the Democratic Party of President Franklin Roosevelt (1933–1945) to the Republican Party, specifically as a supporter of Goldwater's conservative movement and presidential ambitions in 1964. Reagan's political journey was marked by his work for television's *General Electric Theater* when he toured the country, honing what became known as "The Speech," which summarized his criticism of government economic intervention, higher taxation, and failure to stand firm against the Soviet Union.[6] It was "The Speech" that formed the basis of Reagan's national political debut in 1964. Reagan's distrust of government and advocacy of tax cuts was therefore well established.[7] However, Reagan's credibility as a politician still required much work. His support for Goldwater and his 1964 "Time for Choosing" speech catapulted him into national politics, which ultimately led him to the governor's mansion in California (1967–1975) and two failed attempts to win the American presidency in 1968 and 1976 before his successful presidential campaign in 1980. In 1968 Reagan came in third in the Republican primaries—albeit his campaign was part of a broader "stop Nixon" attempt—while in 1976 he nearly defeated the incumbent president, Gerald Ford (1974–1977), in the contest for the Republican nomination.[8]

Reagan visited Britain not just because of his Anglophile-inspired acting career or out of nostalgia for *The Hasty Heart.* His transatlantic visits must be placed in a broader political context. Transnational connections in ideas are not a new phenomenon and have been explored by multiple historians.[9] But the transatlantic movement of politicians also warrants attention as politicians seek visits abroad to strengthen their credibility and claim for government at home. For instance, in recent times, American presidential candidates such as Barack Obama and Mitt Romney have sought to establish themselves as statesmen and thus credible presidential candidates by undertaking visits abroad to meet with significant political figures. Reagan's expeditions echoed Nixon's visits to Britain, first as a member of Congress in 1947, second as US vice president in 1958 (which included a meeting with Winston Churchill), and third in 1963 as a private citizen.[10] Reagan's international tours were partnered by other means to raise and maintain his profile. After leaving the governor's mansion, and until 1979, Reagan gave speeches, wrote a regular newspaper column, and delivered over one thousand radio addresses, offering his views on current affairs.[11] The number of Californian and British press cuttings that Reagan's office kept about coverage of his tours demonstrate their concern regarding how the governor was perceived at this time.[12] However, the extent of coverage by more "national" American newspapers appears to be far more limited, with, for instance, the *New York Times* failing to report Reagan's tours as governor in 1969 and 1972 and as a private citizen in 1975 and 1978. Despite his efforts, Reagan's expeditions were not always necessarily headline news.

1969: Reagan Visits Britain as Governor of California

In 1966, Reagan achieved what Richard Nixon had four years earlier been unable to do and defeated Pat Brown (D) to become California's governor. In Reagan's first term he set out to balance the California budget, which involved tax increases, and controversially confronted the student protest movement at the University of California, Berkeley, using the National Guard.[13] In November 1969, on a visit to London to promote California's trade with Britain, Reagan delivered a speech to the Institute of Directors (IOD), becoming the first American to do so. In his letter of invitation, Sir Derek Pritchard, the IOD president, promised Reagan that a speech ensured extensive publicity and status for him. Pritchard explained that the IOD had "around 50,000 members" and "its annual conference is probably the greatest platform for speaking to senior industrialists that exists in Europe today," with "a great deal of press and TV coverage and publicity," and despite holding "the conference in the largest hall in London (seating 5,500 people)," every year "the demand for tickets far outstrips the available accommodation and . . . the hall is full to capacity."[14] Further appealing to Reagan's political ego, Pritchard added: "In the past we have had three British and one Australian Prime Minister, the Leader of the Opposition, the Chancellor of the Exchequer and H. R. H., the Duke of Edinburgh, so you will be in good company and we are all very delighted in anticipation of your formal acceptance."[15] As discussed below, Reagan took the bait and addressed the IOD.

Reagan had not arranged any formal meetings with British politicians, as his visit to London was purely to promote trade between Britain and California, specifically by addressing the IOD and the British National Export Council. Reagan did enjoy a dinner in his honor, hosted by US ambassador Walter H. Annenberg (but unfortunately it is unknown which British ministers, if any, attended).[16] However, Reagan's position as America's most prominent right-wing Republican and record as governor ensured that his visit was political; as an aging former actor, Reagan was subject to much mockery and ridicule in the British press. Reporting on a confrontation with a former student from Berkeley on his arrival in the UK, the *Daily Mirror* simply did not present Reagan as a serious politician. The *Mirror* sarcastically noted that Reagan had "scintillating hair" and "shiny shoes."[17] For Berkeley students, Reagan had a history of controversy following violent antiwar and antiestablishment protests in 1969 on Berkeley's campus, which prompted Reagan to utilize the California highway patrol and National Guard to restore order, albeit at the cost of injuries among students, reporters, and police, and the death of James Rector, a student who was not involved in the protests.[18] The *Mirror* joked that Reagan was back in London, where he had made *The Hasty Heart* and was making a sequel, *The Heated Exchange*.[19] Continuing the movie theme, the report went on, noting that Mike Smith, who was a former student at Berkeley, was appearing "opposite" the governor and shouted questions about cuts to the mental health budget in California. Reagan replied that the budget was actually at a record high for an individual patient. Smith simply called Reagan a liar, who in turn responded with a "grin" before leaving in a Jaguar.[20] Reagan's domestic difficulties had followed him across the Atlantic.

Indeed, the British press reflected a cynicism toward Reagan and confusion about his political success. Writing in the *Daily Sketch,* Dermot Purgavie observed that Reagan still wore brilliantine in his hair, presented himself as a good and wholesome American who likely lived on peanut butter sandwiches and milk, and watched the western series, *Bonanza*.[21] Geoffrey Moorhouse, writing in the *Guardian,* also mocked Reagan on the basis of his acting past but made a serious point about the governor's ability to play the politician, observing his high level of creativity.[22] Michael Brennan, writing in the *Sun,* identified the simplicity of Reagan's message, which echoed his former career as a Hollywood cowboy, in which his message was a simplistic morality tale.[23] Brennan also identified Reagan's political abilities and potential to become president of the United States.[24] At the press conference following his arrival, Reagan was inevitably asked about the Vietnam War. The governor used this as an opportunity to support Nixon's policies. The *Daily Mail* and the *International Herald Tribune,* for example, reported Reagan's warnings that a failure in Vietnam would be disastrous and lead to "a thousand years of darkness."[25] Reagan's support for Nixon was natural, given his position as a governor abroad, his political affiliation, and his established views about a Communist threat.

Drawing on his experience as governor of California, Reagan used the IOD platform to advocate the dangers of increasing government intervention in the social and economic life of a country. Reagan observed: "For a number of years I have been speaking out against what has seemed to me to be an inexorable march by government, an encroachment on, usurpation of, rights traditionally held to be the proper possession of the people. . . . In almost three years in government I have learned at first-hand how savage can be their resistance to any attempt to reduce the size and power of government."[26] In order to address this problem, Reagan argued that the private sector had an important role to play in public life. The governor explained: "It is time for business to recognize its obligation to participate in public affairs. This means more than just campaign contributions and attendance at political rallies. It means offering government the expertise and management skills of the private sector. It means lending your manpower to government, not your cast-offs. Government by second rate men will be second rate government."[27]

Reagan's lack of trust in government and, concurrently, his faith in the free market were reminiscent of speeches that he had made throughout the 1950s and 1960s. His speech to the IOD was certainly well received. The *Daily Telegraph* reported that Reagan received a standing ovation from the five thousand guests.[28] Peter Hillmore, writing in the *Guardian,* utilized the theme of actor-turned-politician in his report of the speech. Hillmore explained in almost disbelief that the former actor was now the governor of California and delivering a speech about the merits of free enterprise.[29] The audience included Denis Thatcher, whose wife, Margaret, was then in the Shadow Cabinet of the Conservative Party leader Ted Heath.[30] Thatcher would later claim in her memoirs that she had been enthused by Reagan's speech upon hearing about it from Denis, thus retrospectively connecting their intellectual commonality much before Reagan's presidency.[31]

Speaking at the same event as Reagan, Barbara Castle, the secretary of state for Employment and Productivity (1968–1970) in the Labour government, became the first woman to address the IOD and spoke about the role of union power on the shop floor. Despite being photographed on the stage with Reagan, Castle ostensibly did not believe Reagan's speech or attendance at the IOD to be significant enough to be mentioned in her diary, although she recalled that her speech was well received.[32] Reagan seemingly did not impress Castle at all. Writing in her diary, she recalled Reagan's arrival in Britain: "Rushed off to lunch at Thompson House with Governor Ronald Reagan, film star turned politician, who really isn't particularly handsome." (Castle footnoted that she "was astonished when he became President of the United States in 1980.")[33]

Four days after his IOD appearance, Reagan also had the opportunity to further promote California to British industry in a speech to the British National Export Council in London. As governor of one of the largest economies in the world, Reagan sought to ensure that British industrialists understood California's economic value and potential and knew of Californian's love for British products.[34] In his speech, Reagan explained, "Californians, as an average, have the highest purchasing power in the world; the market is one of the most dynamic in the United States. . . . We are, basically, a consumer-state which should be important to your trade ambitions."[35] Reagan's visit to London in 1969 was to promote increased trade between the United Kingdom and California. The governor also met with French government officials in his subsequent visit to France (during the same tour). Despite claims that Reagan made a three-day visit to Paris as a tourist, he met representatives of the French Foreign Ministry, including Maurice Schumann, the foreign minister, and Herve Alphand, the Foreign Ministry's secretary general.[36]

1972: Reagan as President Nixon's Special Representative

Reagan was certainly rising in political stature, and no better examples of this can be found than in the fact that President Richard Nixon (1969–1974) asked him to be his special representative. In some respects, this was a surprising development. The relationship between Reagan and Nixon was defined by political cooperation and competition. Reagan campaigned for Nixon in his 1960 presidential campaign and during his 1962 attempt to become governor of California. However, during Nixon's ultimately successful 1968 presidential campaign, Reagan was an abortive "stop Nixon" candidate in the Republican nomination process. Nonetheless, Reagan remained loyal to Nixon throughout the Watergate scandal and until the president resigned from office.[37] In turn, Nixon recognized Reagan's increasing political strength in the Republican Party and sought to utilize his talents in his foreign policy. Thus, between 1969 and 1973, Reagan, in his capacity as governor of California, made four trips abroad representing the Nixon administration in a ceremonial and goodwill capacity. Although Reagan was more right-wing than Nixon, the president viewed Reagan to be the perfect bridge to allies at home and abroad.[38] For instance, between July 3 and 22, 1972, Reagan traveled to Denmark, Belgium, France, Spain, Italy, Britain, and Ireland on behalf of Nixon.[39] In a White House press briefing, Jerry Warren, who served as Nixon's deputy press secretary, announced that Reagan's "trip will underline the importance the administration attaches to our ties with Europe, to our NATO commitment and to mutually beneficial relations with the enlarged European community."[40] The wider context of Reagan's European tour in 1972 was the 1969 Nixon Doctrine, which envisioned a partnership and burden sharing with Europe in foreign affairs, the end of the Bretton Woods System, and Nixon's visits to China and Moscow.[41] Reagan's mission was clearly one of reassurance to America's allies that they had not been abandoned to fate in the Cold War, although détente ironically encouraged such circumstances. Similarly, it should be viewed in the broader context of the Nixon administration's desire for a rapprochement with Western Europe as he sought to end the Vietnam War.[42] Despite Reagan's utility as an emissary, Nixon did not rate the governor's chances of ever becoming president, telling Henry Kissinger on April 19, 1972: "Reagan never could make president to begin with and he couldn't handle it."[43]

On this occasion, Reagan did have formal meetings with senior British politicians as he was representing Nixon. Before Reagan's reception in Britain in July 1972, the Foreign and Commonwealth Office (FCO) provided 10 Downing Street with a biography of Governor Reagan, written by Patrick Grattin, praising his 1969 address to the IOD and his ability to articulate his opposition to central government interference. Reagan was depicted as having triumphantly shed his image as "a know-nothing right-wing ideologue" and having gained the reputation "as an effective administrator with a relatively pragmatic approach."[44] Reagan the politician had clearly surpassed the FCO's expectations in office. The FCO also sent a short briefing (also written by Grattin) on potential topics that Heath might wish to raise with Reagan. Grattin suggested that Heath could use the opportunity to explain the government's position regarding Northern Ireland so that Reagan might subsequently be able to deal "with any of the wilder accusations put up by the Irish-American Community."[45] Grattin also encouraged Heath to discuss the enlargement of the European Economic Community (EEC): he suggested that Reagan would probably share Nixon's sympathetic attitude and advised Heath to explain that although EEC enlargement strengthened the Atlantic alliance, it would inevitably place strain on American relations with Europe, specifically with regard to trade. The FCO was concerned that the Nixon administration should be reminded that Britain would seek to ensure that the EEC was outward looking, and, subsequently, would not have to succumb to the American protectionist lobby. Heath was also encouraged by Grattin to ask Reagan about Nixon's chances for reelection.[46] By now, the British government, specifically the FCO and Downing Street, knew that there was increasing scepticism toward EEC enlargement in Washington, DC, particularly among Henry Kissinger, the national security adviser, and possibly Nixon himself.[47] The lunch was also attended by a range of officials: Sir Alec Douglas-Home (the UK foreign secretary, 1970–1974), Lady Douglas-Home, Lord Carrington (the UK defense secretary, 1970–1974), Lady Carrington, Sir Douglas Greenhill and Lady Greenhill, Walter H. Annenberg (US ambassador to the United Kingdom, 1969–1974), Mrs. Annenberg, Mr. Robert Scott (UK businessman), Mrs. Scott, Lord Bridges, and Lady Bridges.[48] It is likely that Reagan first met Thatcher (secretary of state for education and science, 1970–1974) at this social occasion as a copy of the lunch's menu is available among the Thatcher papers at Churchill College, Cambridge.[49] Unfortunately, the record of the meeting between Reagan and Heath does not appear to exist, which perhaps betrays how the British viewed Reagan's status. Nevertheless, Heath was grateful for the jade tree Reagan presented to him as a "most handsome present" and "much enjoyed" his conversation with the governor.[50] Likewise, Nixon was grateful to Heath for meeting with his representative. Following Reagan's visit, Nixon wrote to Heath, in accordance with standard diplomatic protocol, "I greatly value every opportunity I have to exchange views with you, whether it be through face-to-face meetings, through our exchange of messages, or through visits by personal representatives such as Governor Reagan."[51]

Reagan met separately with Sir Douglas-Home. Given Reagan's position as representing the American president, the FCO saw this as an opportunity to discuss American foreign policy. The briefing suggested that Douglas-Home should ask Reagan whether Nixon planned to reduce the American military presence in Europe. Furthermore, the FCO wanted Reagan's views on the importance the electorate would attach to Vietnam during the upcoming November elections. Moving on from military affairs, further proposed points for discussion were Reagan's views on the reopening of contact with China (which the British government by and large welcomed) and "the sudden revelation" of possible reunification in Korea.[52] Again, there does not appear to be any record of the actual meeting itself. However, the level of discussions does suggest that there was greater interest in Reagan among British officials than in 1969. Alternatively, the British may have been frustrated with Nixon's secrecy and approach to foreign policy: At this point, nearly all the information that they learned from the White House was from Kissinger's meetings with Burke Trend, the cabinet secretary (1963–1973). Thus, the FCO may have been tired of being ostracized by Nixon's modus operandi.[53] The British clearly had an interest in hosting Reagan to help with this situation.

The visit received some attention in the British broadsheet press. A photograph of Reagan and Mrs. Reagan with Heath was featured in the *Guardian,* which reported the lunch as being Reagan's penultimate visit of his seven-country European tour.[54] *The Times* reported Reagan's European tour as an attempt by Nixon to emphasize the important transatlantic relationship with Western Europe.[55] Hoping to reassure anxious Europeans, Reagan observed that the American military presence in Western Europe would only be reduced when the United States and its European allies were confident that their presence was no longer required.[56] The 1972 expedition to Europe was an opportunity for Reagan to meet senior British politicians, which would lend some weight to his later claims for foreign policy experience. However, at the time, the very fact that Nixon utilized Reagan's skills between 1969 and 1973 demonstrated the president's confidence in Reagan's political prowess, even if he did not believe that Reagan had the political acumen to ever win the White House for himself.

Reagan Visits Europe in 1975 as Preparation for the 1976 Presidential Campaign

Three years later in April 1975, Reagan, now the former governor of California, visited Zurich and London as a private citizen. In London, Reagan was scheduled to meet Thatcher, now leader of the Conservative Party and leader of the Opposition, and key figures in her Shadow Cabinet—namely, Sir Keith Joseph, Sir Geoffrey Howe, and Reginald Maudling. Reagan was also due to meet Robert Conquest, a historian of the Soviet Union, and to deliver a speech to the Pilgrims Society (the Anglo-American society).[57] During this visit Reagan met few other dignitaries. He did not meet any leading figure in the Labour government or even a cabinet minister, apart from a courtesy meeting with Roy Hattersley, a junior minister at the FCO (1974–1976). Reagan clearly was not considered to be a sufficiently important or interesting political figure by the British government at this time to warrant a higher-level ministerial meeting. Indeed, that Thatcher was the only prominent British politician who made the time to meet Reagan was something that the future president would never forget.[58] In his memoirs, Reagan wrote, "I liked her immediately—she was warm, feminine, gracious, and intelligent—and it was evident from our first words that we were soul mates when it came to reducing government and expanding economic freedom."[59] When interviewed by Geoffrey Smith in 1990, Thatcher recalled that the meeting was brought about by her shared political and economic philosophy with Reagan and recollection of his 1969 speech to the IOD. Thatcher explained,

> I think the first time I heard of Ron Reagan's beliefs was when he spoke at the Institute of Directors and right at the end he used words something like this: the background was that the role of government had steadily become enlarged. It has actually and I think there are good reasons for that but it had been swollen and enlarged too much and encroached too much on the fundamental liberties and that we were not doing enough about it to safeguard those fundamental liberties, and I think he said somewhere at the end: *"If our grandchildren ask us in a generation to come 'where were you when liberty was lost and what did you get to put in its place?'"* I think my [Denis Thatcher] husband was probably there.[60]

Reagan again espoused this philosophy in his speech at the Pilgrims Society dinner on April 7, 1975, in London. He claimed that the Soviet Union sought to redraw the political map of Europe following the "communist takeover" in Portugal, in light of the rise of leftism there after the 1974 Carnation Revolution.[61] Reagan argued that Western Europe must remain strong in the face of Soviet diplomacy. *The Times* observed that it was the type of critique of both Western weakness and Republican foreign policy befitting a presidential candidate.[62] Although he did not announce his intentions until November, *The Times* clearly anticipated a Reagan candidacy.

Reagan's letter of thanks to Thatcher after their first formal meeting in 1975 pointed to a discussion about Cold War politics. Reagan observed that "somehow the shadows seem to have strengthened" following the recent fall of Saigon.[63] Reagan offered to return the hospitality should the Opposition leader accept speaking invitations in California, writing that Thatcher had "an enthusiastic supporter" in the "colonies."[64] Their meeting was advertised to the American people. The *Pasadena Star-News* featured a photograph of Thatcher admiring Reagan's silver bear design cufflinks after their meeting.[65] Reagan was so impressed by Thatcher that the Conservative leader was included in his "On My Christmas List . . ." broadcast in December 1977: it included, among others, aspirin for President Jimmy Carter (1977–1981) and a chance for Thatcher "to become Britain's first woman prime minister."[66]

Reagan publicized his European tour during one of his US nationally syndicated radio broadcasts in April 1975. Comparing the failure to confront Nazi Germany in the 1930s with the inaction against the Soviet threat that he claimed could lead to a third world war, Reagan clearly advertised the diplomatic and political meetings he had attended and argued that his views were shared across the Atlantic. Reagan explained, "I had an opportunity to visit with various govt. officials including those concerned with foreign affairs. Inevitably the conversation turned to the world situation & how to maintain peace. . . . And just as inevitably the Soviet U. was automatically accepted as the possible threat to world peace just as 40 yrs. ago it was Nazi Germany that loomed as the storm cloud on the horizon."[67] Reagan was presenting himself as an American equivalent to Winston Churchill, also warning of the dangers of a totalitarian menace while out of office and seemingly in the wilderness years of his political life. However, in the case of the Soviet menace, the British government, according to Reagan, agreed with him. For Reagan's presidential ambitions, it was vital that his views on foreign policy and his diplomatic abilities were taken seriously, and he clearly made every effort to ensure that this was how it was portrayed. Therefore, Reagan was using his "shadow summitry" as a means to enhance the credibility of his claims for the American presidency.

Thatcher's Rationale for Visiting the United States in 1975

Margaret Thatcher unexpectedly defeated Edward Heath in the Conservative Party's leadership contest in 1975.[68] Thatcher's gender, lower middle-class background, and support for New Right economics meant that she was an archetypal outsider.[69] Upon assuming the role of leader of the Opposition, Thatcher initially struggled for credibility in the view of both a male-dominated Conservative Party and the electorate at large. However, by the 1979 general election, Thatcher was able to assert her authority within her party and became Britain's first female prime minister (1979–1990). Many factors determined Thatcher's transformation in the Opposition, but a vital component was how she approached Anglo-American relations. Expeditions to the United States in 1975 and 1977 underpinned her relationship with Ronald Reagan throughout the 1980s. Even in Thatcher's mind, her inexperience and gender were equally her political Achilles heel.[70] Nonetheless, through her visits to the United States, Thatcher was able to transform these perceived disadvantages to her advantage.[71] In sum, Thatcher cultivated an international profile as a means to consolidate her own position as leader of the Conservative Party.

Typically, before Thatcher's visit to America in 1975, British Opposition leaders were broadly ignored when they crossed the Atlantic to the United States.[72] However, no previous Opposition leaders attempted anything akin to Thatcher's North American tours in 1975 and 1977, particularly in regard to her ambition, content, and media coverage. Yet while the coverage of Thatcher was unprecedented, other Opposition leaders had sought to use visits to the United States as a means to prepare for Downing Street. For instance, Hugh Gaitskell (leader of the Opposition, 1955–1963) visited America for a lecture tour (including Harvard) and addressed the Trade Union Congress in the United States.[73] Before his first premiership (1964–1970), Harold Wilson met with President Lyndon B. Johnson (LBJ, 1963–1968). In this meeting, he commented that he was prepared to abandon Polaris when he became prime minister; while this did not ultimately happen, this meeting between LBJ and Wilson was not a mundane courtesy meeting between president and potential prime minister.[74] Wilson, again as leader of the Opposition (1970–1974), met with President Nixon on April 30, 1971, during a visit to the United States in which he gave lectures about labor relations and education in the public sector, and visited LBJ in Texas.[75] Nixon was briefed that this was an opportunity to discuss, for instance, Britain's entry into the EEC, the British economy, and the situation in Northern Ireland.[76] Given Wilson's experience as prime minister, the meeting was an opportunity for a more nuanced discussion than might typically be expected of a meeting with an Opposition leader. Similar to Wilson's post-premiership visit, Heath spent three days in New York City and Washington, DC, which included meetings with Vice President Gerald Ford and the United Nations Secretary-General, Kurt Waldheim, in September 1975.[77] This visit overlapped with Thatcher's American tour and, as he was already an established political figure, Heath risked overshadowing his successor. Yet Heath's American trip did not marginalize his successor. Furthermore, Thatcher's visits to the United States were so successful in achieving her purposes that they have been replicated by subsequent Opposition leaders—namely, Neil Kinnock (1983–1992), Tony Blair (1994–1997), and David Cameron (2005–2010), albeit with varying degrees of success.[78]

Given the experience of her predecessors as leader of the Opposition, that Thatcher's visit to the United States in 1975 proved significant was surprising. The Ford administration did not attach any particular importance to her usurpation of Heath—if anything it was surprised. Thatcher's victory over Heath in the first ballot of the leadership contest only led to the Ford administration's conclusion that the "popular Willie Whitelaw" would secure the Conservative leadership in the final ballot.[79] Reacting to Thatcher's victory, the State Department reported that it "was as surprising as Whitelaw's poor showing. . . . To win a future election she will have to move an appreciable distance from her position on the right wing of her party."[80] The American Embassy in London remained unconvinced by Thatcher's leadership. The embassy informed the State Department that despite "a quick, if not profound mind," Thatcher "tends to be crisp and a trifle patronising."[81] Despite being raised as a grocer's daughter, the embassy noted that Thatcher's political career thus far had cast her in the mold of traditional Tory politician: "Unfortunately for her prospects of becoming a national, as distinct from a party, leader, she has over the years acquired a distinctively upper middle-class personal image."[82]

Thatcher's developing foreign policy ideas were broadly conventional and in tune with her conservative predecessors, and her "Atlanticism" was unsurprising given her wartime childhood and prior visits to the United States (in 1967, courtesy of the US State Department, and an English Speaking Union tour in 1969).[83] Thatcher's participation in an international visitor program in 1967 meant that she was able to meet academics, economists, members of Johnson's administration, and members of the US Congress.[84] This visit was fairly standard for promising politicians. Subsequently, Thatcher had limited experience regarding foreign affairs by 1975. Moreover, foreign affairs were hardly her priority as leader of the Opposition. She once asked Frank Cooper, a retired civil servant, "Must I do all this international stuff?" Cooper's response was succinct: "You can't avoid it."[85] Thatcher's inexperience in the nuances of foreign policy necessitated Reginald Maudling's appointment as shadow foreign secretary.[86] (Maudling had held various posts in government, including chancellor of the exchequer, 1962–1964.) Nevertheless, as the Conservative Party leader, Thatcher did adopt a strong approach to the Soviet Union and communism. She equated the Soviet Union with Nazi Germany and argued against a policy of appeasement. For instance, Thatcher argued that the 1975 Helsinki Conference, which saw Western leaders offer the Soviet Union aid and recognition for a quid pro quo of human rights guarantees, was mistaken. In turn, Thatcher articulated her views on détente and the Cold War.[87] For instance, addressing the Chelsea Conservative Association on July 26, 1975, she warned the West that political retreat would lead to the failure of détente: "If you do something they want without insisting on something in return, the Soviets do not regard it as a kindness to be reciprocated, but as a weakness to be exploited."[88] The speech was an example of Thatcher's characteristic directness.[89]

The First North America Tour: September 13–26, 1975

John Campbell suggests that by mid-1975, Thatcher was concerned about her continued inability to shine in parliamentary performances.[90] Such occasions were vital to her credibility as leader of the Opposition. Consequently, Thatcher changed her approach: as "her voice was carrying little weight at home," she would "be heard in the wider world."[91] The two-week tour of the United States and Canada in September 1975 afforded her an opportunity to establish herself as a substantial politician at home by being received as such abroad.[92] The foreign trip was therefore important as an exercise in shadow summitry and would demonstrate that Thatcher was capable of conducting important diplomatic business as prime minster. Furthermore, if she was received seriously in the United States, it would be indicative of her political prowess for domestic audiences. Thatcher certainly had an opportunity to impress. After all, there was a real fear among political circles in Washington, DC, that the British economic disease would reach the United States. Alan

Greenspan, chairman of Economic Advisers (1974–1977), briefed Ford on the "crumbling financial and fiscal condition" in Britain, and warned that "frightening parallels, with a lag, between the financial policies of the United States and those of the United Kingdom should give us considerable pause."[93] Similarly, Kissinger commented to Ford: "Britain is a tragedy—it has sunk to begging, borrowing, stealing until North Sea oil comes in."[94] Britain was held up as an example of what could happen when a country did not successfully face up to economic problems both domestically and globally—an archetypal cautionary tale.

As American politicians and media were interested in Britain's economic decline, Thatcher's public statements offered an optimistic future for Britain, with the caveat that this would only happen if her Conservative Party was victorious in the next general election and able to shift the emphasis of the British economy away from state intervention to free-market economic policies. Thatcher's speeches, television appearances, and meetings with leading American figures were her opportunity to establish a Thatcherite narrative of Britain's challenges and solutions: only greater "freedom" for the British people would see an end to "socialism" and ensure that British foreign policy would help combat the Soviet Union's ability to threaten the "free world." Writing for the *Daily Telegraph* before Thatcher's tour, Stephen Barber anticipated that she would encounter an understanding audience.[95] He argued that in the United States there was much sympathy to Britain's decline, although there was also concern that America should not fall victim to the "English disease" of poor management and difficult relations with trade unions. Moreover, Thatcher's opposition to an excessive welfare state was shared by Ford—and even leading Democrats who hoped to defeat him in the 1976 presidential election.[96] Thatcher was briefed by the FCO on American politics before she departed.[97] Watergate and the subsequent pardon for Nixon had severely undermined support for the Republican Party, although Ford was judged as a "hard man to beat." However, given conservative opposition to Vice President Nelson Rockefeller (1974–1977), Reagan was "on the verge of challenging the President for the 1976 nomination." According to the briefing, Anglo-American relations were "close and workmanlike on all levels."[98]

A great deal of careful planning was involved in order to maximize Thatcher's chances of capturing widespread positive publicity. Gordon Reece, Thatcher's public relations adviser, traveled ahead in order to cultivate media attention. Thatcher even flew to America by Laker Airways rather than

British Airways, thus underscoring her commitment to free enterprise, while her gender and message emphasized her novelty to the American political audience.[99] Given that Thatcher was potentially the first female major Western leader (although Golda Meir had of course served as Israel's prime minister, 1969–1974), she recognized that the media attention presented aesthetic pitfalls. This was emphasized to Thatcher's staff: "Adequate time must be left between engagements for her to prepare. . . . She did not want to go down as a scruffy female politician."[100]

As per convention, Thatcher's office approached the FCO for advice about the upcoming tour. The FCO's key point was that she had every reason to be optimistic about the country's future resulting from the unwritten rule that British politicians should promote Britain when traveling abroad. G. N. Smith (North America Department, FCO) offered counsel on press coverage and the content of Thatcher's public remarks. Referring to consultations with Sir Peter Ramsbotham (British ambassador to the United States, 1974–1977), Gordon Booth (the consul general), and Ham Whyte (head of British Information Services New York), Smith suggested that the Conservative Party leader should speak about the state of Britain, the EEC, its mixed economy, the importance of America's Western leadership, and Northern Ireland. Smith noted that the American audience wanted Thatcher to "affirm that Britain is going to come through its current difficulties" as the American press had "overdone the gloom." He observed that, for instance, Thatcher would "no doubt wish to underscore the positive side of the picture (relatively low level of unemployment, improved balance of payments, firm action to grasp the mettle of inflation early, etc.)," and "a strong affirmation that the spirit of private enterprise is still strongly alive in Britain."[101] It is clear that the FCO encouraged Thatcher to deliver an apolitical message in the United States even though this inevitably contradicted her own political position.

Given that Thatcher and her staff were inexperienced in such visits, and again in accordance with convention, her office also consulted the FCO about interview requests. The FCO advised that she should do a *Newsday* interview before she departed. Thatcher was advised to meet with the Associated Press (AP) and the *Metropolitan Sunday Newspaper,* which included twenty-six newspapers—including the *New York News* and *Chicago Tribune,* which was to be was to be a photographic feature. *People,* which would produce a feature about Thatcher at work and home, was also recommended. Additionally, Thatcher was advised to conduct an interview with the *New*

York Times.[102] This all promised a significant level of press coverage. For instance, trailing Thatcher's arrival in the United States in the *Chicago Daily News,* Ellen Warren described the Conservative Party leader as one of the most powerful women in European politics.[103] The Institute for Socio-Economic Studies in New York City promoted Thatcher's speech, describing her as "potentially Britain's first female Prime Minister."[104] The press release also described Thatcher as a "staunch advocate of private enterprise" who would "discuss the way the public welfare burden has brought both the national economy of Britain and the finances of New York City government to the brink of collapse."[105] The challenges of the global economy could therefore be seen at a local and national level.

The Central Office of Information wanted a ninety-second interview with her before she left Britain, which would be offered to news networks.[106] Thatcher also conducted an interview with Arthur L. Gavshon, the diplomatic and political editor for the AP, before her departure. The interview (with pictures) was published in thousands of newspapers inside and outside America and was one of the leading foreign stories of the day. The *Daily Telegraph* also printed the interview. The preamble of the AP interview stated that in America, Thatcher would argue that "this country will rise again as a world power" and she would "hammer home" her resolve "to preserve the closest possible cooperation with the United States."[107] A *World in Action* crew from Granada television would follow Thatcher on her tour.[108] Likewise, the BBC's *Panorama* also wanted a crew to accompany her.[109] A great deal of effort was made to promote Thatcher's visit to the United States.

Despite receiving advice from the FCO, Thatcher was still accused by the Labour government that she "talked down Britain" abroad. The September 15 speech at the Institute of Socio-Economic Studies in New York was particularly significant. Here, Thatcher explained that Britain had to avoid repeating the mistakes of the previous thirty years: in pursuit of "the progressive consensus . . . persistent expansion of the role of the state and the relentless pursuit of equality has caused and is causing damage" to the British economy.[110] Thatcher argued that, instead, national wealth could be increased through support for private enterprise and "equality of opportunity" coupled with a "right to be unequal." According to an editorial in *The Times*, this was a direct statement about Conservative Party philosophy under her leadership.[111] Similarly, an editorial in the *Daily Telegraph* observed that Thatcher was right to say this either side of the Atlantic.[112] Writing in the *New York*

Times, Peter Kihss noted Thatcher's criticism of thirty years of an expanding welfare state, which had caused Britain's economic growth to be restricted.[113] Thatcher had clearly contradicted the FCO's guidance. In response, Neil Kinnock, a Labour Party member of Parliament, claimed that Thatcher's Britain would lack opportunity for all.[114] In addition to Thatcher's philosophical statements, her fashion sense was subject to press coverage in Britain. According to the *Daily Express,* Thatcher's pearls and see-through cape marked a transformation in a fashion sense while her speech captured the attention of American leaders.[115]

Thatcher then addressed the Pilgrims Society in New York City. She argued that "whatever our present shortcomings in the eyes of the world we still stand for those fundamental freedoms which are the breath of life to nations who believe in human dignity."[116] She explained that the next Conservative government would abandon "soft options" and return to sound money so as to halt Britain's economic decline, meaning that she would control inflation and government spending. For Thatcher, British democracy was on trial, and if the country "were to break, a well nigh mortal blow would be struck against the western ideal." On foreign affairs, she argued that even though she supported détente, it was important that it led to results.[117]

Before Thatcher addressed the Pilgrim Society, Barbara Walters interviewed Thatcher on NBC's *Today* program.[118] Thatcher argued that policies pursued by successive governments that were designed to create equality had simply taken more of the people's money and increased state expenditure. While Thatcher refused to consider abandoning the welfare state, she noted that British people should instead consider exactly what was expected from government. For instance, higher taxation reduced incentives for people to earn more and create prosperity. Thatcher believed that it was absurd that the rich should be expected to pay for the welfare state: "Before very long you will find that there aren't any rich left, and you are taxing not the rich but the income of the average person." When Walters expressed fears that the United States could replicate British decline, Thatcher responded that "those of us who believe in the free society and the capitalist society haven't been nearly as active in putting forward our view and putting forward the advantages of a free society as those who believe in a Communist society." Walters bluntly asked her guest, "How bad are things in England? Can you pull yourself out of it?" Thatcher's optimistic response would likely have satisfied the FCO. She cited familiar wartime stereotypes, which evoked the British character:

"We have problems. . . . But we are still the same people. We've still the inventiveness. We've still the same sense of adventure. . . . We are still the same people who fought for freedom." However, Thatcher's optimism was contingent upon her own political fortunes: "I sometimes say that I think perhaps we are an 11th hour nation. But you know we wait rather late to take effective action. But we are at the 11th hour now and action is being taken and no doubt Britain can come out of her present economic problems." In response to Walters's comment that Thatcher reportedly knew "very little about foreign policy" and her ostensible opposition to détente, Thatcher explained, "What I have said is that you don't get that just by signing pieces of paper. You really must look and see what nations do. . . . I thought President Ford's speech at Helsinki was a marvellous one. I read every word of it. And he put it beautifully when he said, 'We shall be judged not by the promises we make, but the promises we keep.'"[119] The British press reported on Thatcher's press coverage in the United States. Ian Ball, writing in the *Daily Telegraph,* noted that Thatcher's appearance on the *Today* program was viewed in seven million American households. Thus, Thatcher had been able to reach a large American audience, showing that she was a politician of significant interest and should therefore be viewed in such terms at home.[120] Simon Winchester, reporting for the *Guardian* from Washington, DC, unsurprisingly sought to undermine Thatcher by noting that Heath had upstaged Thatcher when he also appeared on the *Today* program that week.[121]

When Thatcher visited Capitol Hill, she told the Senate Foreign Relations Committee that although Britain was behind America, Germany, and France in tackling inflation, she was confident that the British people would rise to the challenge.[122] According to the British record, "Mrs. Thatcher had *no doubt* of our ability to surmount our problems and survive." Thatcher assigned blame for Britain's economic difficulties to "a few very powerful unions exercising monopoly power in the nationalised industries" and the failure of successive governments to introduce economic constraints. Thatcher praised American policies for tackling inflation.[123] In a meeting with the House International Relations Committee, Thatcher was asked about the future of the welfare state. She explained that Britain "had reached the end of the road as far as redistribution and the pursuit of equality were concerned" and should instead focus "on incentives and opportunities."[124] When she was questioned about her views on détente, Thatcher again spoke of her support for Ford.[125] The *Daily Mail* sought to promote the success of Thatcher's performance. It reported that during the meeting, Representative Clarence Brown (R-OH) passed a note to Ramsbotham, stating that Thatcher would be a welcome addition to political life in America.[126]

After her meetings on Capitol Hill, Thatcher visited the White House for her meeting with President Ford. Kissinger recognized that Thatcher was using the meeting simply as a means of improving her position within the Conservative Party and to promote the impression that she was a capable leader. The secretary of state briefed the president: "Her purpose in meeting with you is to gain further foreign affairs experience and to improve her position within the party and in the public image as an effective leader."[127] The meeting lasted thirty-five minutes, with the discussion focusing on American and British domestic policy. Given common economic problems, Ford argued in favor of coordinated economic action between the United States and Western Europe.[128] Thatcher's subsequent letter to Ford was a combination of diplomatic protocol and her ambition for a close, yet privately candid, relationship with the president. She was "heartened and encouraged" by the meeting and hoped that it would "be the first of many meetings and that we may be able to exchange views frankly, on all subjects, at any time."[129] Fred Emery, writing for *The Times,* observed that Thatcher charmed "part of the political community in Washington out of its cynicism about Britain" and was thought-provoking with "her articulate championing of less government interference with the individual."[130] When one reporter inquired as to whether she was worried that Heath's concurrent visit to America would upstage her visit, Thatcher dismissively replied, "Not at all, is he still here?"[131]

Thatcher certainly believed that her visit was successful. She told Emery that she had succeeded in international affairs, an area that others claimed was her weakness, and no other British politician had enjoyed such a successful tour for a long time. It is perhaps telling that Thatcher's objective for the expedition—that of holding positive meetings with dignitaries and presenting a strong image of leadership—seemed to constitute success in international affairs. Emery reported that Thatcher's visit to the United States was such a success that a former member of Ford's cabinet opined that she could defeat both the president and Reagan for the Republican nomination.[132] The *Daily Mail* quoted an article in the *New York Times* that praised Thatcher's knowledge and political skills.[133] The *Guardian* inevitably lacked such enthusiasm: Simon Winchester argued that Thatcher attracted little attention in the United States among the American people.[134] Naturally, the *Daily Mail* could not have disagreed more. According to Philip Fin, after a five-minute conversation with Thatcher, Private Kenneth Donovan, who served as an officer in the US Park Police in Washington, DC, had been persuaded that he would vote conservative if he lived in London.[135]

However, it was the abandonment of diplomatic protocols that guaranteed British coverage of Thatcher's American expedition. A *Daily Express* editorial observed that although Thatcher's critique of the British economy was correct and appealed to Americans who feared equality driven by mediocrity, she had invited criticism for breaking protocol and undermining Britain abroad. Harold Wilson, the British prime minister (1974–1976), was reportedly excited by this political opportunity.[136] Even the *Daily Mail* conceded that Thatcher's remarks were controversial.[137] James Callaghan (the British foreign secretary, 1974–1976) attacked Thatcher for breaking from protocol.[138] Thatcher recalled in her memoirs that she had been accused of "running Britain down abroad," but she argued that "the message I was bringing to America about Britain was essentially one of hope, namely that the nation's potential was great enough to withstand even the effects of socialism."[139] Thatcher suggested that the Labour government's outrage simply guaranteed that her arguments were taken seriously.[140]

Thatcher and Callaghan continued to disagree over the former's remarks in the United States following publication of an article in the *Spectator* in October 1975. The article suggested that the FCO had not offered the expected advice to Thatcher about her visit to the United States. Callaghan advised Thatcher that this was "difficult to believe" given that appropriate British embassies always advise the leader of the Opposition about visits abroad and, furthermore, Thatcher's office had actually passed on their appreciation to the FCO's North America Department for exactly this assistance. Callaghan wanted Thatcher to publicly deny the *Spectator* article. He wrote: "I should appreciate your letting the Editor of 'The Spectator' know that you regard as unfounded his statement that you had received less than the ordinary courtesy of advice and assistance. If you were so disposed to set the record straight as regards the help you yourself received from the Ambassador and his staff, I should be grateful."[141]

While Thatcher had sought to utilize shadow summitry to further her own ambitions for government, it had clearly undermined the objectives of the current government to portray the British economy in a positive and optimistic light. Regardless of the political row between the leader of the

Opposition and the foreign secretary, the FCO was delighted with Thatcher's tour and believed that her optimism had actually served their own agenda of promoting British prospects. Derek Thomas (North America Department, FCO) wrote to R. M. Russell (British Embassy in Washington, DC): "Mrs. Thatcher certainly seemed to get what she wanted out of her visit. But it seems to me that it also served a useful non-partisan purpose in giving her American audiences a less pessimistic view of Britain than the one which they have been getting from their media in recent months. It was inevitable that Mrs. Thatcher should, as you rightly put it, make no bones about her political beliefs, but it does seem that what was more important for her American audiences was her manifest confidence in Britain's future."[142] Thomas added that even though the FCO initially considered a complaint to Thatcher for remarks that were "seriously knocking Britain," ultimately it was understood "that when the substance of what she had said to the Socio-Economic Club was available, the conclusion was reached that there was no need to complain."[143]

Reagan Announces His Campaign for the Republican Nomination for President

While Thatcher continued to work on her international credentials, Reagan was mustering himself for another campaign for the presidency. Indeed, Reagan's presidential ambitions saw him sensationally almost unseat the incumbent president, Gerald Ford, as the Republican presidential nominee in 1976.[144] As an Anglophile, or more likely due to different time zones, Reagan first announced his candidacy for the Republican nomination in Britain's *Daily Telegraph* on November 20, 1975. Reagan's *Daily Telegraph* article (described by John O'Sullivan as a "modest world scoop"[145]) was entitled "Wanted: A New Dream for America."[146] He explained that since stepping down as governor of California in 1975, he had undertaken lecturing, guest speaking, writing a regular column, and making radio appearances. The purpose of his work had been to express his long-standing opposition to the increasing role of government in people's lives. In an echo of his 1968 IOD speech, he argued that centralized power in Washington had in fact only reduced individual liberty. Based on his tenure as governor of California, he said he believed that he offered a real choice to voters: centralization, or distribution of power. Furthermore, Reagan argued that polls proved that the

American people were losing confidence in the ability of government to solve all problems. Reagan again reached out to public opinion, arguing that he felt that grassroots Republicans did not believe that Ford was subject to the traditional deference accorded incumbent presidents. In other words, the circumstances surrounding Ford's presidency (he was never elected American president or vice president) meant that the Republican Party deemed a national nomination process acceptable, if not preferable. The political arguments here are reminiscent of "The Speech" and the future objectives of Reagan's presidency. The reader is challenged to ask if the issue is not about trusting America's institutions but rather about the people trusting themselves to have a better future.[147] Reagan's uplifting and resolute language was in tune with his later reputation as the "Great Communicator." He was convinced of the American people's spirit as a beacon for individuality and freedom. Reagan claimed to be a conviction politician, promising to stay true to his principles ahead of any political reality.[148]

Aside from the small Republican community residing in Britain, voters in the Republican primaries largely would not have read the article (indeed, British Republicans broadly identified with the liberal internationalist wing of the Party, and few of them were Reagan supporters in 1975–1976).[149] Nevertheless, the developing climate of opinion within the Conservative Party, coupled with the *Daily Telegraph*'s political affiliation, meant that Reagan could comfortably outline his political ambitions there. Writing in the *Daily Telegraph,* Stephen Barber observed how Reagan's views were nearly identical to Ford's, although Reagan believed that he would more likely be true to conservative policy.[150] Jonathan Steele, writing for the *Guardian* from Washington, suggested that Reagan ultimately decided to secure the nomination as he believed Ford would lose the presidential election.[151]

Reagan's candidacy was not widely taken seriously in the British press. The *Guardian* highlighted Reagan's candidacy on its front page by reporting that a college student was in custody after pointing a toy gun at Reagan.[152] In contrast, the *Daily Mail*'s coverage was restricted to Jane Gaskell's more lighthearted news column "America," which reported how, according to a federal communications spokesman, other presidential candidates would complain of favoritism in television coverage should stations broadcast Reagan's old movies and *Death Valley Days.*[153] However, nine months later, in August 1976, an editorial in *The Times* observed that the Republican Party had avoided political suicide by nominating Ford ahead of Reagan. It was argued that if Reagan had been successful in securing the nomination, the Republican Party would have been a hostage to fortune, controlled by a minority grouping of extreme conservatives.[154] If Reagan were to run again, *The Times*'s Washington correspondent suggested that he would move to the center, thus allowing Rep. Philip Crane (R-IL) to outflank Reagan on the right.[155] Reports in *The Times* therefore argued that Reagan could not win a national election. Writing in the *Daily Express* from the Republican Convention, Brian Vine observed that there was no bitterness following Reagan's defeat, merely the devastation felt by his hard-core, right-wing supporters.[156] Similarly, Steele, reporting from Kansas for the *Guardian*, stated that Reagan's political career was over, although the report focused on Ford's choice of Senator Robert Dole (R-KS) as his nominee for vice president.[157] With Reagan's White House ambitions seemingly ended, Thatcher continued her quest for Downing Street.

1977: Meeting Jimmy Carter and the Second North American Tour

Thatcher had a further chance to favorably impress either side of the Atlantic when Carter visited Britain in May 1977 and when she returned to the United States later that year for another shadow summit, both to prepare her for power and underscore her credentials to become prime minister. Thatcher asked to meet the president during his UK visit and Carter agreed, on advice from the US Embassy in London that "there is a real possibility" that she might soon become prime minister.[158] According to the *New York Times*, Thatcher told Carter that she would win the next general election.[159] In September 1977, Thatcher met Carter in Washington, DC, at which point she had served as leader of the Opposition for over two years and sought to repeat the success of her 1975 visit to the United States. However, the Carter White House faced a dilemma as to whether Thatcher would in fact be able to meet the president on this occasion, even though it had already been agreed in principle after their meeting in May. Peter Jay, the British ambassador to Washington (1977–1979), explained to the FCO "that the White House was grappling with a tricky protocol problem." François Mitterrand (the leader of the French Socialist Party) was also scheduled to visit Washington, DC, at the same time, and it would be problematic to explain to French President Valery Giscard d'Estaing (1974–1981) that Carter had been willing to meet

Thatcher but not Mitterrand. The White House attempted to engineer a means of accommodating Thatcher, but, fortunately for her, Mitterrand canceled his visit.[160] Thus, Thatcher was able to meet Carter, although one important caveat was attached—no press photographs inside the White House with the president.[161] Thatcher would be unable to exploit this for her own purposes of appearing to be a prime minister in waiting.

In her other engagements, Thatcher again sought to further her political agenda and enhance her international profile. In 1976, Britain had received international financial assistance from the International Monetary Fund, although the loan was accompanied by strict monetary conditions in an effort to reverse the sterling crisis and ensure deflation.[162] In remarks at the British American Chamber of Commerce, Thatcher observed that the British economy was entering "a period of greater financial discipline," which abandoned economic delusions and embraced a more realistic approach. Returning to the themes of her 1975 expedition, Thatcher argued that wealth and prosperity are the results of incentives, investment, efficiency, enterprise, and lower taxation, and not created by policies of wealth distribution, such as government intervention and nationalization.[163]The *Daily Express* reported that Thatcher was criticized in the Soviet Union for her reception in the United States, as if she were a head of state, and also for her policies. For *Daily Express* readers, such respect in the United States and criticism in the Soviet Union underscored Thatcher's growing stature at home and abroad.[164] In addition to her economic arguments, Thatcher was willing to utilize her agenda to promote herself as an alternative prime minister. Ross Mark, writing in the *Daily Express,* reported that the Conservative Party leader explained on NBC's *Today* program that she was able to maintain her femininity in the political arena "and believed that her nicknames, particularly the 'Iron Maiden,' were undeserved."[165] Thatcher informed millions of viewers that she would become prime minister.[166] Thatcher's image as a strong woman again dominated a visit to the United States. For instance, the *Daily Mail* quoted a *Washington Star* comment that Thatcher would address Britain's economic problems by being the "headmistress" and "nanny" issuing the country's medicine.[167]

Concurrent to Thatcher's desire to again maximize favorable publicity for her visit to the United States, she was eager that some meetings should not be public. The FCO correspondence detailed her meetings with three men who were "all known for their strong right-wing views," and Thatcher did not wish these to be publicized.[168] The private meetings were with "Mr.

John Carbaugh, Foreign Policy Adviser to Senator Jesse Helms (R-NC), General Keegan and Mr. Novak of the Washington Post."[169] The privacy was ostensibly a result of their political positions: Robert Novak was a leading conservative political commentator; John Carbaugh advised Republican senator Helms, who advocated a strong anti-communist foreign policy; and Maj. Gen. George J. Keegan Jr. argued that the West had underestimated the Soviet Union's military capabilities. In some respects, Thatcher's wish to cloak these meetings under a veil of secrecy is ironic due to the influence of American "new right" ideas on Thatcher's policy agenda, particularly those of Milton Friedman and the Chicago School's monetarist theories.[170]

In advance of her meeting with Carter, Thatcher was briefed by the FCO about the Carter administration, US foreign policy, Anglo-American relations, energy policy in the United States, nuclear matters, and American-Mexican relations.[171] According to the *New York Times,* Thatcher discussed a range of issues with Carter, such as potential relations between the Carter administration and a Conservative government, developments in Rhodesia, and British defense policy.[172] According to Ross Mark, writing in the *Daily Express,* Thatcher told Carter that he would be dealing with her as prime minister in due course.[173] She even announced on the White House steps that such meetings were useful preparation for her premiership.[174] In her letter of thanks to Carter, the sentiment of Thatcher's remarks echoed those she shared with Gerald Ford two years earlier: "May I say how good it was to see you, to hear your views expressed so openly and frankly, and how much I appreciated the amount of time you gave me. Your conviction gives us renewed confidence for the future."[175] Establishing a potentially useful relationship with the American president trumped political ideology and commonalities.

The FCO described Thatcher's meeting with the president as "cordial" and noted that it "went on longer than the allotted time."[176] Similarly, Thatcher and the FCO were pleased with her visit to the United States.[177] Despite the "frenetic pace" and being "thoroughly exhausted," the British Embassy noted, "The visit went well and she appeared satisfied."[178] Thatcher received "extensive coverage in the United States press and her press conference in the Embassy was well attended"; her television appearances were also judged to be successful.[179] However, Thatcher had failed to impress Carter in their 1977 meetings. Carter agreed with Zbigniew Brzezinski's (the president's national security adviser, 1977–1981) description of Thatcher after she became prime minister in May 1979, as "a cooler, wiser, more pragmatic person now than the Opposition Leader you met in May, 1977, or the dogmatic lady who visited you in Washington that fall." Brzezinski assured the president that regardless of Thatcher's "hard-driving nature and her tendency to hector," he was "impressed by her courage and discipline." Indeed, Brzezinski was sufficiently impressed by Thatcher's beginning to her premiership that he briefed Carter: "I am sure we can work with her; I am equally sure that she will benefit greatly from the fact and the feeling of your personal attention."[180] The Carter administration clearly saw potential in Thatcher but hoped to influence her on the world stage.

1978: Reagan Returns to Europe

After failing to secure the American presidency in 1976, Reagan's political ambitions remained unfulfilled, but he ensured that his profile was maintained. An important aspect of this was to be viewed as relevant to, and knowledgeable of, international affairs. Therefore, in the period of November 25 to December 3, 1978, Reagan again visited Europe as part of a wider strategy in maintaining and enhancing his political profile through nationally syndicated columns and radio broadcasts. Reagan visited London, Paris, Cologne, Berlin, and Munich before briefly returning to London for a series of meetings with political leaders.[181]

In London, Reagan met David Owen, the British foreign secretary (1977–1979), and Thatcher. Reagan held a breakfast meeting with British newspaper editors, which featured a "who's who" of conservative journalists: William Deedes (editor of the *Daily Telegraph*); Frank Johnson, Colin Welch, and John O'Sullivan (all *Daily Telegraph* journalists); Ronald Butt (columnist for *The Times* and deputy editor of *The Sunday Times*); Ferdinand Mount (political editor of the *Spectator*); Russell Lewis (editorial writer of the *Daily Mail*); and Dudley Fishburn (American editor of the *Economist*).[182] Reagan was clearly satisfying curiosity within the conservative British press in advance of another presidential campaign and possible period in office. A luncheon meeting was later held between Reagan and senior conservatives, such as Humphrey Atkins (the Conservative Party chief whip), Angus Maude (the deputy chairman of the Conservative Party and chairman of the Conservative Research Department), Norman St. John-Stevas (shadow leader of the House of Commons), Roger Moat (honorary secretary of the British-American Parliamentary Association), Tim Renton (vice chairman of the

Conservative Parliamentary Trade Committee), and Derek Howe (Thatcher's press secretary).[183] This was obviously a standard meeting between Conservative members of Parliament and an established Republican politician. Unfortunately, there is no record of these meetings, although that the Conservatives did meet with him shows that Reagan was viewed as a sufficiently significant American political figure by the Opposition. Reagan did not meet with Callaghan, who had succeeded Harold Wilson as prime minister two years earlier, or any government minister, so it was clearly not important for the Labour government to meet a former California governor and failed Republican presidential candidate.[184] Therefore, Reagan was able to cite the visit as an example of his international expeditions but was unable to gain further experience of working with the British government.

In contrast to the British case, Reagan was viewed to still be sufficiently important to meet with government officials in France and West Germany. Furthermore, that the purpose of Reagan's European visit was arguably preparation for a presidential campaign is clearer given the meetings scheduled in France and West Germany. In Paris, Reagan met Olivier Stirn (the French secretary of state for Foreign Affairs) and Francois Ceyrac (president of the French National Business Council), and held luncheon meetings with French business, industrial, publishing, and research organization leaders. In Bonn, as in London, Reagan met Opposition right-wing politicians—namely, Manfred Worner (shadow defense minister of the Christian Democratic Union [CDU]) and Helmut Kohl (leader of the CDU and leader of the Opposition in the Bundestag)—and had a luncheon meeting with scholars at the Konrad Adenauer Foundation, namely, Dr. Walter Heck, Dr. Hans Ruehle, and associates. This foundation is essentially a right-wing think tank affiliated with the CDU. Reagan also met the West German Chancellor, Helmut Schmidt, and the US Ambassador, Walter Stoessel. In Berlin, Reagan received a military command briefing at the US headquarters and visited East Berlin. While in Munich, Reagan met Franz Josef Strauss, who was the CDU-Christian Social Union candidate for chancellor and Bavarian minister president, and dined with Dr. Robert Strausz-Hupe, former US ambassador to the North Atlantic Treaty Organization, and Dr. Fred Ikle, former head of the US Arms Control and Disarmament Agency.[185] Reagan would certainly be able to cite meetings with current, former, and potential key figures in Europe during a run for the presidency in 1980.

A key example of Reagan exploiting his European visits to enhance his credibility as a presidential candidate was his radio broadcast in May 1979, in which he congratulated Thatcher on her general election victory. Romanticizing Britain and Thatcher, Reagan declared:

> I couldn't be happier than I am over England's new Prime Minister. It has been my privilege to meet and have two lengthy audiences with Margaret Thatcher and I've been rooting for her to become Prime Minister since our first meeting.
>
> If anyone can remind England of the greatness she knew during those dangerous days in WWII when alone & . . . UNAFRAID her people fought the Battle of Britain it will be the Prime Minister the Eng. Press has already nicknamed "Maggie."[186]

Reagan telephoned the new prime minister to congratulate her, but the civil service did not prioritize a call from the former governor of California and failed presidential candidate, so he was unable to speak with Thatcher.[187] Yet eighteen months later, Richard Allen, Reagan's first national security adviser (1981–1982), handed Thatcher's congratulatory message to Reagan, who read it to his supporters at his victory party.[188] While Reagan celebrated Thatcher, the Republican Party was equally inspired by her 1979 general election victory. The Republican National Committee (RNC) was in need of a fresh vision since the challenges of the Vietnam War, Watergate, and Ford's defeat by Carter in 1976.[189] William E. Brock III (chairman of the RNC, 1977–1981) sought to gather ideas from political parties abroad. Subsequently, the Republicans adapted the Conservative Party's advertisement that featured a young man leading in a race but who became slowed down by the burden of too much taxation, bureaucracy, and regulation. In the Conservative Party's version, the athlete represented Britain, but in the Republican Party's advertisement, he came to represent America. Brock told the journalist Geoffrey Smith, who was developing his book *Reagan and Thatcher*, "There was nothing that even came close to having the impact that the 1979 election in Great Britain had upon us."[190]

Concurrent to Thatcher's attempts to establish herself as a leading ally for the Carter administration and amid Republican admiration for her electoral success, the New Right in the United States became suspicious of her economic program. Writing in the *Wall Street Journal,* Arthur Laffer, the advocate for supply-side economics, criticized Thatcher after her 1979 budget for reversing a key policy that she espoused in opposition. The new prime minister had previously promoted the advantages of lower taxation as the crucial ingredient to a growing economy. Laffer argued that now she was in government, Thatcher had actually increased taxation by increasing the rate of value-added tax, which meant that her fiscal policies were less favorable than the previous Labour government, and American observers should note this fact.[191]

The Republicans had certainly taken notice of the message used by Thatcher to secure her election victory, but American conservatives were dubious of how her rhetoric had been implemented in practice. Similarly, doubts in Britain about Reagan's candidacy persisted even after he announced his decision to enter the 1980 presidential election. David Cross, writing in *The Times,* questioned Reagan's stamina for a presidential campaign and accused him of offering the standard Republican policies—namely, tax cuts and strong policies toward the Soviet Union to alleviate American woes.[192] During the campaign, the *New York Times* argued that Reagan's abilities in foreign affairs should be questioned.[193] In defense of Reagan, Nixon subsequently wrote to the *New York Times* and argued that he had an impressive range of experience in foreign affairs.[194] While the extent that Nixon could have been a useful surrogate so soon after Watergate and his resignation is clearly debatable, it is telling that Reagan's foreign tours were therefore utilized during the campaign by his supporters to counterattack doubts about his ability to conduct foreign policy. Furthermore, as Cannon notes, Reagan believed that these visits gave him a strong ground in dealing with foreign leaders and, by listing countries he had visited and leaders he had met, it allowed him to address questions of his inexperience in this area.[195] Despite Nixon's optimism in Reagan's abilities, caution among the British press prevailed after his presidential election victory in 1980. Writing in *The Times,* Peter Jay advocated that America's allies would have to adjust to the Reagan era, arguing that Reagan was not a Californian Thatcher.[196] Reagan's taxation policies were condemned, and in foreign affairs he would require careful handling by both allies and enemies.[197] A *Guardian* editorial was pessimistic for the world in the Reagan epoch.[198] In contrast, Thatcher's enthusiastic view of the president-elect as representing "a watershed in American affairs" and "a greater one in world politics" therefore clearly contrasted with some of the British press's opinions of Reagan.[199] The scene was ostensibly set for Reagan and Thatcher to enjoy a "special relationship" in office and act on the rapport established during their previous meetings.

Conclusion

The role of Anglo-American relations to Reagan during his presidency was preceded by the emphasis placed on them while he was effectively campaigning for the Oval Office after 1969. Although the British press consistently underestimated Reagan as an actor and extreme politician, some elements of the press identified Reagan as a potential American president. It is to this end that Reagan's travels must be viewed. Indeed, Reagan was representing California in 1969 and the Nixon administration in 1972, but these expeditions, and that in 1978, can also be viewed in the context of a politician seeking to enhance his profile and relations abroad in preparation for a presidential candidacy. Reagan was able to claim experience in foreign affairs that was important to his credibility as a presidential candidate. The trips also allowed Reagan to cultivate what would prove to be important relationships, particularly that with Thatcher, in advance of gaining power. However, just as many in the British press underestimated Reagan as a failed presidential candidate and Hollywood actor, the British (Labour) government clearly did not consider him to be a serious contender for the presidency. This lack of foresight only contrasted with Thatcher's enthusiasm for meeting the former governor of California.

In 1975 and 1977, Thatcher visited the United States to enhance her international profile. The purpose of these expeditions was manifold, although Thatcher had three ambitions for the visits. First, Thatcher wished to cultivate Anglo-American relations in order to be taken seriously as a potential prime minister by the Conservative Party and the British electorate more generally. Second, Thatcher sought to establish her political and policy directions in a favorable setting, and a welcoming reception in the United States would prompt those speeches to be reported by the British press. Third, Thatcher intended to impress the American political establishment so as to build relations before taking power. For the press supporting the Conservative Party, Thatcher was a strong woman who articulated a clear vision for Britain during her travels. Callaghan's rebuke in 1975 simply highlighted her arguments, and that allowed her supporters the opportunity to clarify that she had criticized the Labour government—not the British people. As far as Thatcher and her allies in the press were concerned, she had demonstrated that she was ready to lead the country. Yet despite Thatcher's efforts, the country remained unconvinced. Even at the time of the 1979 general election, less than one-third of British voters considered her to be a capable leader.[200]

Victory for Reagan and Thatcher in their general elections of 1980 and 1979, respectively, ended their need to engage in shadow summitry; they would now be instigating and participating in bilateral and multilateral summits as heads of their respective governments. In their first telephone discussion as president and prime minister (on the occasion of Reagan's inauguration), they resolved to "lend strength to each other."[201] In February 1981 Thatcher was the first major world leader to visit the Reagan White House—a clear signal that the Reagan administration hoped that the "Iron Lady" would prove to be a valuable and firm ally in international affairs. The FCO anticipated that the administration would listen to Thatcher, as she was "an ally whom they much respect and with whose Government they feel they have much in common."[202] Welcoming Thatcher to the White House, Reagan connected her visit with their previous meetings in London, recalling that he "was impressed by the similar challenges our countries faced and by our determination to meet those challenges."[203] The meetings certainly mattered to Reagan, both politically and personally. Reagan may have been dismissed in Britain by the press and some senior politicians as an extreme actor-politician and failed presidential candidate, but his visits to Britain did allow him to develop his "special relationship" with Thatcher—something that both parties would seek to utilize for their respective domestic political positions during their partnership in power.

Some material in this chapter has been adapted from its initial use in the author's article: "The Foreign Politics of Opposition: Margaret Thatcher and the Transatlantic Relationship before Power," *Contemporary British History* 24, no. 1 (March 2010): 23–42. I am grateful to the Taylor & Francis Group for their permission to utilize the article in this way. The article can be accessed via https://www.tandfonline.com/.

2

A Political "Special Relationship," 1981

When meeting as world leaders for the first time in February 1981, Ronald Reagan and Margaret Thatcher publicly demonstrated a wish that their respective government programs at home and abroad be viewed as having commonalities in detail and purpose. They hoped that such a display of unity would offer each of them political cover in light of their domestic economic problems and an ostensibly resurgent Soviet Union. Nevertheless, Reagan and Thatcher's public diplomacy masked a problematic reality. During the 1980s, the American and British economies differed. For instance, although Reagan and Thatcher both inherited high inflation and high income tax rates, the British economy featured nationalized industries and related trade union influences that did not exist in the United States. Inevitably, Reaganism and Thatcherism would have different details. Consequently, at the summit in February 1981, it was inevitable that at least one side risked a harmonious image of shared philosophy and policy commonalities. As such, the first meeting between Reagan and Thatcher as partners in power raised questions about the nature of summitry, such as realistic ambitions, differences between public and private diplomacy, the relationship between summitry and domestic affairs, and the closeness between Reagan and Thatcher at this stage in their time in office.

Thatcher was fortuitous in the timing of her general election victory. The role of trade union strife in the fall of the successive governments since 1969 ensured that there was a readiness among the general public to accept some action against union activities. Similarly, monetarism had been quietly applied by the preceding Labour government—albeit, at the behest of the International Monetary Fund following its bailout of the British economy in

1976—meaning that the civil service need not have anticipated a radical departure in economic policy after all.[1] Nonetheless, during the first two years of Thatcher's premiership, the fortunes of the British economy worsened. The years 1980–1981 saw unemployment increase to 2.7 million and the gross national product declined by 3.2 percent.[2] This did not go unnoticed in the United States, and it was raised in a telephone conversation between Reagan and Thatcher on Inauguration Day. The president told the prime minster that he and Nancy Reagan were looking forward to welcoming the Thatchers in Washington, DC, and they would discuss international issues and economic challenges that they both faced. Thatcher candidly remarked that as the "newspapers are saying mostly that President Reagan must avoid Mrs. Thatcher's mistakes," she would brief the president "on the mistakes." Graciously, Reagan told Thatcher: "I don't think I have to worry about that. I have just been watching and I know you have got such an uphill battle there but my goodness you've been staying there in the front line without rest or recreation." Clearly touched by the president's encouragement, she likened her political mission to his: "Well, you know it makes it worth it when you are fighting for things we are fighting for then we have to give everything we've got." Sealing the sense of solidarity, Reagan added that they would "lend strength to each other"—and Thatcher unsurprisingly agreed.[3] Despite the president's rhetoric of solidarity with the prime minister, Thatcher's economic program was subject to criticism by members of the new administration, and it was widely hoped that Reagan's program would not repeat the failings of Thatcherism. Criticism of Thatcherism in the United States contextualized Thatcher's arrival in February 1981, and this, in turn, was indicative of the tension between domestic policy and the globalized economy: what was happening in the United Kingdom was again viewed as a cautionary tale in the United States. The importance of domestic politics was also evident in Thatcher's first visit to the United States as prime minister, when she met Jimmy Carter in December 1979, which will be discussed below by way of background.

Thatcher and Carter in December 1979

Thatcher was determined to have a close relationship with the American president, whoever it was, in order to enhance British influence in international affairs. This was evident in her meetings with Ford and Carter in 1975 and 1977, respectively, and continued to be the case when she first became prime minister. In December 1979, Thatcher visited the United States for the first time in her premiership. In this bilateral summit, she offered Carter clear support following the taking of American hostages in Tehran. Given the crisis for the Carter administration, the *Daily Telegraph* editorial believed that Thatcher should cooperate with the president.[4] The hostage crisis engulfed the remainder of Carter's presidency. Upon arriving at the White House, the prime minister did not fail to live up to the *Telegraph*'s expectations: "Our admiration goes to the American people for their patience and wisdom and self-control. You yourself, Mr. President if I may say so, have won enormous respect in Britain for the statesmanship, calmness, and courage with which you have faced an agonizing problem. At times like this you are entitled to look to your friends for support. We are your friends. We do support you. And we shall support you. Let there be no doubt about that."[5]

Nicholas Henderson, British ambassador to the United States (1979–1982), diarized that this statement "was like a trumpet-blast of cheer to a government and people badly in need of reassurance from their allies. It got the visit off to a perfect start."[6] At an evening dinner at the White House, Henderson observed that in his remarks, Carter "was generous about the bilateral relations and about Mrs. T, more so, it occurred to me, than mere courtesy required."[7] Brian Vince, writing for the *Daily Express* from New York, informed his readers of the *New York Times*'s view that Thatcher was Britain's most effective statesman since Harold Macmillan (British prime minister, 1957–1963).[8] In the *Daily Telegraph,* Stephen Baker wrote about Thatcher's support for Carter, yet was candid about the difficult history of their relationship, albeit that it had become convivial.[9] Thatcher's determination to improve Anglo-American relations in this fashion was naturally praised by Conservative Party supporters. For instance, writing in *The Times,* William Rees-Mogg argued that Britain became Carter's leading ally because of Thatcher's unreserved support for the United States.[10] Of course, this success was very much for public consumption. Carter was unable to convince Thatcher to agree to sanctions or military action against Tehran, meaning it was not such a success for his administration.[11] Nonetheless, the response of the British press demonstrated the value of summitry as a means to the prime minister obtaining positive headlines and news coverage.

Despite the international situation and focus on strengthening Anglo-American relations, Thatcher saw the summit as a means to further her own domestic agenda, specifically that of the "Troubles" in Northern Ireland.[12] Before the prime minister's departure, Sir Robert Armstrong (secretary of the Cabinet, 1979–1987) briefed her that she should ensure that the president was "in no doubt about the realities of the Northern Ireland situation."[13] Thus, Thatcher was advised "to apply pressure on the Americans" over their refusal to continue the sale of arms to the Royal Ulster Constabulary (RUC).[14] Northern Ireland was an issue that encompassed American and British domestic politics and added an extra dimension to Anglo-American relations. This was crystalized by the need for the US State Department to approve the sale of American arms to the RUC through the issuing of a license on January 31, 1979, which brought these factors together. The RUC wished to purchase three thousand revolvers and five hundred automatic rifles from Sturm, Ruger, & Company, located in the United States. Some Irish Americans in Congress, plus the Italian American, Mario Biaggi (D-NY), utilized this issue to further their condemnation of the British government and the RUC following the revelation of human rights abuses with the publication of the Bennett Report in March 1979, which revealed abuses by the RUC.[15] In August 1979, Speaker Thomas P. "Tip" O'Neill (D-MA) allowed Biaggi's amendment that was attached to the State Department's appropriations bill to pass through Congress. This effectively prohibited American weapon sales to the RUC. O'Neill's message to Thatcher was clear: her government had to end the Northern Ireland conflict in which he had a long-standing interest to see legal guarantees for Catholics' civil rights and an end to the violence. In addition, the Speaker was able to neutralize Biaggi's claim that in selling arms to the RUC, the State Department was essentially choosing sides in Northern Ireland. O'Neill could not ask Irish Americans to not support the IRA if the United States government was supplying arms to the RUC, which was accused of abusing Catholics. Regardless of the internal politicking among Irish Americans, this Congressional action caused some tensions in Anglo-American relations. Carter, preferring to prioritize his domestic agenda over his relationship with Thatcher, did not oppose Congress's decision.[16]

On meeting with the president at the White House, Thatcher raised the RUC issue.[17] She acknowledged "the difficulties the question of the supply of arms from the United States to the RUC raised for the president." Yet she was also blunt that the issue "also created difficulties for her" at home in the United Kingdom. A decision in the US Congress had therefore complicated her domestic political situation. Thatcher explained that the RUC was not sectarian, that other British police had comparable American arms, and given that the RUC was already in possession of three thousand American Rugers, it was accordingly "very strange to deny them the remainder of the order and thereby to deprive a significant number of members of the RUC the right to defend themselves effectively." The prime minister even attempted to flatter Carter and American manufacturing, commenting that she had "handled both the gun which the RUC at present used and that which was on order" and it was obvious that "the American Ruger was much better." Thatcher asked whether Carter's stance was "one of principle or one of timing." Carter confirmed that it was the timing of the issue and advised her to raise the matter with O'Neill. Carter admitted that he would have sanctioned the arms sale, but he was not prepared to risk a defeat in Congress or even "a major altercation" with Democrats on Capitol Hill. Thatcher argued that the American position risked "a major propaganda victory for the IRA."[18] Nonetheless, Carter organized his own domestic priorities, and that required working relationships with leading members of Congress. Although the meeting between Carter and Thatcher was mostly about international issues—such as those related to the Strategic Arms Limitations Treaties of 1972 and 1979, and Soviet advances into Africa—domestic priorities were clearly an important part of Thatcher's thinking: Northern Ireland and the impact of Congress's decision toward the RUC were significant enough to be raised alongside other issues that are typically associated with international summitry. Nonetheless, as far as public presentation was concerned, the impact of the meeting with Carter had proven to be a positive one for the new prime minister.

Thatcher did indeed discuss Northern Ireland with members of Congress, including Tip O'Neill.[19] She expressed her appreciation for O'Neill's "firm stand on terrorism." Rather than tackle the RUC issue directly, the prime minister instead explained her policy toward Northern Ireland, citing "excellent cooperation" with the Irish government and stressed that the RUC and Irish police "cooperated well." However, in response to ongoing and long-standing Irish American interest in Northern Ireland, Thatcher was forthright: "Ulster was part of the United Kingdom because that was the way its people wanted it. . . . So long as there was terrorist violence, the Army must stay."[20] Thatcher's domestic priorities also proved to be a factor when she returned to the United States to meet with Reagan, Carter's successor, in February 1981, for their first bilateral summit.

Preparing for the February 1981 Summit

Thatcher's position as the first major world leader to visit the new president was a sign that the Reagan administration believed that she would prove to be an invaluable ally. Indeed, her anti-communist stance and advocacy of New Right economic policies suggested that it would be a successful occasion. Nevertheless, there were reservations about the summit. For instance, Alfred Sherman, who was a co-founder of the Centre for Policy Studies, a conservative British think tank, briefed the prime minister. The Centre for Policy Studies was the brainchild of Sir Keith Joseph following the Conservative Party's electoral defeats in 1974.[21] (Incidentally, the briefing paper was ostensibly passed to David Wolfson, Thatcher's chief of staff, who, for unknown reasons, did not plan to share it with the prime minister until after the March 1981 budget.) Sherman commented on the range of Republican attitudes toward Thatcher: "The Thatcher-Reagan similarities are double-edged. Until the [US] elections, genuine and spontaneous pro-Thatcherism was really nationwide, and was used by Reaganites as a portent of victory. Since November, Reaganites have quite brutally differentiated themselves from the Conservative government here."[22]

The British government was certainly defensive toward American attitudes of its economic policy. For instance, the Foreign and Commonwealth Office (FCO) advised Thatcher to inform the president that her government would continue with its economic program, regardless of any American criticism.[23] According to the British Treasury, Thatcher was briefed that some critics in the United States believed that her government had "deliberately engineered a recession" while others claimed that Thatcher's monetarism was "sound, but implementation has not been rigorous enough." David Stockman, the director of the US Office of Management and the Budget (1981–1985), had noted the "very disturbing" results of monetary policy in the United Kingdom.[24] Nonetheless, the Treasury officials believed that British policy could be associated with those pursued by Reagan. They briefed Thatcher that the British government shared Reagan's "economic objectives," and that should "non-inflationary growth" return to the United States, it would be "very important for the rest of the world." Thus, the Treasury sympathized with Reagan's policies of tax cuts and lower public spending as a means to stimulate the private sector. Nonetheless, the Treasury suggested that during her time in Washington, DC, Thatcher should ask about potential difficulties that could be caused by the US deficit if Congress resisted spending cuts or should economic growth be slower than expected. This concern was motivated by European concerns about US interest rates. Although UK Treasury officials readily admitted difficulties in achieving their money supply targets, they were clearly not prepared to be lectured at by their American counterparts.[25] Indeed, the FCO explained that there was continuing debate about whether "the United States has—or can regain—the economic muscle necessary to form the basis of a strong . . . defense posture and a more decisive role abroad."[26] According to this briefing, Reagan sought to restore the American economy concurrent to increased expenditures on defense and a policy in Central America "designed to contain the spread of communism."[27] In sum, these briefings suggest that senior British government officials had no clear expectation as to what would happen at the summit. Thatcher also received a number of other briefings from government departments. She was briefed on East/West relations; defense policy and equipment; regional questions; Vietnamese refugees; Northern Ireland; international economic and monetary policies; the extraterritorial application of US antitrust laws; prospects for the forthcoming Mexico and Ottawa summits; energy; counterterrorism; and United Nations issues (she was also meeting with United Nations Secretary-General, Kurt Waldheim). According to the British steering brief for the visit, Reagan's domestic priorities would be the economy and his foreign policy focusing on the Soviet threat, consultation with America's allies, and other security issues, such as El Salvador. It was expected that the Reagan administration viewed Thatcher as "an ally whom they much respect and with whose government they feel they have much in common."[28]

Regardless of British concern about how Thatcher's economic policy was viewed in America, the FCO did not anticipate it to be a priority for discussions with the Reagan administration. The prime minister instead expected Reagan to focus on how Anglo-American relations would help deliver an organized foreign and defense policy and a firm stance against the Soviet Union.[29] The British objectives for the summit were therefore a predictable inventory for a first official visit with a new president: a formal exchange of ideas and consultation. Thatcher's main priority was to reaffirm the importance of Anglo-American relations, particularly within the context of its obligations to its North Atlantic Trade Organization (NATO) and West European allies. The British government clearly sought an endorsement and political support from the new administration. Thus, the second objective of the summit was for Thatcher to strengthen Reagan's ostensibly positive opinion of her government. The prime minister expected to exchange views on policies toward Poland and the Middle East, defense equipment and policy, opposition to sanctions against South Africa, support for Namibian independence, the president's domestic and economic program, Northern Ireland, and US policy in Central America (particularly El Salvador and Belize).[30] These topics are unsurprising for a bilateral Anglo-American summit.

Despite Thatcher's view that Northern Ireland was a British domestic issue, it was anticipated to be a difficult topic by both London and Washington. Echoing the prime minister's meeting with Carter in 1979, the FCO also advised her "to give the President and his advisers an account of the realities of the Northern Ireland situation."[31] Similarly, the Northern Ireland Office briefed that the new administration would "follow its predecessor in condemning violence unequivocally and taking practical steps to prevent US assistance to IRA terrorists."[32] The political frustration over the RUC issue remained. Indeed, Thatcher was advised that even though the RUC no longer required any Ruger revolvers from America, it was politically "the best position . . . for the Americans to lift the ban" so that Thatcher would be able to "say that this has happened." The British clearly hoped for a political victory for the new prime minister. Nevertheless, it was acknowledged that O'Neill maintained his stance, and consequently, Reagan would continue Carter's policy of not opposing him on the issue.[33] In his briefing for the president, Alexander Haig (secretary of state, 1981–1982) warned Reagan that Thatcher might also raise issues that Reagan should avoid. Such issues included Northern Ireland.[34] He briefed that "our policy has been to prevent Northern Ireland from disrupting our close cooperation with the UK and Ireland by adopting a policy of strict neutrality."[35] Ultimately, Northern Ireland was not raised during Thatcher's meeting with Reagan or when she met members of the US senate on Capitol Hill.[36]

Amid concern for international affairs at the forthcoming summit, domestic economic issues also mattered for the Reagan administration. Martin Anderson, Reagan's chief domestic policy adviser (1981–1982), circulated a memorandum to senior White House staff, which detailed "a brief description between the economic program implemented in England by Prime Minister Thatcher and the economic program proposed by President Reagan."[37] Anderson explained that the Conservative Party entered government in 1979 "with much the same rhetoric that surrounds the Reagan

Administration's economic program" but "the substance of these programs has been very different." The memorandum noted that by almost doubling the value-added tax to 15 percent in order to regain revenue following the 1979 income tax cut, the Thatcher government had simply counterbalanced the supply-side incentives of the tax cut (thus echoing Laffer's 1979 article in the *Wall Street Journal*). This was underscored by the Thatcher government's decision to raise employee "social security" contributions (national insurance) and increase taxation on tobacco, alcohol, and oil petroleum products. According to Anderson, Reagan's program was different: firstly, there would be no tax increase; instead the tax cuts would increase incentives (although Reagan did of course raise taxes). Secondly, while the Thatcher government reportedly increased spending, the Reagan administration sought a significant reduction in spending (although this did not happen). Thirdly, Thatcher's government was judged to have failed to achieve its monetary targets, yet Anderson stressed that the Reagan administration would work with the Federal Reserve System to do so. Finally, Anderson's memorandum stated that any economic comparison was inaccurate as "the two countries are substantially different, including the fact that the US is not so encumbered with money-losing state industries."[38] The White House was determined to stress the differences between Reaganism and Thatcherism.

Alexander Haig, despite being primarily concerned with foreign affairs as secretary of state, briefed Reagan in advance of a discussion of the economy: "Outline your economic strategy. Mrs. Thatcher will want to share her own experiences in dealing with the British economy."[39] Whereas Anderson sought to distance Reaganism from Thatcherism for political purposes, Haig was interested in Thatcherism's fate due to his belief that Britain's economic fortunes were crucial to America's international interests. Haig argued that the Reagan administration "benefited from Mrs. Thatcher's pro-American, anti-Soviet instincts. She believes in a politically active, outward-looking Britain. Her cooperation is limited, however, by a deteriorating economic situation."[40] Yet Haig believed that Britain's economic problems threatened Thatcher's political fortunes and strengthened the possibility of a Labour government, which could weaken American interests: "Mrs. Thatcher's political future may be tied to the economy. Elections must be held by Spring 1984. The Labor opposition is embroiled in a left-right struggle over party policies and leadership. The policies being expounded by the left, which is ascendant, would seriously detract from the UK's role in NATO."[41] Thus, the

State Department's briefing paper suggested that Reagan should "exchange views with Thatcher on her experience, in part to learn from British mistakes. . . . While she is trying to restructure an economy which in many ways is different from the US we share common problems. Thatcher will be interested in your economic program and your plan for implementing it."[42] In contrast to British officials who believed that the Reagan administration was keen to learn from Thatcher's experience, Haig believed that Britain's poor economic performance would mean that Thatcher would listen to American advice about how to improve the British economy.

Despite Thatcher's problematic domestic circumstances, Haig observed that she would wish to reaffirm the "special relationship" and, in turn, Reagan should "demonstrate publicly and privately that Thatcher is the major Western leader most attuned to your views on East-West and security issues." Reagan was advised to urge Thatcher "to continue to support increased Western defense efforts" and "coordinate closely our response to Polish contingencies." Haig encouraged the president to ask Thatcher to delay the European Community's policies for a Middle East settlement (as its members advocated the participation of the Palestinian Liberation Organization) until the administration's policy review was completed. The key issues on which Reagan was briefed to raise at the summit echoed those suggested to Thatcher by the FCO: East-West relations, the NATO defense effort, US-UK-European relations, southwest Asian and Persian Gulf security, the Middle East, arms control and security issues, South Africa and Central America, and the Caribbean. Haig also advised that Reagan should avoid the following issues: the tenure of the NATO secretary-general, a two-way street in defense procurement, Northern Ireland, visa reciprocity, the UK-Canadian constitutional issue, and Breeder Reactor cooperation.[43]

The Reagan administration understood the domestic political advantages to the bilateral Anglo-American summit. Thatcher's visit was an opportunity for the White House to enhance the president's "domestic image" as it was "psychologically valuable to demonstrate that he is putting our relations with our major transatlantic partners on a basis which is different from the one prevailing in the recent past."[44] Therefore, it was suggested that Reagan's "willingness to participate in some follow-up social activity to the official dinner would help underscore the substantive importance he is placing on our relationships with a number of key Allies."[45] The White House wanted to contrast Reagan's image with that of Carter: "The public affairs impact of such participation could be enormous and would signal that we have moved beyond the loose rhetoric of "closer Allied cooperation" (so prevalent in the past) to some visible evidence that US leadership in the person of its president really does have a special regard for our major partners."[46] This was identified in the American press: Philip Geyelin, writing in the *Washington Post,* observed that it was a useful chance for two leaders to meet as Reagan needed Thatcher's support for his economic program and stance against the Soviet Union.[47] Geyelin added that Thatcher could comparably benefit from the president's support for her own economic program, which was proving divisive in Britain.[48] Nevertheless, Reagan's opponents saw Thatcher's visit as a means to further their opposition to the new president's program. This was noted in the British press: it was even reported in the Conservative-supporting *Daily Express* that Rep. James Jones (D-OK), chair of the House Budget Committee, argued America should not repeat Thatcher's economic experiment.[49] Tensions between Reaganism and Thatcherism were therefore underscored.

The Visit and Aftermath

Thatcher was concerned about her visit to Washington, DC, as she expressed to her ambassador, Nicholas Henderson (1979–1982).[50] In his diary, Henderson noted that she "admitted to being nervous about it. She looked drawn—pale and rather distinguished. I did my best to reassure her, telling her how welcoming Reagan would be and how much he was looking forward to her arrival."[51] Journalistic opinion was favorable to the prime minister. John Warden, writing for the *Daily Express,* shared Henderson's confidence that the visit would be a success given American interest in the prime minister.[52]

On a personal level, Thatcher did not need to worry about meeting Reagan again, and she was welcomed to the United States amid a ceremonial flourish, with the president warmly welcoming her to the White House. Reagan referred to their previous meetings and tied them into a common agenda now that they were both in office: "You have said that we enter into a decade fraught with danger, and so we have. But the decade will be less dangerous if the West maintains the strength required for peace, and in achieving that goal, there is one element that goes without question: Britain and America will stand side by side."[53] In response, Thatcher shared her host's warmth and economic purpose: "Mr. President, the natural bond of interest between our two countries is strengthened by the common approach which you and I have to our national problems. . . . We both place our faith not so much in economic theory but in the resourcefulness and the decency of ordinary people."[54] These remarks underscored the importance of mutual endorsement of their domestic program. But that was not the leading public purpose of the summit. According to the minutes, a plenary meeting between the American and British parties was dominated by foreign affairs. Nonetheless, Thatcher and Reagan did have a tête-á-tête meeting in the Oval Office, which overran. The British record of the plenary meeting alludes to a wide-ranging prior discussion and noted Reagan's commitment to Anglo-American relations and "close consultation and cooperation."[55] In contrast to the British account, in his diary, Reagan noted that the private discussion with Thatcher included Cold War politics and American and British economic performance. He wrote: "We had a private meeting in Oval Office. She is as firm as ever re the Soviets and for reduction of govt. Expressed regret that she tried to reduce govt. spending a step at a time & was defeated in each attempt. Said she should have done it our way—an entire package—all or nothing."[56]

After the White House meetings, Reagan and Thatcher addressed a press conference in which they both offered uncontroversial details about what was discussed, albeit there was an emphasis on the common features of their respective programs. Reagan explained: "Our deep ties and perceptions we share give us much to talk about. Together we're confronting an extremely grave international situation. We do so with determination and optimism."[57] The prime minister sought to magnify both her and Britain's role in international affairs. "The President and I had a tête-á-tête for some time. . . . We take the same view in the United States and Britain that our first duty to freedom is to defend our own. . . . I really regard it as the beginning of a process of consultation," she claimed, before it was reported in the British press that El Salvador and fears of Soviet expansionism dominated the foreign affairs aspects of the talks (which was accurate).[58] Thatcher's opponents in the British press were sceptical about the success of the discussions and the ability of both Reagan and Thatcher to manage a bilateral summit. For instance, Anthony Holden mockingly reported in the *Observer* that Thatcher had difficulty swallowing a jelly bean during the meeting and their advisers were invited to join them after forty minutes given their relative inexperience in foreign policy.[59]

Despite Thatcher's public delight at both Reagan's welcome and their discussions, her economic program was subject to criticism away from the

White House. Reagan noted in his diary: "P.M. getting great press. Went up to the hill and was literally an advocate for our ec. program. Some of the Sen's. tried to give her a bad time. She put them down firmly & with typical British courtesy."[60] Nonetheless, it was Donald T. Regan, the US treasury secretary (1981–1985), who was most fervent in his criticism toward Thatcher's policies. As Holden explained, Thatcher's meeting with Reagan was incredibly amicable, but afterward, circumstances became more complex.[61] Concurrent to Thatcher's visit to the White House, Regan's testimony to a Congressional committee about Thatcher's economic policy was scathing, and he criticized the British economy generally. When Regan was asked to explain any mistakes that Thatcher had made, he distanced the president's economic program from what Thatcher had implemented across the Atlantic. Regan's detailed—albeit factually dubious—remarks are summarized by his opening claim that on the advent of the conservative government in the United Kingdom, "practically 60% of the population . . . in one form or another was working for the Government. Luckily we don't have that in this country."[62] (This would later be corrected for Regan's benefit—see below.) Commenting on Howe's 1979 income tax cut, Regan echoed Arthur Laffer's initial criticism in the *Wall Street Journal*. Regan concluded: "We think that our program is much more sensible, much more comprehensive, and with a greater degree of chance of success than the British experience."[63] This was not the only criticism of Thatcher's program from the Reagan administration. During the previous week, Stockman advised the same Congressional committee that Thatcher's program "has failed, as one would have expected."[64] Peter Simmonds, writing for the *Sunday Telegraph*, claimed that even Reagan had told Thatcher that despite their similar economic problems, distinctive resolutions were needed to address them on either side of the Atlantic.[65] The White House added to Regan's criticisms when it distributed a paper (presumably Anderson's memorandum) that outlined the differences between Reaganism and Thatcherism and even held an explanatory briefing, whereby Murray Weidenbaum, the chairman of the Council of Economic Advisers (1981–1982), reiterated the treasury secretary's comments at Congress.[66]

The UK Treasury responded to Regan's criticisms with a personal letter from Sir Kenneth Couzens (second permanent secretary, Overseas Finance) to his American counterpart, Beryl Sprinkel (undersecretary designate, Monetary Affairs, US Treasury). Couzens offered a caveat that his comments were based on a transcription of the testimony available from the BBC, but if it was accurate then "the Committee heard one or two mistakes of fact."[67] Continuing his diplomatic approach, he explained why, with Howe's approval, it was important that Regan's statement be corrected: "[A]s has been repeatedly said during Mrs. Thatcher's visit to the United States, the main thrust of the economic policies of our two governments is so similar, it would be a pity if either side misunderstood what the other was doing."[68] Couzens explained that the population of the workforce that was employed by the British government in any capacity—such as local authorities, the National Health Service, and nationalized industries—was not 60 percent but at most 30 percent. He added that the vast majority were not working for the government directly but rather in the public sector generally. Couzens defended the Thatcher government's economic program—namely, its policies on taxation, abandonment of exchange controls, and its (albeit limited) success in increasing exports. Despite his diplomatic tone, Couzens was firm in his criticism of Regan's remarks: "So there are good structural reasons why the struggle ought to be easier for you than it is for us. But it is unhelpful, and also unrealistic to suggest that we have failed because of policy mistakes whereas you won't because you won't make any. Our Government does not accept that it has failed, as you will have gathered from Mrs. Thatcher. We have after all reduced our rate of inflation faster in 1980 than any other major country."[69] It was clearly unhelpful for the British to have differences between Reaganism and Thatcherism be promoted by a member of the Reagan administration, particularly as there had been an attempt by the British to establish the political cover between the president and the prime minister of a commonality in economic policy.

Despite Thatcher's ardent support for Reagan's firm stance against the Soviet Union, her media appearances in the United States saw much attention to her economic policies.[70] The American media were keen to understand how Reaganomics might affect the American economy. Thatcher sought to dismiss American criticism of her program, but she wanted to endorse Reagan's program—which she, in turn, linked to her own, so as to emphasize its credibility. At a press conference for the Washington Press Club, six out of thirteen questions addressed Thatcher's economic policies (although they were interspersed with questions about El Salvador, the Canadian constitution, the Middle East, the Gulf, and the Ottawa Summit, which would be expected in a press conference following a bilateral summit).[71] When the Associated Press asked her about any differences between her economic policies and those espoused by the president, Thatcher responded by praising Reagan and explaining the different economic circumstances in the two countries: "He's chosen just those very things which we also embarked upon and I think he's chosen to do them very boldly indeed, particularly the programmes to cut expenditure and it is the one thing which I could have wished that we had been even more successful at."[72] Nevertheless, Thatcher was asked about the problems that her government faced. Thus, there was a clear difference between the overall purpose of her summit with the president, namely, foreign affairs, and what their respective advisers and officials initially viewed as a minor area for discussion; yet ultimately, domestic policy shared equal billing to foreign policy. This is indicative as to how the agenda of, and public discussion about, summits are at the mercy of issues related to presentation, media interests, and events. Indeed, Jerry Edwin (Westinghouse Broadcasting) even asked Thatcher whether government should intervene to support weak industries. The prime minister responded: "Well now, we have a whole series of a kind of industry which you don't. We have a number of nationalised monopoly industries and a number of others which are in the public sector but not monopolies."[73] Thatcher used each question as an opportunity to praise the innovatory policies of her government: "One of the endemic problems of Britain has been over-manning and demarcation disputes. And one of the side effects of the really rigorous economic policy or disciplined economic policy which we are pursuing is to get the manning levels where they should be. . . . We do it on the basis that they slim down to a size at which they will become viable and profitable."[74] Thatcher concluded: "We're not just prepared to subsidise yesterday's jobs if they haven't a future tomorrow. We will look at those industries and say—we'll try to help you through the effects of change, but you must in fact make the change. Is that clear? Good."

Thatcher was then asked directly by another reporter (representing Eaton) whether the Conservative Party would remove her from office if her program failed to improve the performance of the British economy. Rejecting such a notion, Thatcher used the question as an opportunity to offer a detailed explanation of her mission to reduce inflation: "But I don't expect political defeat. Look what we are doing economically, its top priority—we have to fight inflation." Bob Clarke (journalist for ABC news), clearly with Reagan's tax proposals in mind, questioned Thatcher's decision to cut taxes and whether tax cuts should happen regardless of economic circumstances.

Thatcher's response noted global economic challenges, such as oil shocks and world recession: "The level of expenditure is higher than one would have wished. But in fact we did take down the direct rate of tax in our first budget. But I'm the first to admit that we've switched some of it, or most of it, to an indirect rate of tax. But there's no way of avoiding the world reality. There just isn't." Aware of her role as a guest in the United States and related diplomatic protocols, Thatcher then refused to engage with a question about a prediction for the rates of American unemployment and inflation. A follow-up question inquired about any backlash toward her policies, to which Thatcher offered a single-minded response that claimed popular support despite increasing unemployment: "Of course when you're getting rising unemployment and a number of bankruptcies . . . and I'm one of the first people to be concerned . . . I know we have to go through with it and I think that one of the worst things a government can do is to take the short term easy popular road."[75] Thatcher finished her response by returning to Simpson's first question: "I must leave President Reagan to take responsibility for his problems."[76] On CBS Morning News the following day, Thatcher's interview was dominated by the possibility that the British economy was a glimpse into the future under Reaganomics.[77]

It is clear that what the American press most wanted to know about Thatcher's premiership involved her economic policies, and the press clearly had some preconceptions about her program. The first question on CBS connected Thatcherism and Reaganism as "almost identical" and asked whether Thatcher had any advice for Reagan and the people of the United States. Thatcher responded: "I think he's started off in exactly the right way and I'm amazed at the speed that they got the package of public expenditure cuts before Congress."[78] When asked whether British experience offered any lessons to the United States, given that it also suffered from high unemployment, Thatcher again defended her government: "We came in at a time of the onset of world recession. . . . So we are in fact laying the foundations for a confident economy for the future."[79] As dry a discussion may be about economics on morning television, it is indicative of the American interest in Thatcherism. Indeed, the apparent commonality between Thatcherism and Reaganism meant that domestic economic policies received equal billing to that of foreign affairs in the coverage of the bilateral summit.

In a speech at Georgetown University later that day, Thatcher again defended her economic policies.[80] Thatcher contrasted her approach with those of successive governments since the Second World War, which had pursued policies such as income control and nationalization. The prime minister then equated her economic agenda to that of the Reagan administration: "The President's goal is a stable price level. Ours too. The President's aim is to free the individual from government restraint. Ours too. The President's objective is to reduce public spending and cut direct taxes. Ours too."[81] In this same speech, Thatcher also argued that the purpose of Reagan's economic program was to essentially "restore people's trust in the dollar." She explained that this was crucial for the global economy as it revolved around the dollar. The prime minister's message was clear: "The dollar is the world's money."[82] Ian Aitken, writing in the *Guardian,* argued that by explaining European concerns about the health of the US dollar, Thatcher had reversed the criticism by the Reagan administration against her policies.[83] Nonetheless, Thatcher's advocacy for Reagan's economic policies should not be underestimated. The following day, in a radio interview with Independent Radio News, the prime minister answered a question about the British and American economies by praising Reagan's program. When asked if she had learned anything from the president's approach, Thatcher observed: "I have been very impressed at the way in which they have put their package together in a few days and presented it to Congress. I think if that goes through it will be a wonderful foundation for the deep cuts in taxation they wish to make which I too would have wished to make."[84]

In the same interview, Thatcher again defended her record: "We had a number of things to which we were pledged and we were not quite as free to move as he is and I just hope that his policy goes through Congress."[85] Given that the Conservative Party enjoyed a majority in the House of Commons, while Reagan had to work with a Democrat-led House of Representatives, it is surprising that Thatcher felt she was more constrained than Reagan. It is possible, of course, that Thatcher envied the president's direct electoral mandate. But it is untypical for a politician to complain about the lack of support they have for their agenda. In Thatcher's case, she was still working with the Tory "wets" associated with the previous Conservative government led by Edward Heath (1970–1974) and, at this early stage in her premiership, relied on their goodwill and support (for instance, Sir Ian Gilmour and Jim Prior).[86]

Reagan and Thatcher publicly established a partnership based on mutual appreciation and respect during Thatcher's visit. Reagan returned Thatcher's support for his economic agenda in diplomatic tones and praise. Reagan, for instance, in a toast at the dinner in the British Embassy, compared Thatcher's agenda to Winston Churchill's preservation of British freedom during the Second World War. Although previous presidents had of course similarly praised prime ministers at similar events, Reagan styled Thatcher as a Churchillian-style politician who would lead Britain to economic recovery and even to victory over socialism and communism: "The British people are once again about to pay homage to their beloved Sir Winston by doing him the honor of proving him wrong and showing the world that their finest hour is yet to come."[87] Simmonds, again writing for the *Sunday Telegraph*, argued that such praise from the president was akin to an apology following his administration's public criticisms of the Thatcherite project.[88] Reagan was clearly determined to publicly support his ally—and it is remarkable that he did so by legitimizing Thatcher's economic revolution with a comparison to Churchill's leadership during the Second World War.

It was Reagan's personal warmth toward Thatcher that enabled her to claim that the summit had been a personal success. She told the House of Commons that the visit had been a triumph: "The reception given to us in Washington was warm and generous, testifying to the health of the Anglo-American relationship and also to the excellent understanding that President Reagan and I had established even before either of us assumed our present responsibilities."[89] In his mocking reply, Michael Foot, the Labour leader of the Opposition (1980–1983), stated: "In the United States the prime minister gave several homilies on our domestic affairs, but does she appreciate that the most friendly advice that she could have given to the United States was not to follow her example?"[90] Labour basked in the tensions between Reaganism and Thatcherism. Foot also criticized Thatcher for not warning the president that his approach to El Salvador should heed the lessons of Vietnam. Furthermore, Foot argued that with regard to the Soviet Union, Thatcher and Reagan were both wrong to challenge détente.[91] Ignoring Foot's criticism, Thatcher believed in Reagan and his agenda. In a letter to Henderson, Thatcher thanked him for his hard work for her visit.[92] She added: "I have great confidence in the President. I believe he will do things he wants to do—and he won't give up."[93] Three days later, Thatcher formally briefed the Cabinet on her visit to Washington.[94] She reported: "There was little sign of any weakening in their support and admiration for the British Government's policies, although they had some doubts about whether public expenditure cuts had been carried far enough at the beginning." In turn, the prime minister praised Reagan's economic agenda, noting that his proposed cuts to public expenditure were "a remarkable achievement" to have been presented to Congress so soon and "would involve an actual fall in public expenditure in real terms." She observed that "there was a sense of purpose and confidence in Washington which should make the tackling of economic problems less difficult that in the past."[95] Yet Thatcher was also a little envious of Reagan's economic good fortune, noting that America's "underlying strength" was based on "enviable features" such as "good competition, active enterprise, the ready availability of venture capital, excellent rapport between universities and industry, the absence of nationalised industries, less unionism and stricter union laws." Thatcher noted that the new administration's foreign policy "had so far received less attention than economic policy," but it was clear that Reagan "intended to delegate matters of detail but he had strong views on individual issues, such as Southern Africa . . . the Middle East . . . and above all the need to resist Cuban encroachment in the Caribbean and Central America."[96] The prime minister clearly believed that she had gained a strong understanding about the new president and his administration.

Despite Thatcher's positive account of her meeting with Reagan, Foot's criticisms, though politically motivated, were not without merit. Reagan's unyielding public confidence in the prime minister masked a political reality that, as Foot observed, was much more problematic for Thatcher. Indeed, the Reagan administration was concerned about Britain's economic difficulties. In July 1981, Reagan was briefed by Richard Allen, the national security advisor (1981–1982), upon the White House's receipt of John Louis's first report as US ambassador to the United Kingdom. Reagan was told of the "troubling political, social and economic drift" that Louis found on arrival in Britain and that the prime minister had "lost her grip on the political rudder."[97] Reagan's administration was alarmed about what this could mean for US interests, as the Labour Party "could prove harmful to our security interests even if reduced to a splinter group." Allen observed: "With no British leader seeming to have a clear idea of where or how to go, some political turbulence is likely, with adverse effect on the country's reliability as a US ally." The ambassador had even suggested to the White House that if Reagan visited Britain, it "could significantly strengthen both British resolve and the Western Alliance itself."[98] The Reagan administration continued to fear for Thatcher's premiership toward the end of 1981. Louis "reported extensively on the growing difficulties Mrs. Thatcher confronts (some of them of her own making) in her domestic program."[99] The White House even considered the "possibility of a Tory defeat, with the present government replaced by a coalition government."[100] Moreover, Thatcherism still haunted Reaganism in popular debate. Alan H. Meltzer, writing in the *New York Times* in August 1981, noted how the president's opponents warned that Reaganomics would lead to the same failings of Thatcherism.[101] Public criticism and private concerns meant that in the first year of the Reagan presidency, there were real doubts in the United States about Thatcher's political longevity.

The 1981 summit between Reagan and Thatcher was certainly a success for the Reagan administration. As the White House had hoped before Thatcher's arrival, the president and prime minister discussed and established a coherent approach to a range of Cold War issues, and Reagan's determination to work effectively with Thatcher was clear.[102] Indeed, Reagan clearly sought to project the image of a strong personal and working relationship with Thatcher. President Reagan and his wife, Nancy, broke with precedent by inviting Thatcher and her husband, Denis Thatcher, to the White House residence for coffee just before they left the United States.[103] This followed the warm and positive remarks that Reagan and Thatcher exchanged about each other during Thatcher's visit. The Conservative supporting press in the UK argued that the summit was a victory for Thatcher. For instance, the *Daily Express* placed Reagan and Thatcher in the tradition of the special relationship: "The omens are good for a close working relationship between the President and the Prime Minister, similar perhaps to that which existed between President Kennedy and Harold Macmillan, and Winston Churchill and Roosevelt."[104] The *Guardian,* a critic of both Reagan and Thatcher, warned its readers that the summit was "a political and diplomatic love-in."[105] James Brady, the White House press secretary (1981–1989), briefed American reporters: "It was difficult to pry them away from each other at the end."[106] Thatcher had reaffirmed the special relationship, which was the key priority of her visit, in order to further her credentials in international affairs. Nonetheless, Thatcher had been unable to leave criticism of her economic policies behind, and despite Reagan's personal support, the Reagan administration and the American media were skeptical about the Thatcherite project. This skepticism was to the extent that while concurrently promoting the closeness of Anglo-American relations, the Reagan administration was able to distance its own economic program from that of Thatcher—its supposedly closest ally—all while Thatcher was publicly advocating Reaganomics. A bilateral summit that would otherwise be expected to be about promoting a common agenda in foreign relations was therefore an exercise in politicking about domestic policy. The White House was successful in this endeavor. It secured the endorsement of the British prime minister for the president's economic policies while also distancing Reaganism from the perceived failings of Thatcherism.

The Ottawa Summit, July 20–21, 1981

In the months between Reagan and Thatcher's meeting in Washington, DC, and their participation at the G7 summit in July 1981, both had begun to establish their domestic agendas. On March 30, 1981, Reagan survived an assassin's bullet and was able to advocate the passage of the Economic Recovery Tax Act through Congress (ultimately signing the bill on August 13, 1981), which reduced the top rate of income tax from 70 percent to 50 percent. Across the Atlantic, Thatcher's March 1981 budget—in which Howe raised taxation despite conventional wisdom urging the opposite amid a recession—prompted national outrage. This included a condemning letter from 364 of the nation's leading economists to *The Times* and a wave of violent protests toward Conservative policies in London, Birmingham, and Liverpool. Nonetheless, the British economic recovery commenced soon after Howe's controversial budget. Unemployment hit a peak of three million in January 1982, but Thatcher could point to increasing outputs and steady falls in inflation and interest rates as evidence that her government was making progress.[107] Yet both Reagan and Thatcher could reasonably expect their G7 colleagues to critique their abandonment of the postwar Keynesian consensus when they gathered in Ottawa. The president, in particular, faced an inquisition from other heads of government due to the international consequences of American interest rates, which averaged at a rate of 17 percent throughout 1981.[108] On the eve of the summit, Steven Rattner, writing in the *New York Times,* noted the differences between Reaganism and Thatcherism.[109] Recalling Regan's congressional testimony concurrent to Thatcher's visit to the White House earlier that year, and Laffer's criticism of Thatcher in the *Wall Street Journal* in 1979, Rattner argued that the two programs were quite different. Thatcher's balancing of direct tax cuts with increases in indirect taxation ensured that her program lacked Reagan's supply-side effect.[110] Domestic economic concerns were at the forefront of the Ottawa

Summit. The growing interconnectivity of global markets and monetary flows meant that there could be no separation between global economics and domestic economic policy. In short, globalization meant that a meeting of the G7 was as much about the economic concerns of individual countries as the fortunes of the global economy.

Just before Reagan's tax cuts were introduced to the House of Representatives on July 23, 1981, the days of July 20–21, 1981, saw the leaders of the G7 gathered for their annual summit. The meeting in Ottawa was Reagan's first with multiple world leaders. The president's surprising nervousness undoubtedly prompted his desire to bring informality to the occasion: Reagan told his colleagues at the conference table, "My name is Ron." Yet Reagan's amiability suggested to his host Pierre Trudeau (Canadian prime minister, 1968–1979 and 1980–1984) that he was unconfident in the company of his world leaders. This, coupled with the opposition of leaders such as François Mitterrand (French president, 1981–1995) and Trudeau to Reaganomics, ensured that it was potentially a difficult summit for the president.[111] The politics were noted in the press coverage of the summit.[112] In his memoir, Reagan recalled that he "was the new boy in school"—a modest statement for the president of the wealthiest country at the G7.[113] Reagan was advised before leaving for Ottawa that "the United States was likely to come under fire . . . for our high interest rates, which several of the countries blamed for their own economic troubles."[114] *The Times* reported that American interest rates were a source of tension among the countries.[115] Similarly, the *New York Times* noted that US interest rates were the leading topic of discussion.[116] Fortunately for him, Thatcher returned the favor of public support that Reagan had offered for her in February 1981 as she steadfastly supported the president in the meetings and advocated his agenda.[117]

On July 20, Reagan and Thatcher met privately over breakfast and were then joined by their respective teams for a discussion before the conference began.[118] They agreed on the reality that "global negotiations" should not actually be that, for instance that aid to the Third World should be given bilaterally rather than multilaterally. Given that they were in the minority opinion among world leadership, the prime minister "did not want to find that the United States and the United Kingdom were put in the dock and held to be against the Third World—not least when the Americans were giving more aid than anybody else." As such, she was willing for the world leaders to discuss "global negotiations" despite her opposition to the term.

Thatcher's willingness to support alternative American language of "a readiness to participate in preparations for a global negotiation process" was tempered by the fact that, as Lord Carrington observed, Britain, holding the presidency of the European Community, had "agreed on a form of words on the global negotiations at the last meeting of the European Council," so any support for this was contingent upon someone else taking "the lead and especially if the French and the Germans were content." Thus, Thatcher's desire to support Reagan was challenged by commitments to the European Community. Political implications of Britain's relationship with European partners thus restricted their flexibility at the multilateral G7 summit, meaning that they were bound to prior agreements with West Germany, France, and Italy, rather than simply the United States.

British industry was a priority for Thatcher in her bilateral talk with the president. Having professed her support for Reagan's view on "global negotiations," she argued "that we had to get over to the Japanese that the practice of concentrating their export efforts on certain narrow fronts—the so-called laser techniques—was likely to kill the industries concerned in the countries importing their products." She noted that Britain "was an open trading nation and wanted to remain so," particularly as Britain "exported 33 percent of our GNP, more than any of the other countries represented at the Summit." Thatcher stressed that her government wanted this to continue to be the case, although "if the Japanese went on trading in the present way, there would be a rising tide of pressure to introduce protective measures against them," so other leaders would "have to work on the Japanese primarily behind the scenes, though we should need some suitable words in the Communiqué." Edwin Meese (adviser to Reagan 1981–1985) argued that even though "the Americans shared the concern expressed by the Prime Minister" it was a problematic issue that they did not wish to appear to be "ganging up against the Japanese." Haig concurred, arguing that a "word in the draft communiqué was satisfactory," despite Regan's scepticism "that the language in the Communiqué would have the desired effect." Thatcher's concurrent complaint and compliment about Japanese industry was undoubtedly rooted in her own frustrations with the British economy, feelings shared by her immediate predecessors in Downing Street: "The *Prime Minister* said that the problem arose largely because the Japanese were very efficient. They were already ahead in many sectors of advanced technology. They had virtually no strikes and their workers enjoyed a lower standard of living than their counterparts in the West. The Japanese labour force was very well disciplined. One-third of all Japanese profits was re-invested. The fact was that most Western countries simply could not match this kind of industrial competition."[119]

Following a discussion of Israel's overnight "ground attack" on Lebanon, to which Reagan added that the United Nations had proven "ineffective," the discussion returned to economic concerns. Thatcher explained that she and Reagan "had touched upon the problem of US interest rates over breakfast." The prime minister argued that her government "had given the highest priority to bringing down the rate of inflation in the UK" as it "was essential for both future investment and the social fabric of the country." Nonetheless, these efforts, that had already reduced inflation from 20 percent to 11 percent, were undermined as "the pound had fallen against the dollar because of US interest rates," which meant that Britain was "in effect, now importing inflation." Thatcher noted that this was also the case for other members of the European Community. In order to avoid a public row, according to the British record, Thatcher essentially offered Reagan a quid pro quo. She agreed to support Reagan in "giving the highest priority to the fight against inflation" and "his policy of cutting public expenditure and taxation," but in return she hoped that Reagan would express his desire for an impending drop in interest rates. The president was silent. Meese replied "that it would be very helpful if the Prime Minister took that line later that day" as Reagan "had inherited high interest rates and they were not a deliberate part of his policy." Meese further explained that while Reagan was instigating measures designed to reduce American interest rates, his tax cuts "were not designed to increase the budget deficit but to deal with the fact that the Carter regime had built in a 22 percent increase in taxation over the next three years." Regan adopted an optimistic interpretation of this economic situation: "The decline in other currencies against the dollar was not due only to high US interest rates but also to increased confidence more generally in the United States and its economic policies."[120] The Americans were clearly defensive about their high interest rates and eager to attribute blame to the Carter administration.

Regan and Howe also discussed the interconnectedness of the American and British economies in their own breakfast meeting.[121] Howe explained that American companies "with the advantage of regulated gas prices were forcing the closure of modern plants in the UK—and particularly in Northern Ireland." Regan's response pointed to an unsurprising concern for American economic priorities. He stated that the new administration "wanted to make progress with deregulation in order to encourage exploration," but the pace of this "was limited by the need to avoid damage to confidence through an upturn in the CPI; the process should nevertheless be complete by 1983." Clearly unsatisfied, Howe "undertook to arrange for Regan to be given further information clarifying the scale of the problems for UK industry represented by US gas prices."[122] It was clearly not just American interest rates that represented a challenge to British economic concerns. The impact of US gas prices on British industry is further indication of the tension between competing domestic economic interests and priorities amid globalization.

A background issue to the Ottawa Summit was the 1981 Hunger Strike in Northern Ireland, which was widely reported in the United States. Irish American interest in the strike demonstrated that the Troubles in Northern Ireland were no longer simply a British domestic matter. On May 6, 1981, the Four Horsemen—Senator Edward Kennedy (D-MA), Senator Daniel Moynihan (D-NY), Governor Hugh Carey (D-NY), and Tip O'Neill (D-MA)—wrote an open telegram to Thatcher whereby they criticized her "intransigence." These four leading Irish American politicians opposed American financial support and gunrunning for the IRA and called for a peaceful settlement in the province. Despite the political influence of the horsemen, Reagan was advised to continue American neutrality on the issue, and he even refused an appeal from Garret FitzGerald (prime minister of Ireland 1982–1987) for him to intervene. Ultimately, the president mentioned the Hunger Strike briefly to Thatcher at the summit: Reagan stressed that his administration would not intervene in the issue.[123] The Hunger Strike was not discussed at the bilateral breakfast meeting, although Thatcher briefed Reagan (on the Sunday evening) when they spoke before the conference formally began.[124]

According to Lou Cannon of the *Washington Post,* Reagan viewed the summit's opportunity to develop personal relations with his fellow leaders as "worth its weight in gold."[125] In his diary, Reagan acknowledged that the summit's "schedule was heavy," although it was "successful."[126] He noted that it was "not divisive although it could have been with regard to our interest rates," which ostensibly coincided with the fact that Thatcher had been "a tower of strength and a solid friend" of the United States. Yet Thatcher had not secured one of her objectives. Reagan wrote in his diary: "We held off what could have been a ganging up on Japan." The president did not mention

Northern Ireland in his diary.[127] Unlike some other meetings with Reagan and G7 summits, Thatcher failed to discuss Ottawa in her autobiography—perhaps indicative of her disappointment with its outcome.[128] Despite his de facto support for the British government on Northern Ireland, the president did not satisfy her economic concerns. Indeed, Thatcher's complaint about American interest rates would continue in subsequent summits with the president. This was also the case with other American allies. For instance, immediately afterward, Otto Graf Lambsdorff, the West German minister of economics (1977–1982), claimed that the United States was too reliant on monetary policy and should utilize fiscal policy in order to reduce inflation.[129] The summit's communiqué left in no doubt the disquiet among Reagan's fellow world leaders, including Thatcher: "Interest rates have reached record levels in many countries and, if long sustained at these levels, would threaten productive investment."[130]

Conclusion

The summits in February and July 1981 highlight the politics that shaped the first year of Reagan and Thatcher's bilateral summitry and co-attendance at the G7 multilateral summit. Thatcher's visit to the United States in 1981 shows that it is simplistic to claim that Thatcherism and Reaganism were the same expression of the New Right. Reaganites distanced themselves from Thatcherites. Thus, the desire of Reaganites and Thatcherites to establish allies was downgraded in favor of the Reagan administration's ambition and anxiety. The president and prime minister certainly shared a broad philosophy, but in regard to specific policies there were differences, and the Reagan administration was prepared to say so. Therefore, the February 1981 summit was driven by tensions between Reaganism and Thatcherism as domestic responses to global economic challenges: politics and policy in one country influenced debate in another. The British economy was subject to great interest in the United States, and that interest subsequently captured attention in Britain. However, despite its criticism of Thatcherism, the Reagan administration was determined to establish Thatcher as a credible partner in international affairs due to the importance of having a strong ally for the United States in Western Europe. This continued to be a concern throughout 1981. At the February summit, Thatcher achieved her wish to be seen as the new president's leading ally, but she failed to convince his administration that there were reasons for total optimism about the British economy and her political future. At the Ottawa Summit, Reagan again benefitted from Thatcher's public support for his economic program. However, in their private discussions, it was clear that Thatcher's concerns for high US interest rates were effectively ignored—as were the more public complaints of other leaders. Thatcher had proven to be a steadfast supporter of the Reagan administration, despite his administration using that to its advantage and distancing its agenda from her when it was expedient to do so. Domestic concerns were at the forefront of either side's list of priorities. After the summits in 1981, it was clear that there was every reason to believe that the relationship in power between Reagan and Thatcher would be as politically centered as their earlier transatlantic expeditions.

Some material in this chapter has been adapted from its initial use in the author's article: "'I must brief you on the mistakes': When Ronald Reagan Met Margaret Thatcher, February 25–28, 1981," *Journal of Policy History* 26, no. 3 (2014): 275–97. Reproduced with permission from Cambridge University Press.

3

Conflicts at Home and Abroad, 1982

President Ronald Reagan's state visit to the United Kingdom in June 1982 was largely contextualized by British domestic concerns. Controversy stalked the government's preparations for the visit with party politicking over the venue for Reagan's address, while the Thatcher government and British press would prioritize Britain's interests in economic policy and the Falklands. For Reagan, the visit came at a time when the American economy was in recession, meaning that the Republicans risked a reversal of the congressional gains they had achieved on his coattails two years earlier. This chapter will examine Reagan's 1982 visit to the United Kingdom and, further underscoring Margaret Thatcher's domestic priorities in foreign affairs, will incorporate the prime minister's visit to the United States later that year. It will show that once again both sides prioritized domestic matters and the impact of foreign policy on those issues. Furthermore, there continued to be a divergence between Reaganism and Thatcherism in addressing the challenges of the global economy.

As detailed below, during their meetings in 1982, Reagan and Thatcher's discussions ranged across a whole series of topics, but they were characterized by cooperation and tension. The Falklands prevailed as the major issue. Another development was Reagan's decision to impose sanctions on the Soviet Union and Poland following the declaration of martial law in Poland on December 13, 1981. The sanctions included a suspension of negotiations for grain sales; the prohibition of flights to America by Aeroflot (the Soviet airline); the postponement of many energy, science, and technology agreements; and a ban on the delivery of high-tech American products to the Soviet Union, including important equipment necessary for pipe laying for work on the Siberian gas pipeline.[1] It was this final sanction affecting trade and economic relationships that, according to Thatcher, "was to be the cause of great anger in Britain and other European countries."[2] The case of John Brown Engineering, a Scottish firm affected by Reagan's decision to apply pressure on the Soviet Union through sanctions, is also discussed in this chapter. Israel's invasion of Lebanon on June 6, 1982, also coincided with Reagan's transatlantic diplomacy and was an inevitable topic of discussion with world leaders, including Thatcher.[3]

Tensions between Reagan and Thatcher in international economic relations were an extension of those within the Western Alliance that emerged as the Cold War developed. East-West trade restrictions during the Cold War were marked by the 1949 Export Control Act, which enabled the US government to prevent exporting of technology and goods to the Soviet Union. The legislation was shaped by concerns for both economic protectionism and national security. American policy was not unilateral. Instead, the United States established the Coordinating Committee for Multilateral Export Controls (CoCom) in 1950–1951, which, until its closure in 1994, was designed to restrict the transfer of some products and technologies to the Eastern bloc. The membership was comprised of Japan, the countries (except Iceland) of the North Atlantic Treaty Organization (NATO), and nations that had received Marshall aid. However, CoCom became a center of tension for the Western Alliance as other countries, in contrast to the United States, sought to explore opportunities for trade with the Soviet Union.[4] Nonetheless, the importance of international trade for the American economy, coupled with détente with the Soviet Union, saw Congress pass the 1969 Export Administration Act. This enabled the US government to encourage international trade or restrict the exporting of technologies and commodities, depending on the president's view of the national interest.[5] This was reinforced by the 1979 Export Administration Act and was soon followed by the Carter administration angering American farmers by putting an embargo on agricultural exports to the Soviet Union as a result of the Soviet's invasion of Afghanistan. The declaration of martial law in Poland in December 1981 meant that the Reagan administration enacted sanctions against both the Soviet Union and Poland, which included prohibiting commodities and technologies from American companies—namely, General Electric and Caterpillar, being used in the construction of a Siberian pipeline. These sanctions impacted European companies involved with the project. In addition to the sanctions focusing on events in Poland, the Reagan administration feared that the pipeline would only ensure that the Western Europeans would become dependent on the Eastern bloc for petroleum and natural gases.[6]

Preparations for Reagan's Visit

The decision-making process in the Reagan administration mired initial plans for the president's visit to the United Kingdom, particularly with regard to whether he would actually address Parliament as Thatcher hoped he would. Following a White House social event on February 11, 1982, Ambassador Nicholas Henderson informed the Foreign and Commonwealth Office (FCO) that according to William P. Clark, the national security adviser (1982–1983), Reagan had decided against addressing both Houses of Parliament—albeit, the decision "had been taken more by those around the president than by the president himself."[7] Henderson had suggested to Clark that the president could make a joint appearance with Thatcher outside 10 Downing Street and "should appear before the public, even for a short time, at some stage during his visit," but did not consider a long prepared speech necessary. Clark agreed that the joint appearance at Downing Street was "a good idea," and he was "tempted to reopen the possibility of some appearance, though a brief one, at Parliament." The uncertainty of this arrangement was clarified by Henderson's admission that after speaking with Reagan himself, it was clear that the president "had only the vaguest knowledge of the program," although the First Lady was "more clued up." This lack of coherency in the White House offered an opportunity to the British to shape the agenda of the president's visit. The ambassador explained that if Downing Street did not believe that progress was being made through Michael Deaver, they "could always get at the President himself through Clark." Deaver, the White House deputy chief of staff (1981–1985), was scheduled to arrive shortly in London in order to agree to the schedule and broader arrangements for Reagan's forthcoming visit.[8]

Thatcher was naturally kept abreast of developments across the Atlantic. On February 12, 1982, the prime minister's private secretary, A. J. Coles, informed her that the White House's explanation for Reagan's refusal to address Parliament or offer any other major address in Britain was that "if he were to do himself justice, he would have to devote a great deal of preparation to this, and he will not have time to do so."[9] Downing Street believed that this decision was "a pity," as a key reason for the president's visit was "to improve his image with the British public" and "lessen the impact of the unilateralists" (meaning politicians and campaigners who wanted Britain to abandon its nuclear deterrent unilaterally). Both Sir Robert Armstrong (the Cabinet Office permanent secretary, 1979–1987) and Edward Streator (minister at the US Embassy, 1977–1984) agreed with this view. Thus, Coles suggested that the prime minister ask Deaver during his preparatory visit to London to request that Reagan reconsider, as his visit "should have the maximum beneficial impact in the interests both of UK/US relations, and in the interests of the Alliance." In a handwritten annotation, Thatcher instead proposed using the Guild Hall for a short speech and a luncheon.[10] A boost was definitely required for the notion of the "special relationship" in Britain. A Gallup poll showed that just as Thatcher was trying to organize Reagan's visit, and between March 1982 and August 1984 more generally, the United States and Britain were moving further apart (disagreements in the subsequent chapters of this book explain why this may have been the case).[11] Three days later, in a meeting with Armstrong, Deaver confirmed that Reagan "was excited about the prospect of addressing the two Houses of Parliament" and planned to speak for around twenty minutes.[12] He added that the White House was keen for the president to participate in an event whereby he would "be seen mixing with British people." Armstrong welcomed this proposal.[13] Believing the matter of the speech to be settled, Deaver informed the *Los Angeles Times,* who reported as front-page news that Reagan would become the first American president to address a joint session of the British parliament at Westminster Hall. Reuters also quoted Larry Speakers, the deputy White House press secretary, as confirming the event.[14]

The proposal for Reagan's Westminster speech was subsequently subject to questions on the floor of the House of Commons from outraged opposition members of Parliament (MPs). Frank Dobson (Labour), for instance, explained that while many of his colleagues and "a substantial number of the British people" could reasonably "expect a number of distinguished American past presidents and existing heads of other states" to receive such an invitation, it was unlikely many "would welcome such an invitation being extended to the present president of the United States of America."[15] These scenes in the House of Commons prompted Secretary of State Alexander Haig to immediately telephone Henderson.[16] Clearly unaware that Deaver's enthusiastic briefing to the American press caused the furor, Haig lamented the situation: "He said it was quite deplorable that there should have been this leak. . . . He entirely understood the indignation that had arisen in the House of Commons from having this piece of news break before they had been consulted." Haig inquired whether he could help rectify the situation as the president's proposed visit "should not create controversy." Henderson suggested to Haig that there may be an American embassy staff member who could tactfully approach the Labour Party, but, regardless, any direct intervention by the secretary of state himself would not be helpful. The potential significance of the Labour Party's reaction was not lost on the British Embassy in Washington, DC. Henderson informed the FCO: "What we want obviously to avoid is the extreme case in which the matter becomes increasingly stoked up in the UK so that the Americans are induced to believe that the only way of preventing further controversy is to cancel the visit. They are not at the moment thinking along those lines but are certainly aware of the extreme embarrassment they have caused in London."[17] It was left to the prime minister to resolve what the opposition Labour Party would claim was a self-inflicted crisis of protocol.

On March 8, 1982, Thatcher and Lord Carrington, the foreign and commonwealth secretary, met Michael Foot, the leader of the Labour Party, to discuss the proposal for Reagan to address members of both Houses of Parliament.[18] Thatcher sought to emphasize the significance of the president's visit. Reagan would be the first American president to be in Britain as the guest of the sovereign since Woodrow Wilson (1913–1921) in 1919. While no American president had addressed both Houses since the Second World War, other dignitaries had, such as Charles de Gaulle (the French president, 1959–1969) in 1960. The prime minster was clear in her stance: "The Government believed that it would be unthinkable for President Reagan, as the leader of our most powerful ally and friend, to have come to this country as the guest of the Queen and not to have been given the opportunity to address both Houses." She stressed that the proposal was in its early stages—the government had hoped to secure Reagan's agreement in principle and then consult Parliament. Thatcher accepted that while other world leaders had spoken at the Royal Gallery, she noted that de Gaulle had been afforded the privilege of speaking in Westminster Hall. She also conceded that the leak in America had been "most unfortunate." Foot argued that the Opposition and House authorities should have been consulted from the beginning of the process and that the prime minister and foreign secretary would not be able to persuade him to change his stance. Foot saw Reagan as a "controversial figure, both in his own country, and in the world at large," due to the domestic and international policies that he pursued, which contrasted with those advocated by many people, not just Labour Party supporters. Furthermore, the Labour leader argued that Reagan was still relatively new in office and the privilege of a Westminster Hall address had only previously been granted to President de Gaulle since the Second World War—someone, Foot claimed, who "was a figure of altogether different stature from President Reagan." Foot insisted that if Reagan wanted to address both Houses, the event would have to take place in the Royal Gallery, as per all other foreign leaders in recent times (except de Gaulle). The Labour leader "was sorry if he was taking a line that was embarrassing the Government, but had they consulted him and the Parliamentary authorities at the right moment, they could have avoided the difficulties they were now in."[19]

Thatcher was determined to salvage Reagan's address in Westminster Hall, clearly an attempt to please the president and promote their close relationship. In a letter to David Owen, deputy leader of the new Social Democratic Party (SDP), on March 9, Thatcher rehearsed the arguments that she made to Foot during their meeting on their previous day.[20] The prime minister apologized to Owen for the reports in the American press that were based on informal discussions with the White House. She wrote: "I am sorry that this has happened and I should like to assure you and the authorities of both Houses that the Government intended no discourtesy whatever. . . . I should like to repeat that it was our intention to hold the fullest consultations at the appropriate moment."[21] An identical letter was sent to David Steel, the leader of the Liberal Party (1976–1988).[22] Foot, in addition to his meeting with Thatcher and Carrington, also received a version of this letter.[23] Deaver was eager to apologize to the government, telephoning Henderson on March 9 to explain that "he was deeply distressed to hear the trouble he had caused."[24] He had simply understood from his meeting in London that the invitation "had been extended to the president" and accordingly "spoken about this to about twenty newspapermen on the West Coast."[25]

Such was the seriousness of the issue, the Cabinet discussed the matter on March 11, 1982.[26] After reviewing events up to that point, Thatcher criticized the Labour Party's objection to the president's speaking in Westminster Hall. In response to the Labour Party's objection that Reagan was "a highly controversial figure," she pointed out that Alexei Kosygin (the Soviet Union's chairman of the Council of Ministers, 1964–1980) was equally controversial yet had previously addressed the Royal Gallery in February 1967 under a Labour government. Thatcher debunked Foot's view that it mattered that Reagan had only been president for a short time on the basis that he had been a head of state longer than De Gaulle had been when he addressed Westminster Hall in 1960. Thatcher described Labour's argument that Reagan should address both Houses in the Royal Gallery as "trivial and small-minded." She admitted that the Reagan administration was "relaxed" about the venue, but "it would be hard to justify according the President a lesser privilege than General De Gaulle; and it would be unfortunate if the Royal Gallery were used and Mr. Foot then chose to represent this as a capitulation to pressure from the Opposition." The prime minister believed that the government could invite Reagan to address Westminster Hall, albeit prompting a boycott by many Labour MPs and peers, or simply hold the event in the Royal Gallery and enjoy wider party participation. Thatcher favored Westminster Hall but agreed to make a decision after further consultation with colleagues and Foot. In turn, the Cabinet agreed that Reagan should receive a formal invitation to address both Houses, albeit this was subject to the result of Thatcher's next discussion with Foot and other concerned parties.[27]

Yet, in a letter to the prime minister later that day, Foot refused to waver.[28] Mocking Thatcher's commitment to Anglo-American relations, Foot wrote that "the embarrassment which this proposal, made without consultation, had caused to the American Administration is the fault of the Government and to continue to lay the blame at the door of the American Administration is quite unjustified." The Labour Party view was the same as if they had been consulted initially: "An address in Westminster Hall to both Houses of Parliament is a special parliamentary occasion and should be offered to foreign statesmen only with the agreement of the major parties and the authorities of both Houses." In order to avoid further embarrassment and "hostility," Foot argued that the government should simply use the Royal Gallery.[29] He was determined to prevent a political victory for Thatcher.

In contrast to Thatcher, the president did not obsess over the grandness of the venue for his speech. Reagan was more troubled by the difficulties that Deaver's briefing had caused Thatcher. In a letter agreeing with Thatcher's view that the recent Trident II sale was "a perfect example" of their governments' "cooperative relationship," Reagan wrote: "May I add how much I regret the embarrassment which premature press reports concerning my visit to London caused you and your colleagues and how much I appreciate your sensitive handling of that issue."[30] But Thatcher was still unwilling to concede on the venue. She discussed the issue with William Whitelaw (deputy prime minister, 1979–1988, and home secretary, 1979–1983), Francis Pym (lord president of the Council, 1981–1982), Cecil Parkinson (paymaster general, 1981–1983), and Michael Jopling (chief whip, 1979–1983) on March 18, 1982.[31] Thatcher summed up the response of the party leaders to her letters of March 9: "The Labour and Liberal parties were clearly against the use of Westminster Hall and in favor of the Royal Gallery. The SDP preferred the Royal Gallery but did not believe that this should be a sticking point: they were anxious that nothing should be done that the Americans would interpret as an affront to President Reagan."[32] The remaining record of the discussion does not attribute any comments directly to the participants, although it is reasonable to conclude that Thatcher argued in favor of using Westminster Hall. In the meeting, the Royal Gallery was described as "not worthy of the occasion" and, due to its uncomfortable seating and poor acoustics, "to allow President Reagan to speak there would be an insult to the United States." Furthermore, if the government agreed to use the Royal Gallery, "it would be putting itself in the wrong by appearing to accept the arguments of Mr. Foot and Mr. Steel." Alternatively, it was suggested that the real question was whether to have Reagan address the more splendid Westminster Hall and risk a Labour boycott that would be obvious or address the Royal Gallery and ensure that at least some Labour Party members would attend. In turn, it was observed that "the occasion should occur with the maximum of good grace and the minimum of controversy." Ultimately the Royal Gallery was decided upon.[33] This was presumably much to the chagrin of the prime minister and to the satisfaction of her opponents. However, this incident is not simply about personal dislike for Reagan among Labour politicians—it is about political advantage and prestige.

Indeed the Anglo-American deliberation over Reagan's address refused to abate. On March 21, Henderson informed the FCO that according to Deaver, Reagan wanted to "abandon the idea of a speech altogether" following "the parliamentary fuss."[34] Deaver claimed that the president wanted to "avoid the prime minister further embarrassment" and that the negative publicity ensured "it would be humiliating to make the speech elsewhere" and appear "a climb down." However, it is clear that the White House was concerned about any residual embarrassment to the president from the saga.

Ostensibly frustrated by American motivations, Henderson candidly told Deaver that "it would look petty for the president to appear to be saying where he must speak." His view was that Foot was playing domestic politics and this outcome might be seen as a triumph for Foot, who "resented the advantage that the PM [prime minister] might get out of it." Thus, Henderson argued, Reagan "would not want to fall into this trap." Admitting that although Westminster Hall would probably "have been best," the ambassador emphasized that the speech promised to still be "a great event and the president could profit greatly from it," whereas, in contrast, abandoning the idea "would seem weak and petty."[35] A couple of days later, the president had changed his mind and settled on delivering the speech in the Royal Gallery.[36] In a meeting with Deaver and Clark, Henderson was assured that Reagan's "aim was to do whatever the prime minister wanted." The president's aides, however, clearly wanted a guarantee "that the opposition parties had accepted the use of the Royal Gallery and would not boycott or interrupt the ceremony," and that it "would be still be televised because this was important for the US as well as worldwide audiences."

When discussing the contents of the speech, the ambassador informed Deaver and Clark that the British government was "ready at any time to help on this," but in the first instance suggested that Reagan should discuss the Western Alliance, Anglo-American relations, East-West relations, and arms control. He stressed that the address "would be extremely widely viewed in the UK and indeed in Europe and it should be seen as an opportunity to check anti-Americanism there."[37] The British were determined that Reagan's speech would be a rebuke to advocates of British unilateral nuclear disarmament and critics of shared Anglo-American policies more broadly. Similarly, the British government wanted to do all it could to help ensure that the visit was viewed as a triumph in the United States. Bernard Ingham, Thatcher's press secretary (1979–1990), arranged for the prime minister to be interviewed by American networks as a priority over meetings with the British press during the president's time in Britain.[38] In accordance with Thatcher's visits to the United States, she clearly relished a favorable opinion of herself in the United States as a benefit to her international credibility. After all, if Thatcher was a popular figure in the United States, she might be able to have more sway of the nation's president. The prime minister accordingly acted on Ingham's advice and made her case for the Falklands War on the American networks.[39]

The Falklands War

The Falklands War was the major issue in Anglo-American relations at the time of Reagan's transatlantic expedition. At the outset of the Falklands crisis, the islands had a population of eighteen hundred people. The Falklands were eight thousand miles from Britain but a mere four hundred miles away from Argentina, which had claimed them since the nineteenth century. On April 2, 1982, in a desperate attempt to regain popular support for the military junta that had ruled Argentina for six years, General Leopoldo Galtieri ordered the invasion of East Falklands. The Argentinian regime did not anticipate a war over their action. That the British were willing to go to war was also a surprise to even some members of the British government. In 1982, Britain's foreign policy focused on the "Troubles" in Northern Ireland and concerns with the Soviet Union.[40] Nevertheless, Thatcher was compelled to act, and her decision to go to war was a turning point in her premiership. As Admiral Sir Henry Loach, the first sea lord, explained: "If we muck around, if we pussyfoot, if we don't move very fast and are not entirely successful . . . we shall be living in a different country whose word will count for little."[41] Argentina surrendered on June 14, 1982, and Thatcher had won her war.[42]

Upon the outbreak of the Falklands War (April 2 to June 14, 1982), the Reagan administration wanted the conflict between a major global ally and a key regional ally to end as quickly as possible. Indeed, as noted in the *Washington Post,* this was a source of great anxiety in the White House and State Department.[43] In his diary, Reagan wrote a few days into the crisis: "Fairly quiet day except in the So. Atlantic. The Royal Navy is sailing toward the Falkland Islands to oust Argentina. Both sides want our help. I'm leaving Al Haig home from Barbados to cope with it. We have to find some way to get them to back off."[44] Reagan's administration was divided by the conflict. For instance, Jeane Kirkpatrick, the US ambassador to the United Nations (1981–1985), believed that the United States should not prioritize the British government over Argentina's anti-Communist regime. Secretary Haig sought to be a peacemaker and was dispatched by the president to London and Buenos Aires in ultimately a failed attempt at shuttle diplomacy. In contrast, Caspar Weinberger, the secretary of defense (1981–1987), ensured that the British benefitted from American intelligence reports about the region and were granted access to the American base on (the British) Ascension Island.[45] Ambassador Henderson diarized that Haig wanted the British to allow "the

Argentinians to find a way out, short of total humiliation." He believed that Haig's view was shaped by American popular and government opinion: "Given the post-Vietnam sentiment in the USA, their dislike of colonialism and their wish to get on good terms with Latin America, we had been very lucky that they came down on our side."[46]

Anglo-American relations during the Falklands War therefore revolved around Thatcher's determination to secure Reagan's support for British action. On April 16, 1982, in the context of Haig's diplomatic efforts, Thatcher wrote to Reagan: "Our aim is to avoid conflict. But it is essential that America, our closest friend and ally, should share with us a common perception of the fundamental issues of democracy and freedom which are at stake, as I am sure you do."[47] But America's divided interests were summarized by Haig's remarks to the National Security Council (NSC) on April 30: "There are growing pressures at home and abroad to support Britain. At the same time, we need to work with Argentina and keep the American community in Argentina protected. Moreover, if this pro-American government falls in Buenos Aires, it may well be replaced by a left-wing, Peronist regime. Therefore, the Secretary said, we need to be careful in how we raise our tilt."[48] Reagan concluded at this meeting that "it would be nice if, after all these years, the UN could accomplish something as constructive as averting war between the UK and Argentina."[49] The president wanted a speedy end to the conflict in order to avoid publicly choosing sides, thus enabling a balancing act between Anglo-American relations and a broader approach to the Cold War. Reagan later admitted that he supported Thatcher "with whatever aid we could," yet he first had hoped to convince Thatcher to agree to some concession to Argentina. The president believed that if the junta fell from power, Argentina would succumb to instability, and another government, one of a leftist view, would take power and be susceptible to Moscow's influence.

Ultimately, Reagan sympathized with Thatcher, given the British cost in "blood and treasure."[50] Thatcher was intransigent on the issue. Haig was subject to the prime minister's clarity during what seems to have been a confrontational working dinner on April 8 in London, in which Thatcher explained that "she had not sent a fleet into the South Atlantic to strike a bargain with an aggressor."[51] When they were leaving Downing Street, Thatcher thanked her guests, noting that "only true friends could discuss such an issue with the candour and feeling which had characterized this dinner exchange."[52] It is clear that the Reagan administration was torn over which ally represented

America's interests: Argentina, a non-Communist country in a region that was a point of concern for the administration, or Thatcher, who was emerging as Reagan's most reliable ally in the Cold War. The British case was underscored by the country's role in NATO and importance in the deployment of Pershing and Cruise missiles. Nonetheless, short of dispatching a fleet to intercept the Royal Navy, the United States simply could not stop the British from undertaking military action. The Reagan administration therefore focused on convincing Thatcher to avoid humiliating Argentina and brokering a successful peace agreement about the Falklands in order to prevent a change in government that could be more favorable to Soviet influence.

Briefing the Prime Minster and the President

In advance of Reagan's visit in 1982, Thatcher was briefed on the objectives for the meeting on foreign affairs, particularly in regard to the Falklands War and the impact of the American budgetary deficit and high interest rates. British domestic concerns were therefore also at the forefront of the prime minister's meeting with the American president. The Reagan administration was anxious that the visit be viewed as a success. The president's transatlantic expedition coincided with a *Washington Post-ABC News* poll that demonstrated Reagan's declining public approval level and the rise in public blame toward the president for increasing unemployment and reluctance to attribute any credit to him for lower inflation.[53] The American people were not alone in worrying about Reagan's economic plan. Geoffrey Howe, the chancellor of the exchequer, told Thatcher that it was in Britain's national interest for the Reagan administration to "settle this matter," and Reagan should accept the need for tax increases, in addition to cuts in expenditure, and "must not shirk them any more than the Prime Minister and the Cabinet had shirked them."[54] Howe clearly believed that Reagan should follow Thatcher's example. Thatcher agreed that the deficit had to be addressed, but "she had difficulty with the idea of urging the Americans to increase taxes" and "had great sympathy with the President's objectives on expenditure." Nonetheless, the prime minister agreed "about the importance to the rest of the world of a declining sequence of US budget deficits," so she was willing to tell the president "that the deficits should decline, and that we wish them every success in their efforts to reduce expenditure."[55]

Alan Walters, Thatcher's chief economic adviser (1981–1983 and 1989), advised the prime minister on American economic policy and its broader implications. A devout monetarist, he wrote that Reagan's policy to "maintain tight control of the rate of growth of the money supply" while "progressively reducing the federal budget deficit" enjoyed the "[w]holehearted approval of the UK Government."[56] Walters observed that by reducing "the rate of growth of the money supply," inflation would be reduced "to the great benefit of the United States and the rest of the free world." Similarly, a reduction in the federal deficit through the reduction of "the rate of growth of federal spending" would "provide capital and manpower for an expansion of the vigorous private sector in the United States—again to the great benefit of the rest of the world." Clearly aware of the prime minister's frustrations with the American deficit, Walters briefed that ultimately it was for Reagan and his advisers to settle on a course of action, dependent on the president's view of the constitutional and legal needs of America and the political and economic situation. Nonetheless, Walters was adamant Reagan was "entirely correct in insisting that the best method of reducing the deficit is to reduce the rate of growth of federal spending."[57] Walters subsequently outlined the debate about the impact of Reaganomics: "The argument of many commentators is that the high US deficits cause high US interest rates which in turn cause interest rates to be high in the rest of the world. In other words, our interest rates are determined by the US deficit."[58]

Although it was "probably correct" that "US deficits cause high US interest rates," Walters warned that the argument is disputed by other economists, such as Milton Friedman (a leading monetarist), as "the *real* deficits as a fraction of GNP are much lower than they appear and are not historically high," meaning "that high interest rates are largely due to erratic monetary policy and high inflationary expectations." Walters added that American interest rates remained high due to the legacy of the 1970s economic experience, which suggested to the markets that "when the going gets rough, governments give up." In turn, according to Walters, the Reagan administration claimed "interest rates have come down and will decline further as markets become convinced that this administration will *not* give up." In regard to ramifications for the global economy, Walters noted that it was difficult "to argue that high US interest rates require high interest rates in the rest of the world." He warned Thatcher that the Reagan administration would respond to such a proposition by "point[ing] to Japanese interest rates of about 6 percent and

German interest rates currently at about 8 or 9 percent—both of these imply real interest rates of the order of 3 percent, not at all high by long historical standards." In addition, they could "powerfully argue that Britain has successfully reduced and indeed can continue to reduce interest rates provided it does not at the same time wish to defend a high exchange rate against the dollar. . . . Freedom of exchange rates implies substantial freedom from the hegemony of American interest rates." In short, according to Walters, the Americans might "argue that . . . we should fix our interest rates according to our domestic monetary policy, and not worry about the exchange rate." Further to the economic nuances for Thatcher's consideration, Walters outlined the political factors that the British had to carefully consider:

> The President is known to his enemies as a very stubborn man and to his admirers as a man of principle. I doubt very much whether preaching to him that we ought to increase taxes, even if he thought the case was being put in good faith, would have any effect on his policy. It would be seen, however, as providing ammunition for the enemies of his policy, particularly in the House. It may do harm to the Alliance and it is very doubtful whether it would do any good. The President has been told by many eminent authorities that he cannot reduce federal spending any more. But this has been the message on each occasion when he has substantially reduced it. In that respect he has a better record than the UK Government.

In contrast to the advice given by the chancellor of the exchequer, Thatcher's economic adviser was clearly concerned that any lecture by the prime minister to the president risked souring Anglo-American relations by problematizing Reagan's domestic position. Walters continued: "It would be very damaging if . . . you tell the President that he should follow the example of Britain: when we found that we could not reduce public spending, we increased taxes in 1981. In the President's circles this is regarded at best as some sort of regrettable necessity in political terms. Britain accommodated the enlarged public sector instead of persisting in reducing it. He believes he must reduce it."

As such, Walters warned that Reagan could reject her advice as "uninformed and unwarranted interference." As recently as 1976, the International Monetary Fund had asked the British government "to reduce the Budget deficit; it did not specify whether that was to be done by cutting spending or increasing taxes." Likewise, Walters advised that Thatcher ought to avoid prejudging any compromise between the president and Congress.[59] Thatcher was therefore also being warned not to emphasize any differences between Reaganism and Thatcherism.

Howe, returning to the issue, disagreed with Walters's analysis. On June 3, 1982, Howe wrote to Thatcher, beginning with: "I am sorry to go on about this. I do so because I am convinced of its importance to our national interest and political fortunes."[60] He explained that "the prospects for renewed growth, and our chance of turning the tide of unemployment, depend on the outlook for lower interest rates—achieved in a responsible fashion," but it also depended "on the prospects of renewed growth in the US." Howe unequivocally connected the American deficit with higher interest rates elsewhere in the world: "But because of the World role of the dollar there is a limit to what we (or other like-minded countries like Germany) can do to get our own interest rates down. And only the US itself can affect its own rates. They have made striking progress in reducing their inflation rate. But markets are not yet convinced that this is permanent. There is no doubt that in this they are powerfully influenced by what they see as the prospect for the US budget deficit."

Echoing Walters's briefing, Howe observed that despite the Reagan administration's progress in reducing inflation, the markets were "not yet convinced that this is permanent." Therefore, it was a pressing concern that Reagan would reach an agreement with Congress on deficit reduction before the 1982 summer recess. This impasse would likely continue until the US midterm elections, in which "no one can be sure that the outcome . . . will make it any easier to secure the necessary reductions after November." Howe reported that Donald T. Regan (the US treasury secretary, 1981–1985) and Paul Volcker (chairman of the Federal Reserve, 1979–1987) were "desperately aware of the need to make progress." Both men appreciated Howe's "restrained but persistent way" in making the case to the US government for deficit reduction. Howe reminded Thatcher that Helmut Schmidt (chancellor of the Federal Republic of Germany, 1974–1982) shared British concerns about the American economy and had even been urged by Secretary Regan to share those concerns with the president. However, Schmidt agreed with Howe that Thatcher was "better placed than anyone else to give the necessary encouragement to President Reagan." He told the prime minister: "He can be in no doubt about the identity of your views and his on the main economic issues." Howe urged Thatcher to "to draw upon our own experience," whereby "only because of our own willingness to 'bite the bullet' in our 1981 Budget that we . . . turn[ed] the tide of expectations in this country." This was a clear divergence from Walters's view. The chancellor conceded that "it is not for us to tell the President how to put his own act together" but argued that "we should leave him in no doubt about the importance, for the political and economic prospects of all the industrial countries, of his displaying firm determination to secure a convincing prospect of declining US deficits." Howe suggested that while Thatcher could not tell Reagan specifically what he could do about the American deficit, the urgent need for action should be emphasized. Thus, he even drafted a statement for Thatcher to express to Reagan, closing with: "We don't suggest that reducing deficits will end all the problems. Nor do we suggest that it would remove all the interest rate problems of other countries, which may be attributable to their own national policies. We all have our own responsibilities. But we do believe it would help substantially to improve the chance of a lasting victory over inflation both in the United States and elsewhere."[61] Howe was clear: Thatcher's approach was superior to Reagan's policies in addressing common economic difficulties.

Questions about Anglo-American cooperation in the Falklands War did not diminish the British government's domestic concerns before Thatcher's meeting with the president. Another cause of transatlantic tension with domestic consequences for Britain was the effect of the 1981–1982 Polish crisis on the interests of a British company, John Brown Engineering. Reagan's unilateral action in December 1981 meant that, due to their use of American technology, John Brown Engineering was unable to sell its turbines to the Soviet Union for the Siberian gas pipeline. These measures prohibited European countries from fulfilling their contractual obligations and, according to the FCO, "John Brown cannot afford to wait any longer."[62] Notably up until June 1982, Reagan had ignored Thatcher's previous two messages about this case, thus indicating his priorities on the matter. Thatcher was briefed to inform Reagan: "If European factories close and workers are dismissed because of your measures transatlantic relations are bound to suffer. Russia would be [the] only ones to benefit from open transatlantic strains. This episode illustrates [the] need for Allies to act together in East-West context." In specific reference to John Brown, the talking points were: "Can you now agree to release the components for our contracts blocked by your measures of 29 December last? If not may I have an answer within the week? Otherwise a good British engineering company will have to show substantial losses in its annual accounts due for publication next month."[63] Thatcher was advised to prioritize British economic interests amid the broader western approach to the Cold War.

According to the FCO, informal discussions with the White House suggested that Reagan would be prepared to talk about the Western Alliance, East-West trade, and the Irish question.[64] On Ireland, the FCO noted that Reagan's "Irish ancestry has not inhibited him from condemning all acts of violence in Northern Ireland and taking a firm line against support for the IRA in the United States." In addition, Reagan continued to resist the Irish government's attempts to involve the United States in the Anglo-Irish process. Regardless of other issues, the Falklands was expected to "dominate the discussion," given American concerns to "reconcile solidarity with its closest ally in resistance to aggression with the preservation of its hemispheric relationship with Latin America." Thus, Thatcher was advised "to urge the President not to weaken in support of the British cause." It was expected that Reagan would "stress the risk of Argentina developing a close relationship with the Soviet Union" and therefore potentially "press us on our future intentions." More generally, the British objectives for the visit included a reemphasis of close Anglo-American relations, factoring in "the conflicting pressures" on both governments during the Falklands crisis; Reagan to appreciate the significance that Britain attaches to Anglo-American relations as part of NATO; and, finally, a desire to "counter any impression on the part of the President and American public opinion that Britain is dominated by anti-nuclear and anti-American elements."

It mattered to the British government what the United States understood about British policy and public attitudes toward foreign affairs. The FCO's assumption of Reagan's objectives underscored the domestic politics of the visit. The leading American objective was viewed as presenting Reagan as the leader of the Western Alliance, showing the American people that their president "is at ease on the international scene and a welcome guest in Britain." Similarly, Reagan would hope to show "British public opinion that America has a responsible attitude to the danger of war, and is working to restrain the arms race." America would attempt to do this by convincing "British public opinion that the Americans continue to regard Britain as their closest ally and attach special importance to Anglo-American relations," as seen in the "common political purpose which the American administration believes it shares with HMG [Her Majesty's Government]."[65] The Reagan administration was clearly determined for the visit to be a success back home. However, it was vital for American interests that Reagan be well received in Britain: a British government that was sympathetic to its aims was dependent on British voters being convinced of the merits of American foreign policy executed through the prism of Anglo-American relations. The extent of cooperation in Anglo-American relations was problematized by the international politics of the Falklands War. The Ministry of Defense advised Downing Street that Washington did not want any public disclosure about the extent of American assistance to the British military effort on the basis that it jeopardized relations between Latin America and the United States. Yet concurrent to the "difficult presentational problems" of denying American assistance, the British government should publicly express "warm thanks" to Reagan, Weinberger, and Haig.[66] While the British were willing to complain about American foreign policy to protect John Brown Engineering, Thatcher's Falklands War was the diplomatic priority.

According to Leonard Downie, writing in the *Washington Post,* Reagan's visit to Britain was intended to be an opportunity for some rest between summits and to help enhance his reputation in Europe.[67] However, the Falklands was also naturally a major component of American preparations for Reagan's meetings with Thatcher. Before the president's participation in the G7 Versailles Economic Summit from June 4 to 6, 1982, Haig briefed him about Thatcher's attitude toward Anglo-American cooperation in the Falklands.[68] The secretary of state suggested that Thatcher "will come to you concerned that you will join with Bonn and Paris in (1) urging a cease fire and negotiations before she has secured the Falklands or, (2) the longer term, a more magnanimous position on the ultimate status of the Islands to avoid a protracted conflict." While admitting that Thatcher would take seriously anything that Reagan had to say, there was some American concern that Thatcher could not be dissuaded from action that would be harmful to American interests in the region: "Basically, Mrs. Thatcher will only really listen to you because, from the outset, she has sought to engage the United States in the role of guarantor for the future security of the Islands. It would be wrong, however, to assume that she would abandon her principles in order to achieve such an American guarantee. At the same time, we must be very careful not to find ourselves in the middle of an arrangement which would be totally unacceptable to Argentina and this led to a permanent state of crisis." Haig was also aware of the domestic implications for Thatcher, which would of course need to influence the Reagan administration's approach. With Thatcher's popularity at an all-time high, the secretary of state thought that Thatcher might be considering an early general election in order to strengthen her own political position. Thus, Thatcher would be "reluctant to deviate from her strong, principled course which has served her well so far, especially in the case of the sacrifices it has entailed."[69]

With regard to Reagan's meeting with Thatcher on June 9, 1982, during his subsequent visit to Britain, the Falklands was again an unsurprising key aspect of Haig's briefings for the president.[70] Haig noted: "Mrs. Thatcher appreciates both our strong support in the crisis, and our earlier mediating efforts. She will welcome your reconfirmation of support." The briefing included material about Lebanon, the Middle East peace process, Anglo-American economic relations, the Versailles summit, East-West relations, NATO, arms control, Anglo-American military cooperation, Northern Ireland, and Africa. Haig contextualized his briefing with the connection between Thatcher's successes at home and abroad. While the crisis had been the focus of her attention, the conservatives had benefited politically, with successes in May's local elections. Thatcher's handling of the crisis, coupled with "the slight improvement in the economy," was a successful political combination. However, if the war continued for too long with an increasing number of casualties, Thatcher would "find her electoral support fickle." Thus, Thatcher was possibly preparing for a general election in the autumn of 1982 following a successful settlement over the Falklands, rather than waiting until the end of her five-year term in May 1984.[71] Despite the briefings on domestic affairs in both American and British preparations, foreign policy would dominate the meeting between Reagan and Thatcher on June 9.

Meeting at Versailles

Reagan and Thatcher met privately in June 1982 during the G7 Versailles Economic Summit (June 4–6, 1982).[72] The Falklands War was the major topic at the meeting. The president "expressed a keen wish to minimize the loss of life" but also "expressed considerable concern about the future course of events." While Reagan understood that it was difficult for Thatcher to pursue diplomacy in the immediate term, he was concerned "about the situation in

Argentina." He was worried that Galtieri could fall from power and that the invasion was authorized by him due to the spectre of widespread strikes "sympathetic to the Peronistas." Thatcher explained that the British also wanted to minimize the loss of life and did not want to humiliate Argentina.[73] Reagan did not want the Falklands War to unsettle domestic politics in Argentina to the extent that it would threaten American interests in Latin America. The president's concern about the future of Argentina was concurrent with his support for Thatcher among other heads of state and government at the Versailles summit. During a discussion about the Falklands, he told the delegation that armed aggression could not be permitted to solve problems: "If so, there were as many as 50 outstanding boundary disputes on the American Continent. So the issue was not so much that of the Falklands as that armed aggression must not be seen to succeed."[74] Reagan's support among fellow world leaders was a diplomatic victory for the British prime minister.

The leaders of the major industrial nations gathered in Versailles in a pessimistic mood. Leonard Silk, writing in the *New York Times,* noted that they feared a difficult decade ahead with regard to unemployment and high inflation.[75] Thus, the G7 summit saw Reagan having to defend America's economic policy and its role during the difficult economic times being experienced by his colleagues in Western Europe. The debate at the summit reflected British briefings about the connection between the American deficit and interest rates in the West.[76] Reagan admitted that the United States economy "was plagued, like others, with unemployment and with high interest rates." Subsequently, his administration had adopted different policies to those of his predecessors and was not trying to implement a short-term quick fix of more spending as previous administrations had, which simply resulted in further recessions, higher unemployment, and increased inflation. Indeed, the 1980 recession had increased to record unemployment levels and interest rates. In response, the Reagan administration reversed the level of increase in federal government expenditure, which meant that spending "was not going up half as fast as when he had taken office." The president admitted that even though this had not been sufficient to reduce interest rates to fully support car industries and building homes, inflation was lower, from 12.4 percent to less than 1 percent during the preceding three months. Reagan claimed to his colleagues that interest rates remained high because of "a pessimistic belief" that Congress would pressure the administration to resort to the old "quick-fix" approach. Reagan said that this would not happen and that he continued to work to reduce the deficit. He noted that Congress had just rejected a budget that would have reduced the deficit by $358 million over three years and therefore established a trend toward a balanced federal budget. Reagan was essentially obliged to explain his domestic policy—given its impact on the wider global economy—although his administration ironically denied the connection between the American deficit and high interest rates elsewhere.

Reagan offered an optimistic view of the economy: "Despite the high level of unemployment, there were more people in jobs than at any time in the history of the United States." Furthermore, the president actually explained that he "recognized the effects of high American interest rates" elsewhere in the world. However, given that they "were being held up for psychological reasons," interest rates would fall when Congress "passed a budget which showed that the reduction of budget deficits was for real." Likewise his tax cuts "would stimulate and thus increase national income and also in consequence tax yield," as was the case with President John F. Kennedy's (1961–1963) proposed tax cuts in his 1963 State of the Union address, which led to the 1964 Revenue Act. Reagan "knew that our economies all affected each other" and so the United States "would stick to its plans." Reagan had admitted the connection, but blamed the Democrats' control of Congress for the world's economic challenges. Not all listeners were convinced. Pierre Trudeau, the Canadian prime minister (1980–1984), mischievously remarked: "President Reagan had said that interest rates would come down if people were convinced that US budget deficits would be reduced, but could we wait? Waiting for lower US interest rates was having disastrous consequences for Canada. We could not wait for the American midterm elections. Could we help President Reagan? He would like to help Canada by helping the United States. Could we help to persuade Congress to agree to what was necessary in order to bring down interest rates?" On the defensive, Reagan responded by stressing his belief that "the United States was on the right track to reduce inflation and, with tax incentives, to stimulate growth and create jobs."

Thatcher supported Reagan in this discussion, although the president's support for the Falklands was matched by her warning against budgetary deficits. According to the British record, Thatcher argued that Reagan was correct: governments had to reduce their deficits and implement policies that they would be lowered in the future in order to increase confidence. The prime minister, drawing upon her own experience in 1981, explained: "There were two ways of reducing a deficit—cutting expenditure or increasing taxes. Cutting expenditure was preferable, but not easy: as politicians they were all to blame for arousing people's expectations of higher living standards." Chancellor Schmidt was obvious in his criticism of American policy. He argued that inflation predated the 1970s oil shocks and instead began with the heavy borrowing necessary for the United States to finance the Vietnam War. Schmidt explained that the dollar's value had again increased because of the relationship between the American budgetary deficit and interest rates: in April, the markets anticipated a budgetary agreement and consequent decline in interest rates, but the failure to reach an agreement in May ensured that such expectations disappeared, meaning that "people were happy to invest in the dollar where they could get 7 or 8 percent real interest." Schmidt argued: "This led to the value of the dollar going up again not as a reflection of the basic position of the US economy but as an expression of expectations about interest rates. . . . If the dollar was more stable, there could be greater cooperation between the United States and Europe. The United States was so strong that they had to bear the responsibility."

Defending his position, Reagan sought to temper the narrative that the fortunes of the global economy rested on the American deficit: "Even if US interest rates went down, that was no panacea." The president agreed with Schmidt's connection of inflation with the Vietnam War: "He agreed that inflation began to accelerate when President Johnson tried to have both guns and butter. He remembered saying 25 years ago that there was no such thing as maintaining a little inflation. Sooner or later it got out of hand. Now we have had the longest period of inflation ever."[77] Reagan clearly wanted his colleagues to believe that finally the western economy had an American president with a credible economic plan. Credibility for his administration's policies—particularly those that connected the domestic and foreign spheres—was at the heart of this transatlantic tension. On Versailles, Reagan wrote in his diary: "We more than held our own and I believe came out on top."[78] In her memoir, Thatcher recalled that the "summer of 1982 saw some useful international diplomacy."[79] On the Versailles summit, her "most vivid recollection of the proceedings is of the impression made by President Reagan." Thatcher gushingly described Reagan as having spoken for around twenty minutes without notes about his "economic vision," which showed the "qualities which made him such a remarkable political leader." She added that French president Mitterrand acknowledged that Reagan could not be criticized for speaking to his convictions, which, given his socialist policies "was almost a compliment."[80] Reagan certainly acknowledged the role of the American economy in the fortunes of those of his allies. However, he sought to assign blame for America's economic challenges on Congress and stressed that his budgetary deficit was not the sole issue at stake. Despite the president's efforts, it is clear that other leaders were more concerned by the economic consequences of the American budgetary deficit rather than if it was the fault of the Democrats or the Reagan administration. Nonetheless, the president was able to overcome a personal obstacle at the summit. According to the *Washington Post,* Reagan struggled to open a bag of jelly beans during the third session, but his treasury secretary, Donald Regan, was on hand with a pair of scissors to open Reagan's favorite confectionary treat.[81]

Reagan's Westminster Speech

Reagan noted in his diary that he was the first American president ever to address what he termed as a "joint session" of the British Parliament.[82] In his memoirs, Reagan recalled that the purpose of his Westminster speech (and a similar speech to the West German parliament) was to demonstrate that he "wasn't flirting with doomsday" by speaking out frankly against the Soviet Union. Reagan was determined to explain how "democracies were up against an expansionist powerhouse that was trying all over the world to peddle its system, yet we who had the system of government that *worked* were doing nothing to sell our vision of freedom and the kind of system in which the people control government, not the other way around."[83] Reagan later described the speech, which led to the "Reagan Doctrine" of support for those fighting for freedom against communism, as "probably one of the most important speeches I gave as president."[84] Thatcher later described Reagan's speech as "remarkable."[85] In her memoirs, Thatcher argued that at the Palace of Westminster, Reagan had "marked a decisive stage in the battle of ideas which he and I wished to wage against socialism, above all the socialism of the Soviet Union."[86] While it is clear that Thatcher shared Reagan's broader foreign policy vision of containing the Soviet Union and the inadvisability of détente, Reagan's call for a firmer stance for freedom was, in Thatcher's view, an endorsement of her domestic and foreign policies to eradicate socialism from Britain and the wider world. In terms of the development of her campaign and presentational style, Thatcher recalled her admiration for

Reagan's delivery and noted how she had made her "first acquaintance with Autocue."[87]

The president certainly appreciated his welcome in the Royal Gallery. A cleaning woman vacuumed the red carpet one final time between the seating of MPs and Reagan's arrival. The red carpet, coupled with the British pageantry of the speaker and lord chancellor wearing wigs and black and gold robes, meant that Reagan, as an Anglophile, said that he felt "at home."[88] In his speech, he told British MPs and peers that despite the need for caution, the ultimate objective of the West had to be to seek freedom for all people; the West should "be staunch in our conviction that freedom is not the sole prerogative of a lucky few, but the inalienable and universal right of all human beings. So states the United Nations Universal Declaration of Human Rights, which, among other things, guarantees free elections."[89] This was achievable if the West fostered "the infrastructure of democracy . . . which allows a people to choose their own way" and "to reconcile their own differences through peaceful means."[90] Reagan stressed that such a policy was "not cultural imperialism" but would provide "the means for genuine self-determination and protection for diversity."[91] Reagan concluded: "The task I've set forth will long outlive our own generation" and would be "a crusade for freedom."[92] However, for Thatcher, the key passage from Reagan's speech for the British press was his support for Britain regarding the Falklands:

> On a distant island in the South Atlantic young men are fighting for Britain. And yes, voices have been raised protesting their sacrifice for lumps of rock and earth so far away. But those young men aren't fighting for mere real estate. They fight for a cause—for the belief that armed aggression must not be allowed to succeed, and the people must participate in the decisions of government—the decisions of government under the rule of law. If there had been firmer support for that principle some forty-five years ago, perhaps our generation wouldn't have suffered the bloodletting of World War II.[93]

Following previous uncertainty over American support, Ian Atkin, political editor for the *Guardian,* observed how Thatcher had secured Reagan's support in the Falklands War, which was her priority during the president's transatlantic expedition.[94] Likewise, Robert Porter, political correspondent for the *Daily Mail,* noted that Reagan's words boosted Thatcher's morale.[95]

Cabinet room talks between Reagan and Thatcher and their teams on February 26, 1981, during Thatcher's visit to the White House. (Courtesy Thatcher MSS digital collection)

Reagan, Thatcher, and Vice President Bush in the Oval Office during Thatcher's February 1981 visit. (Courtesy Thatcher MSS digital collection)

Reagan enjoying Thatcher's toast at her State Dinner on February 26, 1981. (Courtesy Ronald Reagan Library)

The Fourth General Session of the Economic Summit at the Chateau Montebello in Ottawa, Canada, July 20, 1981. From left to right: Helmut Schmidt, Reagan, Pierre Trudeau, François Mitterrand, and Thatcher. (Courtesy Ronald Reagan Library)

In Churchill's shadow: Reagan and Thatcher stand in front of a painting of Winston Churchill at 10 Downing Street in London, June 8, 1982. (Courtesy Ronald Reagan Library)

Economic summit leaders in Williamsburg, Virginia, May 29, 1983. From left to right: Pierre Trudeau, Gaston Thorn, Helmut Kohl, François Mitterrand, Reagan, Yasuhiro Nakasone, Thatcher, Amintore Fanfani. (Courtesy Ronald Reagan Library)

G-7 Economic Summit leaders at Lancaster House in London, June 9, 1984. To Reagan's left, Thatcher, Bettino Craxi, and Yasuhiro Nakasone view a model of the manned space station. (Courtesy Ronald Reagan Library)

A breakfast meeting at 10 Downing Street during Reagan's visit to the United Kingdom on June 9, 1982. Francis Pym and Alexander Haig appear opposite Reagan and Thatcher, respectively. (Courtesy Ronald Reagan Library)

Thatcher visiting the White House on September 29, 1983. (Courtesy Thatcher MSS digital collection)

Reagan and Thatcher at Camp David, December 22, 1984. (Courtesy Thatcher MSS digital collection)

Reagan and Thatcher enjoying the grounds of Camp David, December 22, 1984. (Courtesy Ronald Reagan Library)

Thatcher at a working luncheon at Camp David on December 22, 1984, along with Vice President George Bush, Robert McFarlane, Larry Speakes, Richard Burt, George Shultz, British ambassador Oliver Wright, and other Reagan administration members. (Courtesy Ronald Reagan Library)

Reagan and Thatcher at Camp David, December 22, 1984. (Courtesy Thatcher MSS digital collection)

The *Daily Express* opined that Reagan had simply said what had to be said and in accordance with the expectations of his British audience.[96] A leader at the *Daily Telegraph* praised Reagan for noting that Britain was fighting for his priorities: namely, defense of democracy and liberty.[97] However, there was an element of cynicism in the British press. Andrew Alexander, parliamentary sketch writer for the *Daily Mail,* argued that Reagan's call for a crusade was simplistic and betrayed a vision of the world that understood it in terms of small-town America: a passion for free-market economics, democracy, and a slice of home-baked apple pie.[98] Similarly, an editorial in *The Times* sought more detail in order to clarify Reagan's call to arms with concrete specific policies.[99]

Accordingly, the political reality and importance of state visits in terms of the domestic audience and the American electorate were also duly noted by other press comments. The *Guardian*'s leader reported that Reagan's aides admitted how an important aspect of the president's European tour was to be viewed as a global statesman back home on American television.[100] Likewise, an *Express* opinion piece acknowledged that Reagan was addressing Americans and the British audience.[101] American press coverage noted the popularity of Reagan's remarks about the Falklands. R. W. Apple, reporting for the *New York Times,* noted that Reagan's mentioning of the war stirred the British politicians.[102] Lou Cannon informed readers of the *Washington Post* how before he had finished his last sentence in support of the British soldiers in the Falklands, the president's remarks were punctuated by sounds of approval.[103]

In addition to the reportedly favorable response by British politicians, American interest in the Royal family was evident in the American press. Indeed, the pageantry of Reagan's visit and its importance to the administration's desire to present Reagan as an attractive statesman was not lost on Donnie Radcliffe, who was writing for the *Washington Post.* Radcliffe observed that Reagan made history in Britain: in one day he accompanied the Queen on a horseback ride and then addressed both houses of Parliament.[104] Furthermore, Radcliffe quoted a spokesman for the Queen who confirmed that the banquet was a first for an American president in Windsor Castle.[105] Nevertheless, the efforts of Reagan's aides to take every opportunity to present the president in an advantageous light at home was not always welcomed by Buckingham Palace. Radcliffe reported that the Queen was apparently upset when aides suggested how she might ride her horse to help photographers take their best shot.[106]

The Westminster speech was a clear example of Reagan outlining foreign policy objectives, but he did so publicly endorsing Thatcher's action in the Falklands. This was particularly important given American interests in South America and vital to Thatcher's international credibility in responding to Argentina's action. Thatcher's victory in the Falklands would prove to be an indispensable reason for victory in the 1983 general election. Reagan's support for Thatcher in 1982 was therefore crucial not just to her international policy but also to her claims to be a politician of international standing in her quest for further domestic political successes. Indeed, the voice-over of one of the Conservative Party's political broadcasts during the 1983 UK general election stated: "This government has not only won the respect of the people of Britain, but of the world. Five years ago who would have believed that the President of the United States, the Chancellor of West Germany and the Prime Minister of Japan would not only want Britain at a summit meeting but find that the presence of the British Prime Minister was indispensable?"[107]

Meeting at 10 Downing Street

On June 9, 1982, Thatcher welcomed Reagan to 10 Downing Street. The G7 proved an opportunity for a "stop-over" bilateral summit following the president's speech. The prime minister began their meeting by describing the president's visit as "a triumph" and praised his "superb speech."[108] She enthused: "There was a new feeling here that we could not afford to take freedom for granted" and that Reagan's speech "had chimed in perfectly with this." The prime minister claimed that Reagan's visit had "underlined the closeness of the relationship between our two countries." Despite the briefings about the American deficit and worry for the survival of John Brown Engineering, this meeting focused on foreign policy—namely, the Falklands, the Middle East, and the forthcoming Bonn Summit. This is unsurprising given that Thatcher was on a war footing. On the topic of the Falklands, Thatcher "wished again to thank the President for his magnificent support," although she was saddened that she could "not specify in public the extent of that support." Anticipating victory at Port Stanley, she noted the challenge "in feeding and looking after so large a number of prisoners, and we were grateful for the help that the United States would be able to offer us." Thatcher asked whether it would be agreeable to finalize what help was necessary in due course and "make our request then." According to the British record, Reagan simply "indicated assent."

Turning to the Middle East, Thatcher "feared that the Israeli advance" into Lebanon "would have a fundamental effect on the Arab world." Haig's desire to emphasize the ending of bloodshed in what would become the first Lebanon War with a cease-fire did not meet with approval from Thatcher, who, perhaps with a comparison with the Falklands in mind, "indicated that this might pose a problem for us" as a cease-fire "could leave the burglar in possession." Clearly sensing a potential disagreement, Edwin Meese (counsellor to the president, 1981–1985) said that "it would be important not to be too specific in what was said to the press at the end of the meeting" and they "would be seeking to engineer differences of emphasis between the United States and the United Kingdom on the one hand and the rest of the Alliance on the other." In regard to the Bonn Summit, Carrington argued that the Anglo-American "objective should be to achieve a balance, between the need for strength and the adequacy of deterrence, and the achievement of START." (START, or the Strategic Arms Reduction Treaty, was ultimately signed in 1991 after lengthy negotiations that began in 1982.) Haig explained that the administration was seeking to maintain conventional military strength since they needed "this with Congress, and because it was right in itself."[109] The Reagan administration was clearly more concerned by congressional attitudes toward the Cold War than British desire to prioritize nuclear deterrence over renewed investment in conventional forces.

Unsurprisingly, Reagan and Thatcher promoted the closeness of their relationship and success of the visit in their public remarks. In her speech during the Downing Street luncheon in honor of the president, Thatcher talked fondly about her admiration for and relationship with Reagan.[110] She praised Reagan's Westminster address at length. For instance, she described it as "a new chapter in our history—no longer on the defensive but on the offensive." Clearly aware of the American audience, the president in his response chose to take political cover and focus much on economic affairs. Reagan declared: "These are difficult days for both our peoples. . . . Together and independently, our two countries have acted to renew and protect our way of life. We're restoring incentives and opportunities in our marketplaces by reducing excessive taxation and regulation. By lifting the heavy hand of government, we're placing our faith in the working men and women of Britain and the United States."[111]

On foreign affairs, Reagan simply added that "an important challenge still looms before us namely the protection of our personal freedoms and national interests in the face of hostile ideologies and enormous military threats." Thus, the president sought "the right balance of deterrent forces and arms reductions to secure a lasting peace for generations to come."[112] After their meeting in Downing Street, Thatcher again waxed lyrical about her ally and essentially claimed without justification but in accordance with diplomatic niceties that the president was universally supported throughout Britain: "It's been an extraordinarily warm welcome which I think we must attribute to the way in which President Reagan has appealed to the hearts and minds of our people . . . that reception has been one of great affection and one which recognises that here is a leader who can put to the uncommitted nations of the world the fact that we in Britain and the United States have a cause in freedom and justice that is worth striving for and worth proclaiming."[113] Reagan spoke in agreement on UN resolution 508 for Lebanon (which called for an end to hostilities between Israel and the Palestinian Liberation Organization), expressing American support for British action in the Falklands, noting positive meetings at the Versailles summit, and commenting about a common agenda for the forthcoming NATO summit at Bonn designed to limit any increase in nuclear proliferation and decrease the chances of war. He then offered a diplomatic flourish of his own: "[T]his has been a most important meeting for us and a very heart warming experience every minute that we've been here and we leave strengthened with the knowledge that the great friendship, the great alliance that has existed for so long between our two peoples, the United Kingdom and the United States, remains and is, if anything, stronger than it has ever been."[114] Thatcher's efforts to support Reagan and defend his record and goals in both Britain and the United States were noted by the *New York Times.*[115]

Reagan Welcomes Thatcher to the United States, June 1982

The Reagan administration recognized that Thatcher's domestic support following victory in the Falklands War would contextualize her participation at the second United Nations Special Session on Disarmament (UNSSOD) in June 1982. The American ambassador to Britain, John J. Louis Jr. (1981–1983), informed the State Department: "Thatcher is triumphant and revelling in victory. Public support for her leadership is firm and overwhelming. The shock of the early war losses has long since worn off. The public, reconciled to casualties, credits her boldness that they were not greater. Critics inside and outside the Tory Party are at bay. Parliament, even the Opposition, is paying tribute."[116] Louis noted, however, that Thatcher was conscious of the importance of spending her newfound political capital wisely: "She knows . . . that let-down will follow euphoria, and that to consolidate her political base she must secure peace. She wants, above all, to be Prime Minister for a full ten years, and she knows, despite her patriotic myopia, that protracted conflict in the South Atlantic sooner or later will undercut her." Nonetheless, Thatcher's policy was to "to hold the Falklands for Britain" and, given the casualties and financial cost of the war, the prime minister and her closest aides were clear "that it is wrong to contemplate any Argentine participation in the future of the Islands." Yet American interests were paramount: Louis argued that the Reagan administration needed to guide Thatcher piecemeal toward a settlement with the Argentinians, so as to restore Anglo-American relations with Latin America. Louis stressed that the administration would have to take a longer-term view: "We probably should not press her too hard now, since she will show flexibility only to the degree she sees it in Britain's interest. And she will want gestures of moderation to seem to spring from her."[117]

The process of working with Thatcher to secure a peace in accordance with American interests thus began with a message from Reagan to the prime minister. The president wrote:

> Your victory was both a brilliant military feat and a defense of our shared principle that disputes are not to be resolved by aggression. The minimum loss of life and the generous terms of withdrawal were also in the finest British tradition. A just war requires a just peace. We look forward to consulting with you and to assisting in building such a peace. It must of course take into account the sacrifices of your men in battle. Its elements . . . must include enhancement of the long-term security of the South Atlantic, mitigation of Argentine hostility and improvement in the relations of both our countries with Latin America.[118]

On June 19, Haig briefed Reagan that in the immediate term, the objectives should be to improve relations with Latin America while concurrently "continuing to give the British as much support as possible."[119] Essentially, Haig sought a win-win scenario for the United States. He recommended that Thatcher be invited to the White House after the UNSSOD.[120]

A few days later, the State Department briefed Reagan about Thatcher's continuing concern for John Brown Engineering.[121] The president was informed that European allies were "unhappy" with his decision "to expand export controls on US oil and gas equipment and technology" that had initially been implemented in December 1981. Thatcher was most concerned with the impact that the measures had on John Brown, due to its pipe contracts with the Soviets that were valued at $279 million and dependent on rotors from General Electric (who were, incidentally, Reagan's former employers). The frustration from across the Atlantic was clear to the administration. Thatcher had already written to the president twice as "nonfulfillment of these contracts could force the financially troubled firm into bankruptcy, with politically damaging increases in unemployment." Yet John Brown was part of a broader disagreement between the White House and Downing Street, with the briefing noting how "the British have been among the most vociferous critics of US efforts to apply our laws and regulations in foreign jurisdictions."[122]

Thatcher met Reagan at the White House on June 23. On the Falklands, Reagan offered full assistance to the British.[123] According to the American record, the president "jocularly recalled that in times past mules were used on mine fields, but the animals were very canny and never detonated any of the mines, although it often happened that the troops marching directly in their footprints did so." Thatcher continued the gallows humor of dealing with Argentinian mines. She "laughingly suggested that she would use the Falkland sheep for that purpose." Turning to more serious issues, Reagan suggested that signs of a potential new government in Argentina could help Thatcher to resolve the situation. He was working on the assumption that Thatcher "wanted a peace which did not have the British standing guard duty indefinitely so far from home." Yet Thatcher replied that instead "the British would likely be in the Falklands for a very long time" as having "been caught napping once . . . they would not be caught a second time." Mirroring the Reagan administration's piecemeal approach to influencing British policy toward the Falklands, Thatcher explained that while she would do everything possible to normalize relations with Latin American countries, "we will have to be gentle."[124]

Surprisingly the Falklands was not the main subject of discussion in this meeting. John Brown Engineering dominated the meeting. According to the

American record, half of the time was committed to it (although Thatcher's remarks are largely redacted in the American record).[125] Indeed, despite the pressing issue of securing a favorable peace in the South Atlantic, Reagan "initiated the conversation by raising the sanctions extension decision." The president recognized the potential adverse effect of the sanctions on John Brown and American firms, particularly General Electric and Caterpillar, but the decision was a matter of principle to him. Having "spelled out three criteria which would determine whether or not he could lift those sanctions, keep them in effect, or even impose additional measures" (the abolition of martial law in Poland, freedom for political prisoners, and renewed dialogue between Solidarity [trade union], government officials and the Church), he had no other option but to implement the measures as "soviet repression continued in Poland." Based on replies by Clark and Haig, it appears that Thatcher essentially pointed to the hypocrisy of continuing American grain sales to the Soviet Union. Reagan explained that his decision stemmed from the importance of principle and Western credibility: "Principle is important and is not, unfortunately, cost-free." Moreover, based on a recent meeting between NSC staff and representatives of John Brown, Reagan even suggested that the company "was perhaps in better shape than had been depicted." Having finally exchanged opinions, Thatcher ceased talking about the issue, and the meeting proceeded to discuss the Falklands and the Middle East.[126]

The British record confirms Thatcher's anger about the John Brown situation.[127] Thatcher explained the impact that Reagan's decision would have on the British, particularly the Scottish, economy: "The latest decision would cause us serious problems in an area which already had heavy unemployment." Her fury at the prioritization of American agriculture over British manufacturing was clear: "It would be said that the damage caused to Britain by the American decision was proportionally much greater than that caused to the United States whose main exports to the Soviet Union were of grain rather than of manufactured goods." Yet Reagan was content to prioritize his own domestic concerns. The record noted that, according to Reagan, it was President Carter who "had originally imposed the grain embargo, in connection with Afghanistan" much to the anger of American farmers, to whom he had in turn "promised in his presidential campaign that he would remove this discrimination." Thatcher replied that she "presumed there would be a new grain agreement," which Reagan and Haig refused to confirm. When Thatcher pressed the point, inquiring "whether she could, therefore, say publicly that there would not be a new agreement," Reagan said that "none yet had been negotiated" while Haig added that "even if there were no agreement, grain would continue to be sold on the market." Thatcher bluntly replied: "In that case American farmers would not suffer. But John Brown's employees would." Frustrated, Thatcher explained that John Brown only needed American rotors in order to implement the contract with the Soviet Union, but if this was prevented, "they would be disinclined to buy sophisticated equipment from the United States again." Domestic politics again were a factor: Thatcher candidly told the Americans that she would be under pressure about this issue upon her return home. Seeking to exploit domestic concerns in Britain in order to advance her negotiating position, she even threatened to effectively—and publicly—explain American hypocrisy: she "would say that the latest decision was seen by the Americans as being based on principle but the fact was that US grain would continue to be sold while John Brown could not purchase the necessary rotors from elsewhere."

Reagan was unmoved, stating that "the Americans were prepared to be painted as the villains," but a change in Russian policy in Poland would mean that the "sanctions could be changed." The British and Americans continued to prioritize domestic interests. Thatcher "asked again whether she could state that the Wheat Agreement would not be renewed." This time, Clark replied, stating that "this question had not be[en] discussed, much less decided." Haig argued that the sanctions had affected $850 million of American exports, and their renewal would push this figure to about $1 billion. Not to be outdone, Thatcher claimed that John Brown's contract was worth £400 million, with Ambassador Henderson adding that "British exports to the Soviet Union were on a downward trend while American exports were rising."

Ostensibly frustrated with Thatcher's intransigence, Reagan stated that representatives of John Brown did not share any concern with the American government about his decision. Henderson interjected, suggesting that there had been a misunderstanding as John Brown's comments to the British government "had been quite different." Reagan simply commented that the company could instead acquire the necessary equipment from General Electric's subsidiary in France. After commenting that she would revert to John Brown "because our clear understanding was that they were seriously worried about the situation," Thatcher was clear in her criticism of an ostensibly hypocritical American policy and its impact on European countries and transatlantic relations:

> Meanwhile, there seemed little doubt that the US would continue to export to the Soviet Union by one means or another and thus total American exports to the Soviet Union would continue to rise. European firms would be reluctant to order sophisticated equipment from the United States in the future and would go elsewhere. Existing contracts should have been exempted. The effect of the United States decisions was to prevent the fulfilment of normal commercial engagements. America's word was at stake . . . there would be much resentment in Britain if America's exports to Russia continued to rise while ours went down.

The State Department was proven correct to anticipate broader British concerns about American economic policy. Thatcher added that the British were also concerned about America's recent decision related to steel imports from Europe, which would damage exports to the American market. The prime minister candidly admitted that while it "was a matter for the European Community . . . if the Community did not take it up through the courts, we should probably do so." She warned that the British Steel Corporation would challenge the decision, as it would result in a loss of steel exports worth £50 million and job losses in Scotland (as in John Brown's case). Henderson added that "the matter was a very serious one" as Britain "had reduced . . . steel exports to the United States by an enormous percentage" yet "British Steel was now likely to be badly hurt by the American decision."[128] There was clear tension in Anglo-American relations caused by the impact of American policies on British industry. Apart from noting that he met Thatcher, Reagan did not elaborate on this meeting in his diary.[129] Likewise, Thatcher does not recall the meeting in her memoirs.[130] It had been a tense meeting, with Thatcher buoyed by her success in the Falklands and seeking further victories for British interests. Nonetheless, *The Times* viewed the meeting as a success for Thatcher, with the prime minister making her case to the Reagan administration about the exclusion of Argentina from discussions about the future sovereignty of the islands.[131] The message was likewise noted in Washington. The *Washington Post* quoted Haig as saying after the meeting: "We wouldn't expect anyone to tell us how to deal with our property, and we are not going to presume to tell her."[132]

Thatcher continued to pressure the Reagan administration about John Brown Engineering. In a meeting with Weinberger in September 1982,

Thatcher described the issue as "the only fly in the ointment," after they reviewed Anglo-American cooperation on issues such as the Falklands.[133] According to the US minutes of the meeting, the prime minster explained: "She badly needed some face-saving solution. She noted that she had supported the President at Versailles and that, in fact, she was the only one who did. . . . Mrs. Thatcher said she had some serious problems with unemployment and bankruptcies, and she didn't want her closest friend, the United States, to be blamed by her people." Weinberger responded by trying to assure Thatcher that the administration was "looking for some formula through which our differences could be minimized." Given the potential impact of the sanctions on some British companies, Thatcher observed that Weinberger would "understand what it would be like in a town in the United States with 20 percent unemployment if their main company went out of business." Thatcher was so determined to convince the Reagan administration to change course that she highlighted her commitment to supporting Reagan's economic agenda among allies but also noted that US foreign policy would potentially add to her domestic challenges—and was even prepared for the British public to blame the United States for any subsequent unemployment. Nonetheless, the conversation suggested that there was a path to a compromise given that there was consensus between the two governments on the sanctity of honoring contracts and the sensitivity when it came to the Eastern bloc of any transfer of technology from the West.[134]

Conclusion

Reagan and Thatcher's meetings in 1982 were certainly influenced by domestic concerns and their own priorities. It is clear that there was tension between Reagan and Thatcher, their domestic priorities and the demands of the global economy, and that American and British economic issues superseded those typically understood as foreign affairs. The president was defending his economic record in Europe in the context of concern among his western European partners. The Thatcher government was concerned about the impact of the American deficit and even discussed strongly advising the American president on domestic economic policy. International affairs dominated much of the proceedings, particularly the Falklands. Therefore, although domestic concerns influenced foreign policies of both Reagan and Thatcher, the Falklands War camouflaged Anglo-American international economic differences.

While a victory for Thatcher, the Reagan administration was concerned about the broader implications of Thatcher's success in the Falklands and her renewed mastery of the British political scene. Similarly, Thatcher resented Reagan's policy toward the Soviet Union that threatened the livelihoods of British workers and a long-standing British company in John Brown. Both leaders prioritized their own concerns—foreign and domestic—and were prepared to make the case for them in their meetings. Reagan's visit to Britain and his Westminster speech were even politicized by the British opposition parties, particularly the Labour Party. The Labour Party's threat to ultimately embarrass the American president even prompted Reagan to consider withdrawing from the speech altogether. The domestic and foreign spheres were clearly intertwined at the summits.

The meetings with Reagan did not lead to Thatcher gaining his full support in the key issues. The Falklands remained a source of tension in Anglo-American relations, with Reagan supporting Argentina's desire to negotiate sovereignty through the United Nations before the end of 1982. The disagreement about the Siberian pipeline and its impact on John Brown Engineering continued but was eased when the Reagan administration lifted the sanctions and allowed a single pipeline (not the originally planned two) to be built in 1983 (in return for western European limitations on technology exports to the Soviet Union, who would also receive low-interest loans from Western Europe).[135] Yet Thatcher's concerns about Reagan's economic policy continued and would be a source of many conversations in 1983–1984.

4

Reelections, 1983–1984

The summits between Ronald Reagan and Margaret Thatcher in the period 1983–1984 were contextualized by disagreements in economic policy and foreign affairs. Likewise, 1983 saw Thatcher's emphatic reelection as prime minister and, the following year, Reagan was reelected US president by a landslide. Buoyed by both of their respective political successes, Reagan and Thatcher prioritized domestic issues and ventured to influence each other to further those interests. Given the commonalities in their electoral focus and the continuing debate about some of these issues, the summits of 1983 and 1984 will be examined in one chapter. In addition to ongoing British concerns about the US budgetary deficit, 1983–1984 saw Thatcher attempt to utilize her relationship with Reagan to address issues related to economic extraterritoriality—namely, unitary taxation and the 1979 Export Administration Act, and the Freddie Laker case, which undermined her efforts to privatize British Airways. Likewise, Reagan sought to urge Thatcher to act positively on the Northern Ireland conflict, mainly as a means to foster much needed good relations with US House Speaker Thomas P. "Tip" O'Neill and other leading figures in the Democratic Party. The Democrats still controlled the House of Representatives (and after the 1986 midterms regained control of the Senate). The president, if he desired to pass legislation, had to work with his political opponents in order to implement his agenda. These issues are summarized below and, in turn, discussed in the various Anglo-American summits in the 1983–1984 period. Taken together with the summits between Reagan and Thatcher, it is clear that economic interests and the resulting implications for domestic politics continued to dominate thinking in London and Washington, DC.

During Thatcher's second term as prime minister (1983–1987), her privatization agenda continued with gusto. However, the Conservative government's plans to privatize British Airways were threatened by an American antitrust investigation into British Airways's involvement in the closure of Laker Airlines.[1] The case was ongoing between 1982 and 1985, during which British Airways was subject to twin legal investigations. As explored below, Reagan closed the Justice Department's investigation and later pressured the Export-Import (EXIM) Bank of the United States, which was Laker's main creditor, to facilitate an out-of-court settlement, allowing British Airways's privatization to continue. Likewise, there was tension regarding unitary taxation, meaning that the US companies could be taxed on their global income, not just their revenue from a particular state. Economic rivalry tensions also manifested themselves in Anglo-American relations. Unitary taxation referred to the issue of some American states taxing multinational companies on a level based on their total global income and not just that in a particular state. Extraterritoriality was therefore a cause for concern, particularly for the British.

G7 Economic Summit: May 28–30, 1983, Williamsburg, Virginia

In May, shortly before Thatcher's second general election victory (June 9, 1983), the major industrialized nations held their ninth multilateral summit. While the prime minister was unable to remain at the summit for its duration due to the election campaign, she was still able to meet with Reagan, and Howe was able to attend similarly high-profile meetings in order to promote Britain's economic interests. The US budgetary deficit was again the focus of much discussion, but the British government was also concerned about the impact of other American policies on the British economy—namely, extraterritoriality and antitrust actions taken against British Airways. The Thatcher government prioritized its economic policies and was even prepared to challenge the Reagan administration about its own agenda. This was a fulfilment of discussions before previous meetings with the two governments. Having secured the Falklands, Thatcher was emboldened to secure her government's economic objectives. Indeed, the Falklands victory meant that she was more confident in international diplomacy.

Before the summit, Thatcher welcomed Edwin Meese, counselor to the president, to Downing Street for a meeting on May 4.[2] Beginning the meeting, Thatcher observed how "it was important to damp down expectations about the Williamsburg Summit." For the prime minister, it was unrealistic "to expect new ideas" and therefore the summit should emphasize "the good elements in existing ideas." Indeed, the key purpose of economic summits was, according to Thatcher, "that the participants were encouraged to follow sensible economic policies, e.g., in combatting protectionism and in restraining inflation." Meese concurred, explaining: "President Reagan felt very strongly that we should try to lower expectations" with the summit simply being "an opportunity for meetings between world leaders and not a treaty-signing ceremony." Meese added that Reagan, however, prioritized an emphasis on "increased coordination and communications between the allies on economic policies, for example with regard to exchange rates." The Americans were seeking a coordinated response to the challenges of globalization, albeit on their terms. It was this that marked divergence in opinion between Reagan and Thatcher. The prime minister told Meese: "We must be very careful about referring to exchange rates" as such references might "be highly misleading." Instead, Thatcher argued: "All that we could usefully do was try to pursue stable economic policies. That was the way to achieve stable exchange rates." The United States' focus was therefore on exchange rates, while Thatcher insisted that American interest rates were the leading economic problem. Similarly, another issue of disagreement was Thatcher's disapproval of the support for protectionism in the US Congress. The prime minister commented that while she would be supportive of the Reagan administration in her media appearances in Washington, DC, she believed that "some of the protectionist measures of the United States Congress were objectionable." In reply Meese "suggested that she might make some general public references to protectionism in the United States."[3] The Reagan administration was therefore prepared for Thatcher to be critical of Congress and American economic positions, as long as she remained supportive of the president's agenda. Indeed, the *New York Times* observed that Reagan sought solidarity and vindication at the G7 summit. In addition to Thatcher's acknowledgment about the success of his economic policies, Reagan wanted other leaders to share in his vision for economic recovery.[4]

On arriving at Williamsburg, Thatcher twice met with Reagan bilaterally on May 28. The first meeting was a courtesy call and the second was a more substantial discussion.[5] When Thatcher raised "the question of the US budget deficit," Reagan replied "that he was convinced that the American economic recovery was linked to his tax cuts" and that if the cuts "were not fully implemented, the recovery would be aborted." The president also believed that the economic recovery prompted by supply-side policies would mean "that national income would rise and this process would by itself bring the deficit down substantially in 1985/86." In addition to her unease about the deficit, Thatcher also told Reagan of her fears of the wide-ranging problems that the Export Administration Act would cause in Europe. In reply, Reagan explained that he hoped that the bill before the House of Representatives would pass instead of that before the Senate, preferring the former as it would not ultimately "cause us much trouble" and the president's "powers under this legislation would of course be discretionary." The record states that after the meeting, Thatcher remarked "that there is little point, in the light of these arguments, in pressing the Americans further about the budget deficit." However, she was positive about the president's health as he "seemed much better and he was also much better informed."[6] Sir Geoffrey Howe, the chancellor of the exchequer, raised similar concerns with his American counterpart, Donald T. Regan, during their meeting that same day. The American deficit was therefore an issue in all meetings between senior British and American officials.

After discussing issues related to the summit, Howe moved the meeting on to issues of concern to the British government. Referring to the US-UK consultations on May 23–24 about American antitrust actions against the British airlines, Howe observed that he understood "that these had gone well," which was important for British Caledonian (an airline based in the southeast of England) and the "fundamental principle that inter-governmental agreements . . . should not be called in question by legal proceedings in national courts."[7] Secretary Regan promised to investigate the issue as the US Treasury had not participated in it so far. Just like Thatcher had with Reagan, Howe raised the Export Administration Act with Regan and stressed that extraterritoriality raised "very difficult issues" for the British government. Regan's reply echoed that of his president, albeit with more detail. He claimed that the bill, as had been amended in the House of Representatives, would enable the president "to intervene in respect of sales to the Soviet Union of equipment produced in the United States by US firms." The administration had resisted the original bill, which encompassed all "foreign firms selling to the Soviet Union US-designed products abroad." A rival bill had emerged in the Senate that proposed granting the president "powers to block imports in the US of products produced anywhere, whether or not the sales to the Soviet

Union by the firm in question, which were deemed to affect US security, were of US-designed equipment." The administration wanted a final bill that was "closer to that in the House than that in the Senate."[8]

Without a definitive response from Regan about extraterritoriality, Howe moved on to the US deficit, expressing concern about potentially increasing the deficit and the resulting impact on the markets, particularly with "very high real interest rates." Reagan's optimism when queried by Thatcher was equalled by Regan's refusal to accept the premise of Howe's position. The treasury secretary argued that "the alleged causal relationship between high deficits and high interest rates was a gray area" and he was therefore "unconvinced," although he was happy for his team to host a British economist "to work through the arguments." Clearly dissatisfied with Regan's response, Howe offered an account of his own experience, once again turning to his controversial 1981 budget as an example of the "importance of market perceptions." If markets expected that a deficit would continue to be high, then interest rates would follow suit. Howe explained: "We in the UK had faced a rather similar situation in 1980/81, and had resolved it in the 1981 Budget, when, at the depth of the recession, we had imposed sharp real increases in indirect taxation, and had not increased income tax allowances/thresholds at all." In turn, Regan offered a little more detail, although contradicting the president's explanation to Thatcher that the deficit would be quashed by economic growth caused by his tax cuts: "If the US deficit remained above 3% of GNP in 1985, increases in direct taxation would take effect" and "the proportion in 1985 would in fact be between 3 and 4%." Howe asked whether it would be sensible to envisage higher indirect taxes before then, based on the British experience in 1981, which "had demonstrated the value of convincing the markets of one's determination to put one's borrowing on a declining path." Regan simply "referred to difficulties in Congress."

Whereas President Reagan was convinced by the optimistic forecasts of his supply-side revolution, Secretary Regan grasped the political reality and therefore decided to worry about the economics in due course. Howe was much more concerned about the immediate economic and political situation, with the summit set to focus on the American deficit. He commented that he and his colleagues in Europe and Japan were worried about "the prospect that world-wide real interest rates would remain high, given the dominant influence of US financial markets." Regan again sought to sideline the significance of the deficit, arguing that "the latest evidence suggested that monetary policy would be likely to have more effect on interest rates than fiscal policy." Regan believed that limiting the growth of the money supply might, in turn, "change the picture again." Howe argued that "both fiscal and monetary policy were important," adding that the easing of the global recession would be risked "if interest rates remained high." Nonetheless, Howe ended the discussion in a conciliatory manner, welcoming Regan's offer to host a British economist in Washington. Regan again stressed that this "would be very welcome."[9] Despite the pleasantries, it is clear that there was disagreement between those responsible for the American and British Treasuries over how best to respond to shared economic challenges.

As Howe warned, the president had to defend the US deficit at length during the summit's plenary session on May 29.[10] Reagan argued that in terms of reducing the deficit, "The only answer is recovery." During the discussion, Howe suggested that high American interest rates were "retarding recovery" and affecting "domestic interest rates in Europe." George Shultz, having succeeded Alexander Haig as the secretary of state (1982–1989), defended Reagan: "No need for us to be defensive. Interest rates are down by 50 percent since 1981. We are making progress. Only reason why people react to high interest rates is because the President has been so fantastically successful in getting inflation down. Markets will respond to sound policies pursued with persistence and resolution. Deficits bigger than President wants: but tax increase now would be crazy: stop recovery in its tracks. The President has been very courageous and has been doing a hell of a job."[11] These economic debates continued when Thatcher visited Reagan in September 1983 for a bilateral summit. The meeting was contextualized by the prime minister's 1983 general election victory, in which she received a larger majority in the House of Commons. Reagan telephoned the prime minister to extend his congratulations and described her victory as "a shot in the arm for everyone."[12] On the Williamsburg summit, Reagan wrote to Thatcher and praised her government's economic performance: "The 'Williamsburg Declaration on Economic Recovery' was a victory for the future. Your Government's economic policies have proved the wisdom of the key principles laid out in the declaration. Non-inflationary growth, open markets, adequate liquidity and economic stability. I am certain that under your continued leadership, Britain will experience sustained economic growth."[13]

Yet Reagan refused to follow Thatcher's example in fiscal policy. What would have been particularly promising for Thatcher was Reagan's assurance that the United States would seek to address issues that were of particular concern to the British economic interests: "You have my solemn assurance, so far as the United States is concerned, that I shall now do everything in my power to translate the commitments we made together at Williamsburg into tangible legislative action. With that end in mind, I met with the bipartisan leadership of the Congress on June 8 and urged early progress on anti-protectionist measures, increasing our IMF quotas, and further limits on the growth of federal expenditures as a means to reduce budgetary deficits."[14] Thatcher would seek to ensure that Reagan delivered on these assurances. The British were clearly unconvinced by the president's approach to the American budgetary deficit and his grasp of its impact on his allies' economic fortunes.

Thatcher Visits the United States, September 1983

Unitary taxation was upheld in the United States in June 1983 when the US Supreme Court upheld the right of California to tax a business based on its income from within and outside of the state following an appeal by the Container Corporation.[15] In response, the Reagan administration created a commission to investigate this.[16] But Reagan abandoned the issue and decided not to call for a rehearing of the case at the Supreme Court.[17] Unitary taxation remained a point of concern for British industry.[18] In September 1983, Thatcher twice appealed to Reagan to help legislate a ban on unitary taxation.[19] Charles Hill, executive secretary at the State Department, summarized Thatcher's letters for the president. Thatcher argued that unitary taxation was "totally contrary to international practice" and "involves heavy compliance costs" while undermining "efforts to relieve double taxation," which makes it "a disincentive to investment in the US" and may encourage less industrialized countries "to adopt the same method."[20] Reagan established another administrative working group.[21] However, the president declined to act again, writing to Thatcher and stating politely that her "clear and forthright explanation of British views will be taken fully into account as we continue to review the complex set of economic, legal, and constitutional issues involved in unitary taxation."[22]

There was a clear determination within the Thatcher government to succeed in convincing the Reagan administration of the errors of their economic policies and persuade them to operate in a way that was much more favorable to British economic interests. The relationship between the prime minister and the president was crucial to the achievement of this objective. Ambassador Oliver Wright wrote to the Foreign and Commonwealth Office (FCO) that "the official talks which we have had in the past on issues of extraterritoriality . . . have not yet led anywhere because of inertia, confusion and perhaps deliberate prevarication by the various Washington agencies involved."[23] Thus, as the president was "the sole source of executive power," Wright argued that "the most important outcome of the discussions between the President and the Prime Minister on stress-related subjects should be a directive to our respective bureaucracies to get together."[24] This was factored into the "Game Plan" developed in Downing Street by Robert Armstrong and A. J. Coles.[25] For the hour-long tête-à-tête with Reagan, Thatcher was to be advised to cover East-West relations; follow-up on the economic summit at Williamsburg and forthcoming 1984 summit in London; Central America, Belize, and the Falklands; and bilateral issues. These bilateral issues included the Export Administration Act, unitary taxation, and the role of antitrust laws in the Laker case. Armstrong was clear in the ambition for the meeting: "An important objective here is to strengthen our hand in the follow-up with US officials." This was echoed in Armstrong's advice for the working lunch for the American and British parties: the prime minister might wish to revisit the tête-à-tête topics during the more widely attended lunch so that members of the administration would know what was on Reagan's mind.[26] Thatcher was therefore armed with a cogent plan for the summit.

The Reagan administration anticipated British priorities in its briefings for the president. Memoranda from both Shultz and William Clark reflected a report dispatched by John Louis, the US ambassador to Britain (1981–1983), to the secretary of state on September 15, 1983, about Thatcher's forthcoming visit to Washington. It was Louis who passed on the much-repeated comment in American briefings from Thatcher's Cabinet Office foreign policy adviser (Charles Powell) that "to an extent, the trip itself is the message."[27] Clark warned Reagan that while Thatcher "remains among your strongest supporters," she "will have much on her mind."[28] Similarly, Shultz advised: "In her customary style, Thatcher will speak plainly about British interests and concerns, expecting us to respond in a similar fashion."[29] In addition to briefing the president on Thatcher's approach to issues such as the East-West relationship, the Middle East, and Central and South America, Shultz summarized the economic issues that would be raised. The president was briefed that Thatcher would "underline the fragility of the European economic recovery in the face of what she considers to be high US interest rates." In addition it was expected that the prime minister would express her concern about unitary taxation (and seek Reagan's support for forthcoming legislation against it) and wish to discuss "extraterritoriality," specifically the importance of "legislation to limit the use of export controls for foreign policy purposes." Shultz advised Reagan to "reiterate that we are mindful of British concerns regarding extraterritoriality, which is extraordinarily complicated and involves questions of basic national interest."[30] Before Thatcher's arrival in Washington, both sides therefore anticipated the subsequent disagreements between the two governments.

The day before meeting Reagan and other leading American political figures, Thatcher dined with some American industrialists and politicians. After the dinner, the party discussed economic policy in Britain and the United States. The prime minister defined her approach to the economy as one "based on the principle that expenditure had to be paid for."[31] Therefore, given that her government had not succeeded in reducing public expenditure to the level it had wished at the start of its term, they "reluctantly increased taxation." Thatcher believed that it was vital not to "mislead people into thinking they could have something for nothing." She was equally candid in her remarks about American economic policy. Thatcher's criticism of unitary taxation and its "damaging consequences" for the interests of American business was greeted "with particular enthusiasm by the American industrialists." Two prominent guests equalled Thatcher's candor. Martin Feldstein, who served as chairman of the council of economic advisers to Reagan (1982–1984), shared his criticism of Reaganomics. He argued that even though "the American economy had exceeded the best expectations of the Administration," he recognized that the budgetary deficit was causing "tremendous damage. . . . I don't know what the Administration's position is any more." Senator Peter Wilson (R-CA), also in attendance, offered a comment on the broader political picture, which was naturally not a priority for an economist such as Feldstein. Wilson blamed the Democrats for being unwilling to control expenditure. He claimed that if the White House followed the British example of raising taxes, it would only lead to increased spending by Congress, just as it had done in the past. Despite the politics of the deficit, it is clear that its economic significance was a cause for concern by both Reagan's leading international ally and his leading economic adviser.[32]

The following morning, on September 29, 1983, Thatcher met with the Senate Foreign Relations Committee for a breakfast meeting.[33] After discussing East-West relations, arms control, British and French nuclear forces, and Lebanon, the prime minister addressed the Falklands War. Thatcher was clear that she would not negotiate sovereignty with the Argentinians, as the Falkland islanders "were all British and wanted to stay British." She added that she hoped the United States "as a democracy, fully understood this." After a discussion about international trade, the meeting turned to the US budget deficit. The prime minister explained that the deficit would be tackled through taxation or lower public spending and that her government had enjoyed some success in this. Nonetheless, Thatcher was clear that "she would not presume to give the US Administration advice; but the US deficit was a worrying factor which affected the prospects for economic recovery for us all." On unitary taxation, Thatcher welcomed Senator Charles Mathias (R-MD) calling it an "abomination in the tax system." She argued that the recent American decision was "disastrous, not least because of the example it would set to other countries" and she "would continue to press for it to be reversed." When quizzed by Senator Paul Tsongas (D-MA) about developments in Northern Ireland, Thatcher "stressed the overwhelming wish of the majority community to remain British," adding that her government valued its close cooperation with the Irish government.[34] Domestic issues were discussed in a meeting that was ostensibly dedicated to foreign relations.

Thatcher subsequently met with Paul Volcker, chairman of the Federal Reserve, and then Donald Regan. According to the British record of her meeting with Volcker, it became clear that he differed with the Reagan administration on the point of the US deficit.[35] In response to Thatcher's admission "that she was worried about the deficit," Volcker concurred: "The deficit was a time-bomb." He disagreed with the administration's view that "economic growth would itself reduce the deficit" or with the administration's belief that should Congress be "starved of revenue" it would act to bring down expenditure."[36] The prime minister was clearly trying to cultivate Volcker as a key ally in Washington on economic issues who could, effectively, support the British position. Rather than dwell on the deficit when meeting Regan, Thatcher focused on unitary taxation "because she was desperately worried about it."[37] The prime minister argued: "If governments could not reach agreement on double taxation arrangements, they could not reach agreement on anything." She added layers to this argument: "There was a basic principle that countries taxed only the income arising in their own territory. If the United States Government went beyond this, it would play into the hands of those in Great Britain who were arguing for wider action against multi-national companies, and also into the hands of developing countries who would try to make up their aid receipts through taxation of multi-national companies." Thus, Thatcher believed that the administration's decision not to intervene in the Container Corporation case was actually "a bad decision in political terms," and it could therefore "be an own goal." Accordingly, "it was essential" that the designated working group (comprised of stakeholders, such as heads of multinational companies and representatives of groups opposed to unitary taxation) "reach conclusions quickly and consult a representative range of interests." The prime minister continued to advocate stronger intervention by the White House, explaining that "it would be helpful" if the administration would issue a strong public statement against unitary taxation. In response, Secretary Regan argued such a statement was problematic for the president as the Supreme Court decided that it was a legal action by states, although "there were other forms of pressure upon the states." Indeed, as Regan explained, "States were banned by the US Constitution from taking action which interfered with international relations, and it was clear from the present conversation that unitary taxation *was* damaging international relations." After again emphasizing "the urgency of the matter," Thatcher remarked "that she was worried about wider developments affecting the management of the United States economy." Referring to the deficit, she observed that American fiscal policy was almost tantamount to "a reversion to Keynesian," although she was content for this issue to "be pursued at the working lunch" (after her one-on-one meeting with the president).[38] The prime minister had gone beyond being a proponent of the British national interest—she was directly challenging the competence of the Reagan administration to manage the American economy.

The day's first meeting between Reagan and Thatcher focused on events in Lebanon, East-West relations and arms control, the Intermediate-Range Nuclear Forces (INF) negotiations, and Central America (particularly Belize and Nicaragua).[39] According to the British record, the subsequent working lunch—featuring the broader parties—turned to economic matters.[40] The British clearly wanted all relevant protagonists, including the president, in the same room in order to further their economic concerns. Indeed, Thatcher shared with the meeting that—as per the game plan—she had earlier discussed her "serious objections" to unitary taxation with Secretary Regan and that heads of US multinationals, with whom she dined the night before, agreed with her stance. The record notes: "At this point the President left to take a telephone call," although Regan replied that he understood Thatcher's view on unitary taxation. Thatcher asked the treasury secretary to comment on the American economy. He admitted that "the question which preoccupied the Administration was when a sizable deficit began to affect investment and slow down recovery." Regan argued "that this would not occur in the next twelve months" and that, in contrast to others, he did not believe the US deficit "would reach $200 billion." The treasury secretary then offered both an economic forecast and policy proposal:

> If real growth of 4½–5% could be maintained over the next twelve months, then 10% nominal growth in GNP should be achievable. A deficit next year of $165–$170 billion dollars could be reasonably prophesied. If money supply were kept within the intended bracket of 5–9%, then it should be possible to sustain real growth of 4½–5% without inflation. However, the deficit was huge and it would be necessary to come to grips with it eventually. If growth did not deal with the deficit then it would be necessary to cut spending or raise revenue. He preferred the former.

Thatcher observed that if Regan's analysis was correct "then interest rates should soon fall." Regan elaborated that "we should not look at prime rates. Large corporations were borrowing at 10–10½%. Brokers loans were paying only 10–10⅛%." The prime minister responded that such high interest rates, which particularly affected small businesses, "were our worst problem and were reining back recovery." Attempting to shift the focus of the discussion, Regan claimed that "the increase in the American trade deficit was due to global factors," such as the Iraq-Iran War's impact on the oil supply. Thatcher returned the conversation to interest rates, advocating an aim "to get interest rates down to 3–4% in real terms."[41] According to the American record, Thatcher outlined the importance of the US deficit in connection to international security. She argued for the importance of sustained European recovery as otherwise the "political pressures against defense spending will become enormous." This was because slow economic growth meant that defense spending simply increased as a proportion of GDP. For Thatcher, the economy connected the domestic and foreign policy, as "a sustained recovery is necessary both to improve the standard of living and to increase defense spending." Yet the prime minister was determined to associate this issue with that of the US deficit as, for the British economy, "high interest rates are the worst aspect of the current situation" as international debt is hurting exports as "Third World demand had dropped."[42] Having returned to the working lunch, the president contributed to the discussion on interest rates:

> The *President* said that certain banks were now making available large sums for home mortgages at 9.9%. He had recently seen a TV advert offering car loans for 8.8%. Another factor keeping interest rates high was the fear that artificial stimulation might be used, as in the past, to bring the economy out of recession. People were not yet quite sure that it was possible to obtain growth without inflation. But inflation had been 2.6% in the last twelve months and this was the lowest for twenty-three years. The need was to convince people that the recovery was real.[43]

In response to Reagan's now familiar explanation, Howe simply stated that "the very size of the deficit posed the risk of inflation taking off again."[44] According to the American record, Howe caveated his contribution by jokingly remarking that "he had promised himself that the ex-Chancellor of the Exchequer should stay out of this discussion."[45] Howe underscored that "the size of the US deficit causes Britain great anxiety" as "longer term repercussions could be severe." The debate was closed: the president interjected that it was time to meet with the press and thanked Mrs. Thatcher for the useful discussion. Wanting to have the last word, Thatcher "expressed great appreciation for the President's warm hospitality and the valuable discussions."[46] The British contingent was determined to emphasize their argument about the importance of the American deficit—but the president was clearly unwilling to do more than politely listen.

The British government was certainly pleased with Thatcher's visit to Washington. The British Embassy informed the FCO that it was "a highly successful visit" in which the prime minister "pulled no punches on bilateral and other problems."[47] The embassy noted: "The strength of the UK/US relationship and the rapport which the Prime Minister has with the President and senior members of his Administration mean that the Americans expect forthright discussion of contentious issues."[48] Thatcher's receipt of the Winston Churchill Award in Washington, DC, on September 29 was viewed to be a highlight, particularly as a letter of congratulations from the president was read during the ceremony.[49] The audience included leading figures in the Reagan administration: Regan, Volcker, Jeane Kirkpatrick (US ambassador to the United Nations, 1981–1985), and Shultz.[50] There remained a desire to publicly celebrate Anglo-American relations and the commonalities between Reaganism and Thatcherism. After their White House meeting, Reagan offered an unsurprising description of the talks, focusing on international affairs: "Our conversations reflected the superb relations that exist between our two countries and our determination to broaden our cooperation and consultation."[51] The president added: "We'll carry out our commitments to the alliance, moving forward in the modernization of NATO's conventional and nuclear deterrent. At the same time, I have pledged America's best efforts to reach acceptable agreements on arms reduction with the Soviet Union."[52] On economic affairs, Reagan offered a sweeping summary: "We reaffirmed the course set out at the Williamsburg summit as the best blueprint to sustain economic recovery and counter protectionism," and "agreed on the need for continued close consultations as a means of resolving any differences between us in matters of trade and commerce."

However, clearly buoyed by the victories in the South Atlantic and the recent general election, Thatcher essentially claimed to be representing the wider western world and not just the United Kingdom in what she described as "a very important" visit that included talks about issues that are "extremely vital for the future of our peoples in our several countries." Confident in her brief and certain in her beliefs, Thatcher first commented on the economic issues that were her clear priority: "I've also seen, earlier this morning, Secretary Regan, when we discussed economic matters and, in particular, the problems of unitary taxation. I saw, too, Mr. Volcker, because naturally we are all concerned that the great international debt position should find a solution which enables trade to continue and those countries to come out of their grievous debt problems."[53] Issues in which she offered complete support to the administration were tied with the president rather than others in the administration, particularly the president's approach to East-West relations: "Our purpose in having military strength is entirely defensive—to defend our way of life." Thatcher closed her remarks with her unsurprising commitment to the "special relationship," saying, "It's not surprising that we find common views and we pursue them with common purpose in the wider world."[54]

Still, Thatcher continued to raise the economic differences between her government and the Reagan administration during her press conference at the British Embassy after she had left the White House.[55] The prime minister was clearly frustrated by the lack of progress on the issue. When asked whether anything could be done about unitary taxation, the prime minister replied: "I think something will have to be done about it. That is very much the message we put across and it is very much the message which American businessmen also put across to me." On the Export Administration Act, Thatcher commented: "We are very anxious, as you know, about it. It can cause immense troubles and, as you know, we are absolutely against extraterritorial jurisdiction and we made those views known." The prime minister continued to be forthcoming. Asked if she was encouraging Reagan to raise taxation in response to the American budgetary deficit, Thatcher offered an account of the British experience: "We got our expenditure down a certain way but we are not able to get it down further and it meant higher taxation than I otherwise would have wished, but the higher taxation was necessary, we thought, if we were to carry on with those levels of expenditure."[56] This echoed Thatcher's remarks to the administration. She continued: "I believe it has to be brought home to those who demand more public expenditure that it must be covered in large measure by taxation." Nonetheless, this philosophical response was insufficient for the journalists. A follow-up question inquired whether this approach should also apply to the United States. Thatcher's reply was both a justification of her economic policy and a critique of Reagan's—although he was not named once:

> That is a matter for the US to decide. We in fact did, in the 1981 budget, decide that we were not going to go the way of big budget deficits; that had we gone that way it was a problem for the future and we did not wish to have that great problem hanging over our heads. I think that because the United States has a big deficit, that the interest rate is a good deal higher than it would otherwise be, because although inflation is lower and therefore you would expect the interest rates to be lower, people believe that the existence of a big deficit will lead to renewed inflation and therefore they are not going to lend money on long-term loans to the government based on

> the present rates of inflation, but on what they believe will happen in the future and therefore they are demanding higher interest rates. That is bad from the viewpoint of prolonged recovery and it is particularly tough in Europe because we want recovery and our interest rates are higher than they otherwise would be because of the American interest rates.[57]

Thatcher's criticism of American policy—and the damage it was doing to Britain's economy in Britain—continued. Asked about Britain's economic recovery, the prime minister argued that "all recoveries are affected by high interest rates."[58] The American press noted that despite the declarations of the closeness in Anglo-American relations, the prime minister remained concerned about Reagan's economic policies, particularly the deficit.[59] Thatcher's message to the Reagan administration about extraterritoriality was also included in her report to the British Cabinet. The prime minister explained that she had told Reagan and Regan "that the American position on unitary taxation was unacceptable and would in the long run damage United States interests" while European allies were anxious "about the United States deficit and the damaging effects of extra-territorial legislation."[60] After two years in planning, Thatcher had chosen her time to raise concerns about the impact of the economic policies of her political "soul mate"—but she did so privately and publicly. Thatcher wanted British voters to be aware of her efforts. Yet within a few months, it would be Thatcher who would be embarrassed by her claims of a "special relationship" when the United States invaded Grenada, a member of the British Commonwealth, without consulting the British prime minister.

Grenada and the Visit of Kenneth Dam, US Deputy Secretary of State

On November 7, 1983, Thatcher welcomed Kenneth Dam, the deputy secretary of state (1982–1985), to Downing Street. The visit proved to be part of the Reagan administration's strategy to maintain positive relations with the prime minister following the United States' military intervention in Grenada on October 25, 1983. The meeting proved to be an opportunity for Thatcher to continue to express her frustration about the lack of consultation about the action and forensically dissect the American account of events.

The Reagan administration was startled by a violent coup on October 16, 1983, by a radical Marxist faction inside the Grenada government. Maurice Bishop, the prime minister, was murdered and replaced by his former deputy, Bernard Coard. The new regime was a short-lived: Coard was executed after just three days and a new military government, led by General Hudson Austin, assumed power. The president was greatly alarmed by these developments. Reagan believed that Grenada risked becoming a new Cuba, ensuring that the east-Caribbean region would be a crucial Cold War battleground. An appeal from the Organisation of East Caribbean States (OECS) and concern for American students in Grenada prompted American military action.[61] The administration also pointed to the need to secure the safe return of American medical students to the United States as a justification for the intervention. The British government did not share these American worries. Sir Geoffrey Howe, the British foreign secretary (1983–1989), stated that he was unfamiliar with Grenada before the American action. In fact, Thatcher was not consulted on the planned intervention despite Grenada's membership in the British Commonwealth. The foreign secretary even confidently informed the House of Commons that he did not anticipate any American action on the issue.[62]

When Reagan spoke with Thatcher about her views on the possibility of American action, at the same time as the decision for such action was taken, the prime minister was adamant that it would be a mistake. The president left a meeting with the chairman of the Joint Chiefs of Staff, George Shultz (US secretary of state, 1982–1989), Caspar Weinberger (the US defense secretary), and congressional leaders, in order to speak with Thatcher, who had telephoned to plead her case. It was a one-sided conversation. Reagan's contribution was limited to: "Margaret . . . but Margaret." Unsurprisingly, Reagan informed the meeting that "Mrs. Thatcher has strong reservations about this."[63] However, the president's decision had already been made. Reagan diarized: "She was upset & doesn't think we should do it. I couldn't tell her it had started."[64] Thus, in reality the president had not consulted the prime minister. Recognizing Thatcher's embarrassment, he telephoned her on October 26, 1983, in order to apologize for not sharing his plans. Reagan even compared himself to a cowboy who was expecting a stern greeting upon returning home: "If I were there, Margaret . . . I'd thrown my hat in the door before I came in." The joke was unsuccessful and Thatcher's reply was short: "There's no need to do that." He then offered a lengthy version of events which had led to the decision to undertake military action, explaining that she was not told because of his administration's fear of a leak. Thatcher remained silent and did not interrupt the president's exposition, although she finally lost patience. When Reagan said that he hoped the United States would be able to help Grenada reinstall the former constitution since its suspension by the coup, the prime minister noted that it was suspended in 1979 by the former government. Despite Reagan's apology for causing any embarrassment, Thatcher clearly wanted to finish the conversation.[65] Grenada underscored the political reality that the president would always prioritize his own interests over those of her government, but this incident saw Britain clearly downgraded in American thinking. Grenada is a Commonwealth country and Reagan did not even inform Thatcher as a courtesy of his intention to invade. Thus, Thatcher's much vaunted special relationship with Reagan had not afforded her any special access or influence in Washington.

The incident certainly strained Anglo-American relations. Shultz recalled in his memoir that he and Reagan "felt that she was just plain wrong" and the president "had supported her in the Falklands. . . . He was deeply disappointed."[66] When Reagan was asked in the future by a senior British politician why he had not warned Thatcher about American action, he simply explained: "Because I didn't want her to say no."[67] Thatcher was politically embarrassed. Neil Kinnock, the leader of the Labour Party (1983–1992), declared in the House of Commons that "the relationship that was said to exist between the right hon. Lady and the President turned out to be not so special."[68] Kinnock was right; however, Thatcher did not remain quiet on the issue. During a BBC world-service interview on October 30, 1983, Thatcher argued that if western countries, including the United States, simply invaded countries that had embraced communism internally, it would lead to countless wars around the world.[69] The American press reported on the embarrassment caused to Thatcher by the incident, and her opposition to American military action.[70] However, there were other reasons for Reagan's decision to intervene in Grenada that were simply beyond any influence that Thatcher might have mustered, and arguably beyond saving American students or acting on a leftist coup. The president was determined to exercise painful national memories of Vietnam and show the wider world that the United States was prepared to act militarily and would do so successfully. The situation in Grenada coincided with the bombing of Beirut in Lebanon. As H. W. Brands observes, "The complexities of the Middle East prevented him [Reagan] from responding in Lebanon as forcefully as he wished he could, but these constraints simply rendered more necessary a demonstration of American power elsewhere."[71]

Thatcher and Sir Geoffrey Howe met with Deputy Secretary of State Kenneth Dam to discuss a variety of issues, including Grenada, the INF, Iran-Iraq, Lebanon, the Middle East, and the Falklands.[72] Grenada was inevitably the first topic of conversation. Thatcher was candid in her opening remarks, stating that "the basic question she needed to ask about Grenada was whether it was a one-off operation" or whether there was "a new policy which might embrace other crisis areas such as Nicaragua." Dam explained that while "he could not predict far into the future," Grenada was viewed by the administration "as a very special situation." The United States government "certainly wished to limit the implications of Grenada as a precedent, not least because the Soviet Union might exploit the precedent," although he admitted that the White House would offer statements "designed to make the regime in Nicaragua more uncertain." According to Dam, the uniqueness of the situation in Grenada stemmed from the "chaos on the island and much concern about the US students there." Upon the students' return to America, "it had become clear that they had considered themselves to be in danger," and a subsequent visit by a bipartisan Congress group to Grenada confirmed "that there had been danger to US students." Thatcher's candor continued. She commented that "it was puzzling that the American citizens had not left Grenada if they had felt themselves in danger." The prime minister noted that according to the deputy high commissioner from Barbados, British citizens had not appeared to feel under threat when he visited Grenada on October 23. He did not request intervention when he contacted the British government at this time. Defending the administration's stance, Dam argued that the US consular staff had contacted four hundred American students at that time, "many of whom said that they did feel insecure," with some even "trying to leave in small boats." After Dam claimed that there had been "a curfew in operation and no functioning Government," Howe "pointed out that the curfew was being relaxed in Grenada on 24 October."

Clearly not convincing his hosts, Dam argued, "It was the request of the OECS countries together with the Governor-General's request which had largely prompted US action." Thatcher explained that according to the Jamaican prime minister, there was "no written request before 26 October." Dam attempted to play down this fact on the basis that "the Governor-General was in a hazardous position," although Thatcher again disputed this. Despite the

British protestations, Dam was adamant that "the US Government had learned from Barbados that the Governor-General had made a request." The prime minister clearly remained angered by the intervention in Grenada. She told Dam that "all the signals we had received had pointed to the fact that the United States was not likely to intervene." Therefore, the government told Parliament on October 24, that there was no forthcoming American invasion and nothing to suggest this had changed when she had exchanged messages with Reagan that evening. Thatcher wryly suggested that Reagan's decision to act on Grenada subsequently "put us in difficulty . . . to put it very mildly."[73] The prime minister may not have directly lambasted the president's decision to intervene in Grenada, but she did not hide her frustration from Dam. Thatcher's American guest was being subjected to a forensic questioning about American policy.

Reagan's decision to not warn Thatcher of the military action was clearly an open wound for the prime minister. Dam's explanation represented continuity with the administration's explanation but was also a subtle criticism of the British government's naivety. He noted that while Washington "very much regretted this," Dam would not "defend the lack of consultation" as the Americans had been in communication with the British Embassy in Washington "throughout the weekend and the newspapers had been full of invasion stories." Furthermore, as Dam explained, the British were the only government that they had consulted. Repeating Reagan's explanation about leaks in his administration, Dam added that the decision to invade "was very closely held" due to "a terrible problem of leaks."[74] The prime minister and foreign secretary remained skeptical. Howe offered a subtle criticism based on the workings of the bilateral relationship. He observed that "the worrying feature was that, despite our close relationship and good secure communications, we had received no indication on 24 October of the shift in American thinking. The closer cooperation was the more one relied on it." Thatcher was typically much more direct. Referring to her recent experience with the Falklands War, she argued that "she was the first to understand that where the lives of soldiers were at stake, one had to be very careful. But all the information had tended to support the view that America would not intervene." Furthermore, Thatcher suggested that the Grenada incident had undermined the credibility of Anglo-American relations and her ability to support American foreign policy. She noted that, due to the implications of Grenada, "we had decided to have an early vote in the House of Commons on Cruise missile deployments. . . . People argued that if the Americans did not consult us over

Grenada, why should they do so over the firing of missiles." Similarly, Thatcher noted that "it was now more difficult for her if asked, for example, whether the United States would go into Nicaragua, to defend the Administration's actions. She would simply have to say that she did not answer for the United States." Dam's reply was timid and was clearly designed to move the conversation on: "Grenada and Nicaragua were two totally different situations." After discussing the INF, and the situation in Lebanon and the Middle East, Thatcher again criticized the Reagan administration, this time on its plans to sell arms to Argentina. Thatcher stated that "this would put us in acute difficulty" as it would be viewed in the public arena "as having one purpose—to build up the Argentine potential to fight the United Kingdom." In turn, the prime minister "would have to be vigorously critical—and the decision could have other repercussions on public opinion."[75]

Thus, Thatcher's message to the Reagan administration was clear: recent events had problematized her ability to advocate in her country, and beyond, the merits of British support for American foreign policy. This undermined Thatcher's credibility as a partner for Reagan in foreign affairs and the credence of the president's agenda more generally. Unsurprisingly, the meeting closed with a resolve to focus on future policy making, with an agreement that in subsequent press briefings about the meeting, "both sides would emphasise that, with regard to Grenada, it was the future that was important and that it was for the legitimate authority in Grenada and for the OECS to consider the next steps."[76] After Grenada, the Reagan administration made a concerted effort to offer Thatcher meetings with a variety of officials to maintain consultation on US foreign policy. As discussed below, this continued into 1984 and, in return, Thatcher maintained her pressure on the Reagan administration about economic issues that impacted on British policy making. Yet Thatcher had mixed success. In May 1984, Reagan informed Thatcher that a solution had been agreed by the Worldwide Unitary Tax Working Group in the form of a "water's edge" approach that would limit how unitary taxation would be applied in future.[77] He explained it would apply to American and foreign-based companies and should satisfy Thatcher's "concerns about the taxation of British multinationals in the United States," and assured her that he would "argue that the States implement this recommendation as quickly as possible."[78] This "water's edge" solution limited unitary taxation to income generated in the United States.[79] Although this agreement relied on individual states' acquiescence, the president was "confident that competition between the states for new investment will spur them to act quickly on this issue," and noted that many "state officials, as you have probably heard, have recently expressed reservations over continued use of the unitary method."[80] Despite Reagan's sympathy toward Thatcher's frustration, he did not act any further than to provide a state-by-state solution or try to convince Congress to legislate on the issue.

June 1984

The G7 summit in June 1984 and the fortieth anniversary of the Second World War D-Day invasion of France by the Allies provided the White House with ample scope to gather material for Reagan's reelection campaign. The Republican campaign focused on Reagan's achievements in office, which they claimed, led to a rediscovered positive view of American prospects. In 1984, Reagan enjoyed high approval ratings while his potential Democratic challengers were in disarray. In June 1984, Reagan visited Francc for D-Day commemorations and declared June 6 as a "day of national honor." In contrast, the Democrats were divided between the former US vice president Walter Mondale (1977–1981) and Senator Gary Hart (Colorado, 1975–1987) as they sought the party's presidential nomination. Aside from extensive media coverage of Reagan's visit to France, a political advertisement was inevitably released by his campaign, which showed the president's address to veterans at ceremonies and his description of them as "products of the freest society in history."[81] Perhaps unsurprisingly, Reagan enjoyed a job approval rating of 54 percent at the end of June 1984.[82] Thatcher, hosting the G7 summit, ensured that it was an uneventful gathering which would not undermine the economic claims of Reagan's campaign. Nonetheless, British concerns about the American deficit remained. For instance, Nigel Lawson, Howe's successor as chancellor of the exchequer (1983–1989), briefed the Cabinet about recent turbulence in the financial markets: "Stock markets had fallen in the United States, the United Kingdom and elsewhere as a result of concern about the banking system following the difficulties of Continental Illinois Bank. The underlying problems remained the size of the United States' deficit, the effect of high interest rates in the United States and the problems of some debtor countries, particularly those in South America."[83] British complaints about economic issues were included in the National Safety Council briefing for the president about his European trip. However, the public relations dimensions were also prevalent as the White House turned its attention to the November presidential election.[84] Reagan was informed: "The settings for the visits are both dramatic and colourful. The return home to Ireland, the lessons and sacrifices associated with Normandy, and the historical stability of London provide an ideal backdrop for your central themes of peace, prosperity, and Alliance solidarity." He was warned that during his bilateral meetings with Thatcher, she "may complain about unitary taxation, protectionism and extra-territoriality, but overall our views on international issues are in step." Normandy was described as "the public affairs highlight of your trip."[85] Shultz's briefing for the president noted that since his last meeting with Thatcher in 1983, Anglo-American relations had "come under severe strain from several sources."[86] The secretary of state attributed this to Grenada, British opinion that the US government favored Israeli interests in the Middle East, British disapproval of the mining of Nicaraguan ports, and American opposition to Britain's ongoing arms sales to Iran. However, Shultz argued that "bilateral economic issues constitute the most chronic irritant in the relationship." He noted that the administration was "actively working to overcome the bilateral frictions," such as "extraterritoriality." On Thatcher's request, there had been more informal and frequent political consultations, such as visits from George H. W. Bush, Weinberger, Regan, Meese, Shultz himself, and various subcabinet officials. Likewise, British ministers were "frequent visitors in Washington discussing everything from monetary policy to the Middle East." The administration's approach to easing Thatcher's concerns was, at least according to Shultz's briefing, a success. Nevertheless, tensions over economic policy loomed over the summit. Shultz advised Reagan that the prime minister would "probably express her concerns about the link between the US deficit, interest rates, and the world economy" and comment on unitary taxation if it has still not been resolved to her satisfaction. The president was encouraged to "reiterate our position that the US deficit does not determine world interest rates and outline our reasons for optimism about the US economy."[87] The same central issues therefore continued to dominate the economic aspect of Anglo-American relations.

Hobart Rowen, writing in the *Washington Post,* reported that Reaganomics was likely to be subject to criticism by the president's fellow world leaders at the G7.[88] However, Downing Street fully understood the campaign politics that contextualized Reagan's visit. In turn, the British were willing to play their part in ensuring a smooth summit for Reagan and his electoral ambitions. The

British embassy briefed the government that Reagan's priority for his time in London was "an outcome that will play well in his election campaign."[89] Reagan wanted to be seen as "presidential" and receive an endorsement that the "domestic policy objectives which the President (and indeed most of his summit partners) has been pursuing have paid off in terms of economic recovery." Aware of continued concern about the American deficit and interest rates, the White House would brief the president to address those issues, but hoped that his G7 colleagues would be "content to handle the issues in as noncontentious and low-key a manner as possible" and were already "appreciative of the efforts of the President's British hosts have been making to achieve this."[90]

The G7 certainly obliged the president in downplaying their concern for the US deficit. In its conference declaration, deficits are referenced once—and even then, it is halfway through the declaration and without any specific reference to the United States. The G7 agreed to continue strengthening policies designed to lower inflation and interest rates, reduce deficits, and control monetary growth. The declaration focused on inflation and job creation (which were highlighted in Reagan's campaign as successful issues for his economic program), and other issues included developing countries and trade liberalization.[91] Thatcher sought to deflect questions about the American deficit during her press conference at the summit. Asked whether the communiqué referred to the American deficit, the prime minister explained: "I think you should address that question to the United States. I think, if you look at the percentage of GDP which is represented by the deficit, you will find quite a number of countries may wish to reduce their deficit, so it does not necessarily apply only to one country but to quite a number. We have, after all, taken strenuous steps to reduce our own deficit, thank goodness. . . . I am not going to mention any countries. You must ask each of them."[92] This was a markedly different emphasis to those Thatcher made at her press conference after meeting Reagan at the White House in 1983. The prime minister was clearly trying to avoid any criticism of the economic policies of the Reagan administration. The president followed suit during his press conference on June 10. The president also—unsurprisingly—pivoted the discussion back to his campaign agenda by stressing the success of Reaganomics and its inspiration for other countries: "In '81, the economies of the seven major industrialized nations represented here at the summit had an average growth rate of 1.8 percent, with an 8 ½ percent inflation. Today, our average growth rate has risen to 4 percent, while inflation has been cut in half. And in our own country, we've created more than 6 million jobs in the last 18 months."[93] Defending his administration's record and rejecting the connection previously made by other leaders between the American deficit and interest rates, the president argued that "the connection between deficit and interest rates cannot be established at all." In addition, Reagan claimed: "Right now our deficit as a percentage of gross national product is lower than that of three other nations that were present, and one nation alone was lower than ours, and one nation was tied with ours."[94] Thatcher discussed the protection of Reagan's economic record in a Cabinet meeting on June 14, 1984. Again, she was ensuring that the emphasis on discussions about American policy was kinder than in previous debates. The prime minister explained: "It had been a businesslike and successful occasion, although firm action had been necessary to deflect some unjustified criticisms of the United States."[95] Unfortunately, records of Reagan and Thatcher's bilateral summit and the G7 meetings are ostensibly unavailable at the time of writing. Likewise, the Reagan-Thatcher actions to protect the president's political interests are excluded from their own accounts. Thatcher fails to discuss the 1984 G7 summit in her memoir. Reagan offers a cursory overview in his memoir, while his diary is a brief summary in praise of Thatcher's chairing of the proceedings and allusion to semantics. For instance: "Margaret handled the meetings brilliantly. As expected, P.M. Trudeau of Canada & Mitterrand were usually with a different viewpoint on some subjects—lot of it nit-picking. We overcame them with some compromise word changes."[96] Kathleen Osborne, Reagan's personal assistant at the White House, recalled that at economic summits, the president would tell Thatcher how sorry he was if one of their colleagues were disrespectful to her—to which the prime minister would remark "Oh, Ron, don't worry about that. Boys will be boys."[97]

The Reagan administration was certainly delighted with the outcomes of the president's transatlantic expedition. The British embassy informed the FCO: "Coverage of the entire Reagan European tour in the US media has been massive. The exercise has been presented as a considerable success for the President, with many commentators pointing to the contrast between his performance, speaking for America, and the continuing feuding in the Democrat camp. He is seen as, 'acting presidential': the Democrats as 'playing politics.'"[98] American coverage followed official press briefings, noting that Reagan did not defend his economic record to the extent that he had at Williamsburg. For instance, it was noted in the coverage that the official communiqué did not include any "specific criticism of the impact of the US budget deficit on interest rates" and some reports even "stress[ed] the Prime Minister's role in preventing a 1:6 confrontation on the issue." Similarly, the communiqué's inclusion of the necessity to limit "rigidities in the labour market" was widely viewed to be an acknowledgment of the greater effectiveness of the American economy in job creation. Indeed, the influence of briefings by Regan and Undersecretary Beryl Sprinkel were viewed to be clear "in a number of reports." The demonstrations in London, such as that of the Campaign for Nuclear Disarmament on June 9, did not enjoy prominent coverage, while those in Ireland received more coverage, albeit "because there was less substance to cover as well."[99] A *Washington Post* editorial commented that the reluctance of world leaders to dwell on the American budgetary deficit and interest rates in the summit's formal statements meant that there was little ammunition for Reagan's political opponents at home.[100] The Reagan campaign had much cause to view the expedition as a political success, and the president certainly held Thatcher partially responsible for this. On June 14, 1984, US Ambassador Charles Price wrote to Thatcher: "I know the President appreciated fully your sensitivity to his concerns."[101] Reagan appreciated Thatcher's managing of the summit to the extent that he avoided an extended discussion about the American deficit, which helped ensure that the summit was an electoral advantage for the campaign.[102] There would not be any footage or briefings of other world leaders condemning the president's economic policies that could be used by the Democrats. Reagan ultimately won reelection and defeated Mondale by a landslide. Thatcher was so excited that she twice sent her congratulations. On November 6, she wrote: "It must be a matter of great satisfaction to you that across the land the American people have given such a strong endorsement both of their confidence in you personally and of the values for which you stand."[103] The next day, Thatcher telegrammed Reagan: "I cannot tell you how delighted I am. It will be a great tonic and reassurance for all America's friends who can continue to have the fullest confidence in your nation's leadership."[104] However, reporting to the cabinet meeting on November 8, Howe noted that despite Reagan's "remarkable achievement" in his electoral success, it was unclear "what action, if any, President Reagan would take to curb the United States' budgetary deficit."[105]

Thatcher's congratulations to Reagan were expected. However, in accordance with Howe's concerns at Cabinet, she was quick to press Ambassador Price on the need for Reagan to act on issues that she believed to be of concern to British interests. In a meeting with Price on November 8, 1984, the prime minister informed the US ambassador that there remained "concern in Britain and elsewhere in Europe about the continuing high budget deficit in the US and the effect of this on interest rates."[106]

Another issue that continued to be a source of tension in Anglo-American relations, overlapping both domestic and foreign affairs, was the Laker case. In November 1982, a civil action for Laker Airways (Sir Freddie Laker's transatlantic airline) claimed that the company was bankrupted by collusion between other airlines, including British Airways. Laker's creditors argued that this breached America's antitrust laws.[107] Thus, the US Department of Justice opened a grand jury investigation, which would involve some of British Airways's current and former employees.[108] It was impossible to privatize British Airways in these circumstances because a stock offering could not be issued amid the resulting financial uncertainty, and such investigations by the Justice Department were effectively outside of the president's authority.[109] The American and British governments came to an impasse: the United States expected British Airways employees and former employers to testify while the British claimed that the 1980 Protection of Trading Interests Act empowered them to prohibit its citizens from participating in foreign legal investigations.[110] During the president's first term, Thatcher sought to convince Reagan to end this investigation: "I want to take up with you personally and urgently my deep concern at the proposed antitrust investigation" as it may "have the most serious consequences for British Airways."[111] She argued that the "matter is urgent which is why I am contacting you immediately. I am most disturbed about it and so hope you will feel able to take it up personally and very quickly."[112] Thatcher further argued,

> Aviation has always been handled on a basis of close cooperation between governments and our relations in this field have been governed by our bilateral aviation agreement which is of long standing. My people have therefore pressed for this latest matter to be tackled on an agreed basis. So far this has unfortunately not been accepted. We believe that the right course is for formal consultations to take place as provided by our aviation agreement and our Ambassador has informed the State Department of this. We would expect that meanwhile the Department of Justice investigation will be deferred, so as not to prejudge the consultations.[113]

Thatcher's request was rooted in broader Anglo-American cooperation in aviation affairs, yet the Reagan administration knew that the antitrust investigation was difficult for British Airways's privatization.[114] Reagan responded to Thatcher with disappointing news for the British, "I am afraid that we cannot defer any longer the antitrust investigation by our justice department of British and other air carriers. There are substantial allegations involved . . . it is my clear obligation to see that our antitrust laws are enforced."[115] But the president did not want British Airways to cloud Anglo-American relations, such as its bilateral security cooperation: "I value our personal relationship and the unique cooperation between our countries on important matters. However in this case I feel that I do not have the latitude to respond to your concerns. . . . Knowing your personal interest, I will stay abreast of developments in this case."[116]

With regard to the Laker case, Price reported back to Washington following his meeting with Thatcher on November 8, 1984, that "the issue should not get out of hand or emotions run riot." Yet Thatcher "said that she took a very grave view of the matter." She argued that "if the Department of Justice were to bring indictments against British airlines and former British Airways employees, we should face a very difficult situation." The prime minister attached such significance to this issue that she essentially warned any indictments would be a cause of serious tension: "It would be worse, distinctly worse, than the Siberian pipeline dispute. She very much hoped that the Department of Justice would exercise its discretion not to indict."[117] Bilateral consultations a week before this meeting led Downing Street to believe that in response to a more liberal arrangement for fares and fresh arrangements for inter-airline discussion, the United States government was willing to propose to Congress that it pass legislation "to relieve airlines of civil anti-trust liability."[118] Parallel to this, the US Department of Justice was willing to consider British arguments that British airlines should not be indicted for alleged previous offences against antitrust law. However, it was emphasized that Washington would "deny the possibility of linkage affecting their duty to enforce their law."[119] Whereas Reagan might have sought to use the momentum of his reelection for his own domestic and foreign policies, Thatcher was determined to lobby him about a number of British concerns. Regardless of any hope of progress, the British resolved: "It is important to give the US Government no grounds to think that we might be ready to compromise on this issue."[120] The combination of these two points ensured that the Laker case would be a divisive issue when Thatcher visited Reagan at Camp David in December 1984. Indeed, the extent of Thatcher's concerns was underscored by her mentioning of the Laker case in a meeting with Shultz in November 1984 in New Delhi at the funeral of Indira Gandhi (prime minister of India, 1966–1977 and 1980–1984).[121] At the end of the meeting, Thatcher told Shultz that a settlement for the Laker case was of "great importance to the UK" and the US Department of Justice "must avoid prosecutions." The British record notes that Shultz simply "nodded but made no comment."[122] It was an obvious priority for Thatcher but less so for the Reagan administration. The British refused to accept that Reagan's position was intransigent.

Suddenly, on November 19, 1984, the investigation was canceled. This development was almost unprecedented, angering the Justice Department and surprising the British Embassy. Justice Department officials leaked that this had been Reagan's decision.[123] Reagan diarized just once on this saga: a reference to the grand jury investigation. He noted: "We had a session with Carol Dinkins of Justice & Shultz of St. Justice is pursuing a case—criminal charges of anti-trust violations with England's Laker airline. P.M. Thatcher has really dug in her heels. . . . Hearing both sides I came down on the side of foreign relations—case closed."[124] The development shocked the American and British press.[125] Senator Howard M. Metzenbaum (D-OH), a member of the Senate Committee on the Judiciary, wrote to Reagan and criticized his "extraordinary, perhaps unprecedented, decision to close down a Department of Justice investigation into possible antitrust violations by American and British air carriers."[126] Metzenbaum further added: "The only . . . explanation for your action is a vague reference to 'foreign policy reasons.' I cannot believe that a foreign government, whether friendly or unfriendly, can dictate whether or not our government enforces our laws."[127] Reagan had been prepared to anger his domestic rivals in order to further Thatcher's domestic objectives—he clearly saw the larger picture in foreign affairs and the value of Thatcher's support and defense of American interests at summits that she attended with and without him.

December 1984

Following Reagan's reelection, Thatcher visited the president at Camp David before Christmas 1984. As anticipated in the American and British press, Reagan's Strategic Defense Initiative (SDI) was the major topic of this summit, although domestic affairs remained a significant factor.[128] Noting their commonalities in philosophy and European concerns over SDI, the *Washington Post* quoted a State Department official, claiming that Thatcher was the only ally who could "lean on" Reagan.[129] Recording the visit in his diary, Reagan wrote: "Sat. dawned clear & bright which was fine because P.M. Margaret Thatcher was coming in for a visit. I met her in a golf cart."[130] Writing in her memoir, Thatcher recalled that her visit marked "the first occasion on which I had heard President Reagan speaking about SDI."[131] Reagan "did so with passion" and "was at his most idealistic." Thatcher noted with apprehension that in their talks, Reagan "reaffirmed his long-term goal of getting rid of nuclear weapons entirely." Despite disagreeing with the president on this point, Thatcher resolved to concentrate on "areas of agreement" in her discussions.[132] Indeed Reagan believed that nuclear weapons and the resulting policy of Mutual Assured Destruction were repugnant. Reagan wrote in his memoir that, through his policies toward the Cold War, he hoped to "give the world a greater chance of survival."[133] Thus, $17 billion was spent on the SDI (or, as more widely known, "Star Wars"). The president sought to create a defense shield that would protect the United States against any Soviet nuclear missiles. Opponents of the research argued that such a new antimissile system actually broke the terms of the 1972 Anti-Ballistic Missile Treaty. Furthermore, the Soviet Union claimed that SDI undermined deterrence, therefore only increasing the risk of an American-first nuclear strike.[134] While SDI was never actually created, it remained close to Reagan's heart and helped break down talks between the president and Gorbachev at Reykjavik in 1986, in which there was a near breakthrough in the arms race between the two superpowers.[135]

Northern Ireland would also be on the agenda for Thatcher's visit to Camp David. The Northern Ireland conflict and the Anglo-Irish process were of particular interest to Irish Americans in Congress, including the "Four Horsemen": Speaker Thomas P. "Tip" O'Neill, Senator Ted Kennedy (D-MA), Senator Daniel Moynihan (D-NY), and Governor Hugh Carey (D-NY). Since the Carter era, the Horsemen had advocated a peaceful solution to the "Troubles" in Northern Ireland and called for Irish Americans to cease financial support and gunrunning for the Irish Republican Army. These calls came to be challenged by a rival grouping, the Ad-Hoc Committee for Irish Affairs, led by the Republican-sympathizing firebrand, Rep. Mario Biaggi (D-NY).[136] As two Irish Americans, Reagan and O'Neill would share jokes and stories from the "old country" while the president resisted American intervention in what most members of his administration considered a domestic British matter and therefore an issue that demanded American neutrality.[137] Yet O'Neill's concern for the Anglo-Irish process represented a political opportunity to the White House. Thatcher's public and fierce opposition in November 1984 to the conclusions of the New Ireland Forum (which proposed either a unified Ireland, a confederation of two states, or joint Anglo-Irish authority over Northern Ireland) saw O'Neill urge Reagan's intervention in the issue. The Speaker would prove to be successful in this endeavor.[138]

The State Department reviewed Thatcher's domestically driven interest before the prime minister's arrival in the United States. Shultz was informed that "Thatcher's position on the British domestic political scene remains secure."[139] Yet Thatcher was determined to exploit the close Anglo-American relationship to strengthen the British economy. Richard Burt (assistant secretary of state for Canadian and European affairs, 1983–1985) observed: "Economic issues remain the chronic irritant in the bilateral relationship." In particular, "civil aviation is the source of our most bitter differences." The memorandum detailed that after the two-year dispute, Reagan decided that the Department of Justice should end its grand jury investigation into the antitrust violations that were linked to the bankruptcy of Laker Airlines. (This was to the benefit of British Airways.) In return, the Reagan administration had urged the British government "to take some positive steps to liberalize the current civil aviation regime." Despite the best efforts of Ambassador Price and the State Department, Burt argued that the British government had "been singularly unhelpful." The British simply refused to do this until the United States government eliminated the private remedies provision from the 1914 Clayton Act, which was part of American antitrust legislation, designed to prevent practices that harmed competition. Due to Reagan's intervention in the Laker case, Congress was unlikely to be willing to revise the Clayton Act, which ultimately meant that Reagan was "now politically vulnerable on the issue and British policymakers appear unwilling to take any liberalizing actions to help." Thus, the State Department believed that Reagan should convince Thatcher of the need to "liberalize the civil aviation regime."[140] Reagan's briefing cards reflected the frustration of his advisers on this issue: "Disappointed with your government's response to our decision to close the grand jury investigation. A one-time approval of winter fares is not an adequate step. Congress would reject proposal to waive treble damages. Understand procedures exist to provide British firms ample protection against antitrust suits. Urge you to have your ministers explore these procedures rather than wait for changes in our legislation. Liberalization of the aviation regime would be in both our interests and would demonstrate benefits of more competition."[141]

Similarly, economic issues raised previously by the British continued to comprise the president's briefing.[142] Bud McFarlane, the national security adviser, noted: "Interest rates have come down across the board since early June." In addition, he briefed on another point of concern for Thatcher: "US budget deficit in FY 1984 was $175.3 billion, 4.9 percent of GNP; down from $195.4 billion, 6.1 percent of GNP in FY 1983. (However, it appears that the FY 1985 deficit will exceed the FY 1984 level.) Currently developing budgetary plan for the future with heavy emphasis on control of expenditures." Furthermore, unitary taxation was identified as an issue that Reagan needed to be aware of before the meeting with Thatcher. The president was briefed about the "favorable developments" on the issue—namely, the decision of the Florida legislature to repeal unitary taxation; the Massachusetts Supreme Court ruling that it was illegal; Indiana officials had pledged to repeal such taxes in January 1985; and Oregon had also recently ended unitary taxation. The Reagan administration therefore hoped that the British would be patient while waiting for the eight remaining states using unitary taxation, such as California, to attempt to resolve the situation.[143] Macfarlane clearly hoped that Reagan would be able to address Thatcher's dissatisfaction with unitary taxation so that the meeting would turn to other issues.

The significance of domestic issues at the Reagan-Thatcher summit in December 1984 is underscored by Shultz's briefing for the president, in which half of the content might be considered domestic concerns.[144] The secretary of state explained: "Mrs. Thatcher will want a frank exchange of views on major political and economic issues; there are several important matters which you may wish to raise in order to stress USG concerns about current British positions." In addition to East-West issues, Shultz advised that the meeting would include discussions about aviation antitrust issues, the global economic outlook, and Northern Ireland. On aviation, Shultz noted Thatcher's gratitude toward Reagan but also her unwillingness to abandon British interests. He expected Thatcher to "express her appreciation for your November 16 decision, based on foreign policy grounds, to close the Department of

Justice's Grand Jury investigation of criminal antitrust cases connected with the Laker Airlines bankruptcy." However, it was noted that Thatcher had previously written to Reagan to explain that she could not "take any further steps to liberalize the civil aviation regime" without a commitment from the United States "to remove private treble damage remedies" as per the Clayton Act's antitrust provision. Shultz believed that Thatcher would emphasize this view in the meeting with the president. While the British had "offered to lower winter fares, which is mutually beneficial," it was "not enough to meet our needs," and the British government remained unconvinced by the efforts of the State Department and Price to convince them of the need for "more, not less, competition." Thus, Reagan was advised to stress his "disappointment at the lack of a positive British response and the need for some significant steps in a market-oriented direction, such as longer term liberalization on airfares and increased frequency of flights." In the meantime, the prime minister had already been warned "that there is little chance that Congress would find the elimination of private treble damage remedies in the Clayton Act to be in the public interest."[145] The Laker affair was an important economic issue as it was trumped by the politics of the special relationship. Whereas other sources of economic tension in this study have reflected a commitment to domestic economic matters over foreign affairs, on Laker, Reagan facilitated a "win" for Thatcher. The United States had once again conceded to the British in bilateral aviation affairs. Given that Reagan had already secured reelection, this was at the cost of relatively little political capital and could not be used against him in a future presidential election. In contrast, the privatization of British Airways was an important dimension of Thatcher's domestic economic and political narrative while also serving as an indication of representing British interests abroad.

The relationship between the fortunes of the American and British economies, particularly Thatcher's interest in this, was subject to Shultz's briefing. Reagan was advised that Thatcher would be "interested in your views on the current economic situation" as she believed that Britain's economic recovery relied heavily on America's economic performance. The president was warned to expect an inquiry "about deficit reduction and tax reform plans." Therefore, he might "wish to reassure her that we see a revival of growth to a sustainable pace early in 1985, supported by lower interest rates and continued low inflation" and outline his administration's "efforts to reduce the Federal deficit and discuss possibilities for tax reform." In addition to economic issues, Shultz advised Reagan to comment on the Anglo-Irish process, particularly the concerns of Irish Americans in Congress. Following Thatcher's public condemnation of the New Ireland Forum, Reagan was advised to emphasize that American policy toward Northern Ireland was unchanged, yet the administration was "concerned that unless there is an appearance of progress at the next summit, there may be a radicalization of Irish-American opinion which would endanger our current bipartisan policy."[146] McFarlane's national security briefing underscored the domestic component of the Reagan administration's interest in Northern Ireland: "Tip O'Neill has sent you a letter, illustrative of the attitude of many in Congress, urging you to encourage Mrs. Thatcher to intensify the Anglo-Irish dialogue. There is a feeling in some quarters that Mrs. Thatcher is inflexible and you will want to underline the need for real progress if we are to maintain bipartisan support for our policy toward Northern Ireland."[147] The Democrats ostensibly considered Thatcher to be as dogmatic as she had been when first meeting President Carter in 1977—despite Carter changing his mind at the advent of her premiership.

In a tacit acknowledgement of Thatcher's determination to express her views, the administration hoped to avoid a lengthy discussion about civil aviation at Camp David. Reagan wrote to Thatcher about the issue:

> I remain hopeful that we will be able to improve the competitive conditions of international air transportation between our two countries. We are deeply disappointed, however that you appear to condition new steps towards this goal on legislation that would eliminate private antitrust actions, especially since you and I share the goal of increasing competition in trade. I believe that more competition will serve both to benefit our consumers and to strengthen our airlines. This should not, in our view, be linked to a specific change in US legislation which is at present unrealistic.[148]

The president was clear in his desire to reach an agreement with Thatcher on this issue. He added that, further to Shultz and Price's briefings to British ministers, "We do not believe legislation to eliminate treble damages is necessary in order for our airlines to operate free of litigation in a more competitive environment," particularly as "adequate means are currently available under US law, and our Bermuda II aviation agreement to provide any necessary protection from antitrust suits." Reagan noted this protection was "demonstrated by British Airways' long and favorable experience with US antitrust law." The conclusion stressed that his administration would not repeat the intervention that had benefitted British Airways: "I am hopeful that . . . you will conclude that we can open up the aviation regime without legislation on private antitrust suits . . . we view such movement as essential if we are to be able in the future to contemplate any legislative action regarding private suits." Despite this clear dispute, Reagan warmly signed off the letter: "I look forward very much to seeing you Saturday at Camp David."[149]

Reagan and Thatcher's first meeting at Camp David was restricted to them and two notetakers. The discussion focused on Thatcher's recent meeting with Gorbachev and then turned to SDI. On her meeting with Gorbachev, Thatcher remarked that he "was an unusual kind of Russian" who "spoke with authority" and "was able to discuss and debate easily" about issues that would otherwise "offend other Soviet leaders." On SDI, Reagan argued that if it proved successful, "it could lead to the elimination of nuclear weapons" and he was "ready to internationalize it so that it was at the service of all countries."[150] The wider meeting included the anticipated discussion about civil aviation, the US economy and the Anglo-Irish process.[151]

On civil aviation, both governments had inherited a problematic state of affairs. Airline pricing was in flux following the policies of Alfred Kahn, Carter's chairman of the Civil Aeronautics Board (1977–1978), which deregulated commercial airfares and therefore challenged the fare conferences of the International Air Transport Association.[152] The issue was further complicated by the Anglo-American Bermuda II Agreement negotiations on civil aviation relations in 1976–1977 and again in 1980. In short, in both rounds, the Americans were out-negotiated by the British and accepted a much more regulatory regime than they have wanted, which was in contrast to domestic moves toward deregulation.[153] This was in contrast to the Bermuda Agreement reached in 1946, which was a model for bilateral liberalization.[154] Indeed, the Americans never did a Bermuda II negotiation with any other country—it was viewed as a model for what not to do in bilateral aviation negotiations.[155] The uncertainty over airline pricing, coupled with angst and resentment on the American side following the Bermuda negotiations, was not helped by the disagreements about the Laker case.

On aviation issues, Thatcher began by stating that she was "immensely grateful for the President's courageous decision to drop the indictments over

Laker" and expressed her relief "that the press reception of his decision had been favorable." Nonetheless, "she wanted to explain the problems which remained for the British Government." The British also wanted "new arrangements for competition and deregulation" but this would have to be "in return for legislation to remove liability to private triple damage suits against our airlines." Since Reagan's decision on Laker, his administration "had ended these discussions and the British Government was faced with two major difficulties." The first was that Thatcher wanted to privatize British Airways early in 1985, but despite the preparations having been made and financial projections of "substantial receipts," it was impossible to proceed due to "the liability to triple damages." The second difficulty was that, essentially, (the British understanding of) the terms and arrangements of the Bermuda Agreement approved British Airways's prices, which were the focus of antitrust actions. Thatcher's frustration was clear. The British had thought that the Bermuda Agreement overruled any liability for triple damages, but Thatcher recognized that as the agreement lacked treaty status, it would not override triple damages in the United States. This meant that British airlines, which did not have an automatic right to provide a service within America, faced challenges when offering a transatlantic service, and there was not a framework for satisfactorily discussing liberalization and competition.[156] Reagan was unmoved, explaining that "there had been a procedure in place for fifteen years which had effectively prevented antitrust suits." Unfortunately, it had not been followed in the current cases. In present circumstances, he saw no realistic prospect that Congress would pass legislation to remove liability to antitrust actions. Thatcher's frustration continued. She argued that "the arrangements for avoiding anti-trust actions had been followed in the case of the recent negotiation of winter fares and had taken three months," yet this "would not result in less regulations and greater competition: indeed they would make them more difficult." Over cocktails, Price suggested that Thatcher should simply overcome these challenges to the privatization "by granting an indemnity in respect of the triple damage suit." The prime minister simply argued that British Airways was "in an unacceptable position" and the situation "obstructed the cause of competition and deregulation." Yet the Reagan administration prioritized domestic politics over further support for Thatcher's privatization agenda.

Turning to the American economy, Reagan explained that "the United States discount rate had just been reduced to 8 percent, the lowest in six years, and the prime rate was bound to come down in consequence," while the administration "would be announcing an austerity spending," which, over the next two years, would mean that "the budget should be approximately in balance." In sum Reagan assured Thatcher that America's interest rates and budgetary deficit would be falling—two issues that had previously troubled the prime minister. Thatcher "welcomed the fall in US interest rates and expressed her admiration for Mr. Volcker" and "welcomed the Administration's efforts to reduce the deficit." In contrast, the prime minister criticized her political opponents at home and abroad:

> She recalled the Budget deficit in Britain had risen to an alarmingly high proportion of GDP in the mid-70s. In consequence, the proportion of the UK budget which had to be devoted to debt interest was very high when her Government had taken office. This was one of the reasons why it had been essential for the British Government to reduce the deficit. There was always a danger that, if a socialist government were elected again in Britain, the deficit would increase. This vulnerability to socialist policies was one of the reasons why Europe did not attract the same financial confidence as the United States.[157]

Likewise, Reagan eagerly condemned the economic performance of his political opponents: "Between 1965 and 1980 the US budget had increased 4 ½ times but the deficit had increased 38 times. There had been deficit spending over the last 50 years in the United States and for almost all of them Congress had had Democratic majorities."[158] Reagan was speaking accurately: there had not been a surplus in the federal budget since 1960 and, indeed, this was not achieved until under the Clinton administration in 1998, with a surplus of $236 billion in 2000.[159] However, Reagan did act on behalf of his opponents in regard to the Anglo-Irish process. According to the British record, Thatcher told Reagan that she was on "very friendly terms" with Garret FitzGerald, the Irish Taoiseach (1982–1987), and discussions about Northern Ireland would resume in the new year. Reagan remarked that "what the Prime Minister had said would be very helpful to him," as Speaker O'Neill had written to him, "asking him to appeal to the Prime Minister to be reasonable," and "it was apparent that she was being reasonable."[160] FitzGerald believed that Reagan's comments on Northern Ireland "must have been a factor contributing to the more positive approach the British adopted," which led to the signing of the 1985 Anglo-Irish Agreement.[161] Nonetheless, it was actually Shultz, who recognized congressional concern for the issue, who advised Reagan to raise it with Thatcher. The Speaker's opposition to republican violence and Irish-American support for the Irish Republican Army (IRA) required political cover from Reagan. Thus, Reagan negotiated the necessity of placating O'Neill but did not allow it to detract from his meeting with the prime minister. Reagan simply waited for Thatcher to raise Northern Ireland and then merely pointed out O'Neill's letter. The president therefore avoided direct criticism of Thatcher, cooperated with O'Neill, and did not risk tension at the Anglo-American summit over Northern Ireland.

The American record of the meeting is revealing of Thatcher's candor, particularly in regard to civil aviation and the American economy.[162] The prime minister defended the British negotiations over developing "a more competitive" Anglo-American civil aviation arrangement. She noted that her government "was told that the US would be able to introduce legislation seeking repeal of the treble damage clause," but then "learned that you did not plan to introduce such legislation and believed that should you do so, Congress would reject it." Subsequently, the potential treble damage clause was "hanging over British Airways like a dark cloud," making it "very difficult to denationalize British Airways in such a climate." She noted that there was "still great confusion over the pricing arrangements" as the Bermuda II Agreement "does not override US anti-trust law," which, coupled with the fact that the British faced "a total monopoly in the US," meant that the situation "seems very unfair." The American record notes that Reagan observed: "Increased competition is in both our interests and we do favor the denationalization of British Airways," although he then said "it was time to break for lunch." Reagan supported privatization but was unwilling to do any more to help. According to this record, Thatcher's response to Price's suggestion of an indemnity fund to protect British Airways was direct and to the point: "her budget did not have room for such funding and once it was known that government money would be behind a settlement, this would surely open the door to a large settlement in favor of the private parties." On the American economy, Thatcher's criticism of her European allies included a reminder to Reagan about the importance of his promised economic performance:

> Praising US economic performance, Mrs. Thatcher said that the strength of the dollar is a sign of weakness in Europe. She opined that the overall political situation in Europe is not especially encouraging. There is a socialist government in France; neither Holland or Belgium seem to be able to get their act completely together; Germany is a question mark; and the Italians lack guts. There is a socialist government in Spain; Greece is a pain in the neck and certainly no friend of the US; but Portugal did have the guts to fight communism. In Great Britain, the opposition Labour Party is espousing more and more socialist causes. None of this bodes especially well for Europe, but America's huge deficit and its need for such heavy borrowing to finance the deficit is keeping interest rates up too high.

On Northern Ireland, the American record shows that the conversation was brief, although the president did underscore the importance of progress, particularly for those in Congress. The president then closed the meeting ending what he described as highly valued discussions.[163]

Unsurprisingly, foreign affairs, particularly the SDI and Gorbachev, dominated the subsequent press conference at Camp David. Yet, when asked whether they discussed the American trade deficit, Thatcher replied: "We did talk about the interest rates which, as you know, are recently down . . . and also we did discuss the deficit and the desirability to have a smaller proportion of the national income taken in deficit, but I am sure you will be hearing a good deal more about that in the coming months or so."[164] The prime minister was publicly raising the expectation that the Reagan administration would reduce the deficit. Thatcher was asked about whether she had discussed with Reagan the difficulties in extraditing William Quinn (an American citizen and member of the IRA who murdered an off-duty police officer in London in 1975). She immediately sought to limit any discussion about Northern Ireland: "No, I did not discuss the extradition problem with the United States. I told him what in the United Kingdom they already know, that we did have talks with Mr. Fitzgerald, bilateral talks, and that we should be continuing those talks during the New Year, so there is no question of having a gap. Those talks will continue." Quizzed about the president's response to the update on the Anglo-Irish process, Thatcher again offered a curt response: "It was really rather a case of my briefing the President because I felt that he would like to know and should know on the state of relations between the Republic and the United Kingdom." When she was further pressed about Reagan's view on Northern Ireland and even his reaction to her infamous rebuke to the New Ireland Forum, Thatcher replied: "We were not getting into that kind of detail," but she was happy to have briefed Reagan about the continuing talks, given the false impression of "problems between the Taoiseach and myself."[165] Economic issues and Northern Ireland contextualized a major summit that was committed mostly to next steps in the Cold War. Thatcher was certainly pleased with the outcome of her discussions on the SDI. In her memoir, Thatcher wrote that it was a "reassuring" discussion as the president "did not pretend that they yet knew where the research could finally lead," but Soviet attempts to compete with American technological research "would impose an economic strain on the Soviet Union," which showed that "he had instinctively grasped the key to the whole question."[166] Reagan's reassurances on the SDI, coupled with the prime minister's desire to avoid any perception of a schism in Anglo-American relations on the issue, were noted as successes for Thatcher in the American and British press, which were the focus of coverage of the summit.[167]

While Thatcher was pleased with the discussions on the SDI, she once again did not succeed in convincing Reagan to act on the US deficit. However, Reagan did act again on British Airways as the civil actions threatened its privatization. Thatcher raised this issue in a meeting with Reagan when she returned to the United States in February 1985. On British Airways's negotiations with the EXIM Bank, the American record notes that Thatcher "hoped the President could be helpful," with her explaining that the British were "trying to persuade the bank to settle for a reasonable sum, and the airlines have agreed to the proposed settlement" and also stressing that "her government wishes to move toward liberalization and the denationalization of British Airways, and this matter stood in the way."[168] Reagan clearly wanted to close the issue entirely. The American record noted: "The President observed that the EXIM Bank has autonomy of operation, but we are in communication with the Director. Ambassador Price, in particular, has been trying to work something out, and he (the President) would weigh in if it seemed necessary."[169] As Laker's largest creditor, EXIM was willing to wait to settle with British Airways. However, EXIM received instructions to settle.[170] Thus, the civil action against British Airways ended in July 1985, allowing Thatcher to privatize the airline in 1987. Interestingly, Thatcher does not recall the incident at all in her memoirs.[171] Reagan's decision to pass on

O'Neill's concerns about Northern Ireland to Thatcher was intended to assist the White House's congressional relations. Yet, while Thatcher signed the Anglo-Irish Agreement in 1985—much to the celebration of Irish Americans in Congress—Reagan's public support for the agreement and resulting American contribution to the International Fund for Ireland could not persuade the Democrats to end the ban on American funding for the Nicaraguan Contras.[172]

Conclusion

Anglo-American summitry in 1983–1984 encompassed disagreements about economic policy, Grenada, Northern Ireland, and Reagan's approach to the Cold War. Yet the impact of foreign policy on domestic concerns—particularly reelection and the economy—was still an important theme. Both Reagan and Thatcher prioritized their electoral circumstances and, buoyed by their success at the ballot box, sought to maximize their political capital at home and abroad. While Reagan was unwilling to alter his economic agenda for Thatcher, he was prepared to assist her in cases of unitary taxation and British Airways. The president did not need to worry about reelection after November 1984, so he therefore had the political freedom to do so. Likewise, Anglo-American consultation escalated following the embarrassment caused to Thatcher by the American intervention in Grenada. Reagan clearly sought to support his ally and ease any rumblings in Anglo-American relations. He also saw an opportunity, for instance, with Northern Ireland: being able to claim credit for any progress in Anglo-American relations would, he hoped, endear him to O'Neill, which could help his own domestic agenda. Both leaders continued to broadly publicly support each other, particularly with Thatcher even ensuring that the 1984 G7 summit was favorable to Reagan's reelection campaign. The public diplomacy ensured that each leader was willing—and able—to support the other in issues that mattered to each, albeit only when intervention was "low risk" and "potential high gain" for themselves. Nonetheless, Thatcher's support for Reagan on the deficit in 1984 quickly transitioned to pressuring him to act on the issue, albeit without success. However, this period saw a continuing divergence between the Reagan administration and Thatcher government in regard to economic policy, particularly the extent of the American deficit and Thatcher understanding Reagan's electoral circumstances.

Conclusion

In an address to a gathering of Conservatives in London in 1922, Lord Curzon (the British secretary of state for Foreign Affairs, 1919–1924) remarked that "foreign affairs are really domestic affairs—the most domestic of all our affairs, for they touch the life, the interest and the pocket of every member of the community."[1] Indeed, if politics is essentially a word to describe the managing of interests—whether that be national, international, or a combination of the two—foreign and domestic affairs are so interconnected that they are essentially two sides of the same coin.

The summitry meetings between Ronald Reagan and Margaret Thatcher, and other supplementary discussions between Thatcher and members of Reagan's administration, highlight the clear divergences in Anglo-American relations in the period 1981–1985. Amid a time of economic uncertainty and, on occasion, great difficulty, these differences were motivated by domestic political concerns. In turn this meant that both sides largely prioritized their own agendas over any commonalities in their New Right partnership. This domestic motivation reflected the reasons behind the transatlantic expeditions both leaders undertook before power. Thus, Anglo-American relations at the highest level were sharpened by considerations outside of the diplomatic travails of the Cold War.

These summits further illustrate that regarding domestic interests, one's allies can be just as great a challenge—albeit subtler—than one's enemies. This work has demonstrated this challenge through three themes: first, that the importance of domestic policies and politics could be paramount at summits notionally focused on international affairs; second, that there were clear differences between Reaganism and Thatcherism; third, that these issues arose from inevitable tensions between economic policies and the globalized economy. For Reagan and Thatcher, even one's "best friend" could "let them down."

The dichotomy between the public diplomacy of the Reagan-Thatcher "special relationship" and its tensions are reflected in the accounts from those who were key actors in this period of Anglo-American relations. For many, the Reagan-Thatcher epoch was a period of commonality between two kindred political spirits. Richard V. Allen, Reagan's national security adviser (1981–1982), recalled that Reagan meeting Thatcher before they became heads of their respective governments "started a beautiful intellectual romance."[2] William P. Clark, who held various positions, including national security adviser (1982–1983), argued: "They were so much of the same vision and philosophy and the same policy of peace through strength, Great Britain being our primary ally in both war and peace."[3] Caspar Weinberger, US secretary of defense (1981–1987), noted that Thatcher was "in every way and also was very much the same as President Reagan in being willing to challenge—and challenge very successfully and very effectively—the conventional wisdom" by "decreasing the power of the government to increase the power of people, and so forth."[4] On the British side, Lord Lawson of Blaby (the UK chancellor of the exchequer, 1983–1989), recalled: "[B]eing a head of government is a lonely job and if you find that there is an opposite number, as it were, with whom you are on the same wavelength, then I think . . . there is a kind of mutual support mechanism that happens."[5] Those close to the two leaders' conversations recollected that there were discussions about economic issues. Lord Powell of Bayswater, who served as Thatcher's private secretary (1983–1990), noted that they were among the "meat and drink of regular conversations" between the prime minister and president.[6]

Of course, as this book has shown, discussion about the special relationship demands more nuance than that sometimes suggested by recollections of some former statesmen, diplomats, and advisers. Lord Heseltine, who served as the UK secretary of defense (1983–1986), argued that the United States has "many special relationships."[7] On Anglo-American relations, he cited interests as the key to understanding them: "[T]here were great coincidences of interest between the United Kingdom and the United States. There's often very warm personal relationships across the Atlantic. In the end, America pursues American interests. . . . I think that talk of a special relationship is attractive nostalgically but doesn't actually deliver practical results of significant consequence in the hard clash of national self-interest. . . . Our job as British politicians is to represent British self-interest. Now sometimes that will coincide with America and sometimes it won't."[8] Heseltine's summary is certainly reflective of Thatcher's approach to Anglo-American relations. She chose carefully the time to raise concerns and express frustrations—particularly when American actions impacted on her domestic agenda or British economic issues—but, ultimately, such complaints inevitably fell on deaf ears as British interests did not align with those prioritized by the White House. Power and interests, not sentiment, would determine the course of American actions. For Sir Colin Budd (who served as assistant private secretary to Sir Geoffrey Howe, then the British foreign secretary, 1984–1987) this was to be expected given that "the special relationship wasn't, and certainly isn't, something which applies in all conditions and all circumstances."[9]

Interests are therefore the key components of Anglo-American relations, rather than any personal sentiment or shared history, meaning that the special relationship is "special" when it is based on aligned interests. The ability to exercise power to further self-interests, even with an ally, is significant. Classical realists would claim that such a cynical interpretation would even apply to a celebrated example of specialness in Anglo-American relations as that of Reagan and Thatcher.[10] An alignment of interests was clear, for instance, at economic summits, where Thatcher keenly supported Reagan. Sir Bernard Ingham, who served as Thatcher's press secretary (1979–1990), argued that at the 1981 G7, Reagan and Thatcher, as a partnership, "shifted significantly economic management throughout the world from the sort of spend a lot, tax a lot, to the much more rigorous, Thatcherite, if you like, approach to economic management."[11] Yet Ingham rightly noted that it was "a very complicated relationship, both economically and diplomatically." When it came to disagreements with the president about economic policy, particularly the American deficit, the prime minister recognized "she wasn't going to be fighting him economically—well, she couldn't fight him economically—but for economic ideas. There wasn't going to be a fight there at all."[12] However, as shown in this book, it is clear that while Reagan and Thatcher promoted a common cause when dealing with other world leaders at multilateral summits, Anglo-American bilateral summits would often feature tension due to differences in the practical implementation of a broadly shared conservative philosophy. Indeed, whereas the above comments from members of the Reagan administration focus on common cause, the candor of British interviewees emphasize the bilateral tensions. This is perhaps indicative of how seriously British concerns were taken by the Reagan administration—British priorities were not the same as those of the Reagan administration. Despite the rhetoric of public diplomacy, the British had limited influence, with the Reagan administration ultimately doing what was based on its own interests. For instance, Thatcher was concerned with the impact of deficits—namely, the US budgetary deficit. Reagan did not recognize the broader implications of that issue for the global economy, or chose to ignore it, prioritizing US economic growth (albeit growth predicated on deficit financing).

This book was motivated by three central claims: domestic issues are the key influence in international summitry; there were clear divergences between Reaganism and Thatcherism; and globalization impacted the American and British response to economic pressures during the 1980s and, in turn, Anglo-American relations. In the period 1981–1985, Reagan and Thatcher were both willing to support each other's interests in the short term—namely, Reagan's reelection and Thatcher's privatization agenda, but ultimately, domestic concerns trumped their decision-making in the midterm to long term. In short, Reaganism and Thatcherism were different approaches to government, and both leaders were very different personalities. Anglo-American summitry could not be divorced from domestic matters. Furthermore, the interconnectedness of the global economy was a source of tension between the Reagan administration and its allies—even with its allegedly most special ally, the Thatcher government.

Thatcher never stopped trying to convince Reagan of the value of her ideas for governing and public policy. However, Thatcher's close relationship with Reagan garnered criticism and accusations of a one-sided relationship with America. Thatcher was characterized as a "poodle" of the Reagan administration. More importantly, Thatcher's poodle status needlessly damaged relations between Britain and Europe, which according to "Europeanists" would have better promoted Britain's interests.[13] Nonetheless, each side could—and often would—claim "wins" in the aftermath of Anglo-American summitry. The notion of "winning" is important as international events can be manipulated and exploited by political leaders for domestic gain. For democratically elected leaders conscious of the election cycle, this was not some peripheral concern. Thatcher was able to convince the Reagan administration to act in accordance with her interests on issues such as the Falklands War, British Airways, and John Brown Engineering but not the US deficit. Subsequently, for her domestic audience, she could claim to have secured British interests in her relationship with Reagan while being able to point to global circumstances, such as higher interest rates in the United

States, to account for other economic issues that she could not mitigate. Thatcher's success was rooted in her importance as an ally in international affairs and as a proponent for the president's agenda in the United States and abroad. For Reagan, the ongoing "win" was the ability to utilize Thatcher and the British experience of a common New Right philosophy for both political cover and cynical political distancing, depending on whether the administration wanted to be viewed as similar to or different from the Thatcher government. For instance, the prime minister's visit to Washington, DC, in February 1981 was an example of such contradictory uses of her policy agenda. Yet the similarities and differences between Reaganism and Thatcherism on display at these Anglo-American summits also reveal the different characteristics of Reagan and Thatcher themselves. Whereas Thatcher showed a mastery over detail and a desire to advocate her positions personally, Reagan was content for others to address points of tension—and to even be addressed by the prime minster instead.

Despite the ongoing British frustration toward Reagan's deficit spending, polling between November 1984 and August 1987 showed that the British people increasingly saw a tightening in Anglo-American relations.[14] This coincided with a deteriorating approval among Britons toward America's role in world affairs during this period.[15] After all, Reagan was hard-line in his Cold War rhetoric toward the Soviet Union, particularly during his first term. The special relationship was therefore not necessarily viewed as a positive thing by the British electorate. On the other hand, during the first two years of Reagan's second term, he comfortably enjoyed the support of over half of Americans (the Iran-Contra affair prompting a low of 48 percent before over half of Americans approved of Reagan again before he left office).[16] Reagan and Thatcher did not stop trying to enhance each other's standing as they left office—and after.[17] Welcoming Thatcher to the White House for the last time as president, Reagan claimed that due to Anglo-American leadership, there had been "an almost Newtonian revolution in the science of economics."[18] Reaganism and Thatcherism were apparently as powerful as gravity. In response and despite her previous criticisms of Reaganomics, Thatcher claimed that the president's economic success had "restored faith in the American dream," a comment clearly designed for domestic consumption in the United States.[19] They unquestionably shared a broad political philosophy—namely, that it was vital to roll back the influence of government at home and challenge—and defeat—communism around the world. A final rhetorical flourish in their relationship was left to Thatcher, who in her eulogy for Reagan in 2004, reminded mourners that he had "won the Cold War . . . without firing a shot," and reassured them that "we here still move in twilight, but we have one beacon to guide us that Ronald Reagan never had. We have his example."[20] Yet the public appreciation society does not diminish the real, albeit mostly private, arguments and differences of opinion about key areas of policy that mattered for their domestic concerns.

Reagan and Thatcher rarely made distinctions between domestic and foreign policy. Rather, each sought to further their own political interests generally at Anglo-American summits. Reaganism and Thatcherism impacted on each other and, in turn, the differences between them. Ironically, underneath Thatcher's protestation was a little hypocrisy: for instance, her government did not achieve a budgetary surplus until 1989.[21] However, the size of the British deficit and its impact on the global economy could not be compared to that of the United States. Other aspects of British economic affairs were clearly influenced by American politics too. These were Thatcher's priorities at the Anglo-American summits. But statements of public support and political cover masked the tensions between the two governments and the frustrations experienced by Thatcher. She put aside her dissatisfaction with the budgetary aspects of Reaganomics in order to help secure her ally's reelection in 1984. British criticism did not stop Reagan's political support for Thatcher, as he wanted his ally in 10 Downing Street while he wrestled with the broader challenge of the Cold War. Summitry was therefore not simply a mechanism for diplomatic agreements but another means to achieve broader political objectives.

Acknowledgments

With the publication of this book, it dawned on me that I have spent fifteen years—on and off—in the company of Ronald Reagan and Margaret Thatcher. I began researching their "special relationship" with my PhD at Aberystwyth University and maintained my interest in them while academia took me to Westminster College in Fulton, Missouri, then on to Oxford Brookes University, and now York St. John University. I am indebted to all the colleagues, students, friends, and archivists who have contributed to my research, the development of my ideas, and the maintenance of my sanity during this time. For this particular project, I am very grateful to the University Press of Kentucky for their encouragement and patience, particularly Melissa Hammer and Natalie O'Neal. Similarly, my thanks go to the reviewers of the initial draft of this work—their insights have undoubtedly strengthened the final version. Special thanks must go to Thomas Robb, for his comments on drafts of this book and his invaluable advice.

I have always been fortunate to have the love and support of my wonderful parents, Bernard and Eileen. My life has changed dramatically and continues to do so for the better since I began my life with Ron and Margaret. Academic life took me on a Fulbright fellowship, which took me to Danielle. I was lucky that she returned with me to the United Kingdom as my wife. We have been blessed with two sons (Macaulay and Fox), two dogs (Grover and Henry), two chickens (Maggie and Nancy), and a pigeon (Eddie). This book is dedicated to Danielle, Macaulay, and Fox. I trust that the dogs and the birds will be satisfied with an acknowledgment, with the dedication going to my wife and our boys.

Notes

Introduction

1. "No. 10 Telephone Conversation, Margaret Thatcher and Ronald Reagan," January 21, 1981, http://www.margaretthatcher.org/document/114254.

2. Ibid.

3. For Churchill's speech in Fulton, Missouri, see Winston Churchill, "Sinews of Peace, 1946," *The National Churchill Museum*, https://www.nationalchurchillmuseum.org/sinews-of-peace-iron-curtain-speech.html, accessed January 7, 2016.

4. John W. Young, *Twentieth-Century Diplomacy: A Case Study of British Practice 1963–1976* (Cambridge: Cambridge University Press, 2008), 115.

5. For a discussion about summitry, see David H. Dunn, ed., *Diplomacy at the Highest Level: The Evolution of International Summitry* (Basingstoke: Macmillan, 1996); Jonathan Colman, *"A 'Special Relationship'?: Harold Wilson, Lyndon B. Johnson and Anglo-American Relations 'At the Summit,'" 1964–1968* (Manchester: Manchester University Press, 2004); Peter I. Hajnal, *The G8 System and the G20: Evolution, Role and Documentation* (Aldershot, UK: Ashgate, 2007); David Reynolds, *Summits: Six Meetings that Shaped the Twentieth Century* (London: Penguin, 2007); Emmanuel Mourlon-Druol and Federico Romero, eds., *International Summitry and Global Governance: The Rise of the G7 and the European Council, 1974–1991* (London: Routledge, 2014).

6. Alan S. Alexandroff and Donald Brean, "Global Summitry: Its Meaning and Scope Part One," *Global Summitry* 1, no. 1 (2015): 3.

7. A variety of scholars across disciplines, including law and political science, consider such questions. See Chris Brummer, *Minilateralism: How Trade Alliances, Soft Law and Financial Engineering are Redefining Economic Statecraft* (New York: Cambridge University Press, 2014); Alan S. Alexandroff and Andrew F. Cooper, eds., *Rising States, Rising Institutions: Challenges for Global Governance* (Washington, DC: Brooking Institution Press, 2010); Thomas G. Weiss and Rorden Wilkinson, eds., *International Organization and Global Governance* (London: Routledge, 2014).

8. David H. Dunn, "What is Summitry?," in *Diplomacy at the Highest Level: The Evolution of International Summitry*, ed. David H. Dunn (Basingstoke, UK: Macmillan, 1996), 19.

9. Young, *Diplomacy,* 116–18, 132, 163, 171–73.

10. Sir Geoffrey Howe, *Conflict of Loyalty* (London: Macmillan, 1994), 394.

11. Margaret Thatcher, *The Downing Street Years* (London: HarperCollins, 1993), 464.

12. Lou Cannon, *President Reagan: The Role of a Lifetime* (New York: Public Affairs, 2000), 37.

13. There is a vast historiography about the "special relationship." See John Baylis, *Anglo-American Defence Relations 1939–1984: The Special Relationship* (London: Macmillan, 1984); David Reynolds, "A 'Special Relationship'?: America, Britain and the International Order Since the Second World War," *International Affairs* 62, no. 1 (1985): 1–20; C. J. Bartlett, *The "Special Relationship": Anglo-American Relations since 1945* (London: Longman, 1992); Alan P. Dobson, *Anglo-American Relations in the Twentieth Century: Of Friendship, Conflict and the Rise and Decline of Superpowers* (London: Routledge, 1995); Alex Danchev, "On Specialness," *International Affairs* 72, no. 4 (1996): 737–50; Richard J. Aldrich, "British Intelligence and the Anglo-American 'Special Relationship,'" *Review of International Studies* 24, no. 1 (1998): 331–51; Ritchie Ovendale, *Anglo-American Relations in the Twentieth Century* (Basingstoke, UK: Macmillan, 1998); Thomas Robb, *A Strained Partnership? US–UK Relations in the Era of Detente, 1969–1977* (Manchester: Manchester University Press, 2013). For broader transatlantic studies, see Kenneth Weisbrode, *The Atlantic Century: Four Generations of Extraordinary Diplomats Who Forged America's Vital Alliance with Europe* (Cambridge, MA: Da Capo Press, 2009); Luke A. Nichter, *Richard Nixon and Europe: The Reshaping of the Postwar Atlantic World* (Cambridge: Cambridge University Press, 2015).

14. Kathleen Burk, *Old World, New World: The Story of Britain and America* (London: Abacus, 2009), 561.

15. Young, *Diplomacy,* 132.

16. Burk, *Old World, New World,* 659.

17. See Geoffrey Smith, *Reagan and Thatcher* (London: Bodley Head, 1990); John O'Sullivan, *The President, the Pope, and the Prime Minister* (Washington, DC: Regnery, 2006); Nicholas Wapshott, *Ronald Reagan and Margaret Thatcher: A Political Marriage* (London: Sentinel, 2007).

18. Sally Ann Treharne, *Reagan and Thatcher's Special Relationship: Latin America and Anglo-American Relations* (Edinburgh: Edinburgh University Press, 2015), 260.

19. Richard Aldous, *Reagan and Thatcher: The Difficult Relationship* (London: Hutchinson, 2012), 7.

20. For Reagan and his presidency, see H. W. Brands, *Reagan: The Life* (New York: Doubleday, 2015).

21. For an introduction to Reaganomics, see James H. Broussard, *Ronald Reagan: Champion of Conservative America* (London: Routledge, 2015), 117–22, 135–37. For a wider discussion about the development and implementation of supply-side economics, see Brian Domitrovic, *Econoclasts: The Rebels Who Sparked the Supply-Side Revolution and Restored American Prosperity* (Wilmington, DE: ISI Books, 2009), 203–52.

22. Michael Schaller, *Reckoning with Reagan: America and Its President in the 1980s* (Oxford: Oxford University Press, 1992), 45–46.

23. James Cooper, *Margaret Thatcher and Ronald Reagan: A Very Political Special Relationship* (London: Palgrave Macmillan, 2012) 31, 63–70.

24. Richard Vinen, *Thatcher's Britain: The Politics and Social Upheaval of the 1980s* (London: Simon & Schuster, 2009), 6–9.

25. Arthur Laffer, "Margaret Thatcher's Tax Increase," *Wall Street Journal,* August 20, 1979, 12.

26. Robert Blake, "Monetarism Attacked by Top Economists," *The Times,* March 30, 1981.

27. Cooper, *Thatcher & Reagan,* 43–47.

28. Ibid, 51, 66.

29. Hugo Young, *One of Use: A Biography of Margaret Thatcher* (London: Macmillan and Pan, 1993), 250.

30. Joe McKinney and Alan P. Dobson, "The Anglo-American Economic Relationship: Special or Not?," in *Anglo-American Relations: Contemporary Perspectives,* ed. Alan P. Dobson and Steve Marsh (London: Routledge, 2013), 141.

31. Jorgen Rasmussen and James M. McCormick, "British Mass Perceptions of the Anglo-American Special Relationship," *Political Science Quarterly* 108, no. 3 (Autumn, 1993): 515–41, 526.

32. Daniel J. Sargent, *A Superpower Transformed: The Remaking of American Foreign Relations in the 1970s* (Oxford: Oxford University Press, 2015), 5.

33. Ibid, 299.

34. This is a long-standing literature on globalization; see Chris Bayly, "'Archaic' and 'Modern' Globalization in the Eurasian and African Arena ca. 1750–1850," in *Globalization in World History,* ed. A. G. Hopkins (London: Pimlico, 2002), 45–72; Robert O. Keohane and Joseph S. Nye Jr., eds., *Transnational Relations and World Politics* (Cambridge, MA: Harvard University Press, 1972); Richard J. Barnet and Ronald E. Müller, *Global Reach: The Power of Multinational Corporations* (New York City: Simon & Schuster, 1976).

35. For defenses of diplomatic history, see Karl Schweizer and Jeremy Black, "The Value of Diplomatic History: A Case Study in the Historical Thought of Herbert Butterfield," *Diplomacy and Statecraft* 17, no. 3 (2006): 617–31; Karl W. Schweizer and Matt J. Schumann, "The Revitalization of Diplomatic History: Renewed Reflections," *Diplomacy and Statecraft* 19, no. 2 (2008): 149–86.

1. Before Power, 1969–1980

1. Ronald Reagan, *An American Life: The Autobiography* (New York: Simon & Schuster, 1990), 186.

2. Fred Emery, "Mrs. Thatcher Feels She Has Won International Acceptance," *The Times,* September 26, 1975.

3. For the American case, key works include M. A. Bernstein and D. E. Adler, eds., *Understanding American Economic Decline* (Cambridge: Cambridge University Press, 1994). For the British case, see A. Gamble, *Britain in Decline: Economic Policy, Political Strategy and the British State* (Basingstoke, UK: Macmillan, 1994); R. English and M. Kenny, eds., *Rethinking British Decline* (Basingstoke, UK: Macmillan, 2000), 1–22; Jim Tomlinson, "Thrice Denied: 'Declinism' as a Recurrent Theme in British History in the Long Twentieth Century," *Twentieth Century British History* 20, no. 2 (2009): 227–51.

4. See Alan P. Dobson, *Anglo-American Relations in the Twentieth Century* (London: Routledge, 1995), 146–47; Ritchie Ovendale, *Anglo-American Relations in the Twentieth Century* (London: Routledge, 1995), 143. For Anglo-American relations in this period, see also Catherine Hynes, *The Year that Never Was: Heath, the Nixon Administration and the Year of Europe* (Dublin: University College Dublin Press, 2009); Thomas Robb, *A Strained Partnership? US-UK Relations in the Era of Détente, 1969–1977* (Manchester: Manchester University Press, 2013); Thomas Robb, *Jimmy Carter and the Anglo-American "Special Relationship"* (Edinburgh: Edinburgh University Press, 2016).

5. Lou Cannon, *President Reagan: The Role of A Lifetime* (New York: Simon & Schuster, 1991), 463; see also Ronald Reagan, *My Early Life, or, Where's the Rest of Me?* (London: Sidgwick & Jackson, 1981), 37.

6. Cannon, *President Reagan,* 89.

7. Ibid, 90–91.

8. For the development of Reagan's political views during the 1950s, see Thomas W. Evans, *The Education of Ronald Reagan* (New York: Columbia University Press, 2006). Reagan's presidential election campaigns in 1976 and 1980 are covered, respectively, in Craig Shirley, *Reagan's Revolution: The Untold Story of the Campaign that Started It All* (Nashville: Nelson Current, 2005) and Andrew E. Busch, *Reagan's Victory: The Presidential Election of 1980 and the Rise of the Right* (Lawrence: University Press of Kansas, 2005). Reagan's career as an actor, governor of California, and presidential candidate is the subject of Lou Cannon, *Governor Reagan: His Rise to Power* (New York: Public Affairs, 2003), although Reagan's transatlantic expeditions are excluded from this work. Excellent, albeit biographical, accounts of Reagan's presidency are Garry Wills, *Reagan's America: Innocents at Home* (London: Heinemann, 1988) and Cannon, *President Reagan.*

9. See, for instance, James T. Kloppenberg, *Uncertain Victory: Social Democracy and Progressivism in European and American Thought, 1870–1920* (Oxford: Oxford University Press, 1986) and Daniel T. Rodgers, *Atlantic Crossings: Social Politics in a Progressive Age* (Cambridge: Harvard University Press, 1998).

10. Richard Nixon, *The Memoirs of Richard Nixon* (London: Arrow, 1979), 49, 50, 200–201, 250.

11. The radio broadcasts were titled "Viewpoint" and produced by Harry O'Connor, and although Reagan did not draft all of the newspaper columns, he did write the radio broadcasts. In 1976 the broadcasts were being used on 226 radio sta-

tions, and columns were printed in 226 newspapers. It was estimated that Reagan was able to deliver his views to twenty million Americans every week through this use of the media. See Kiron K. Skinner, Annelise Anderson, Martin Anderson, eds., *Reagan in His Own Hand: The Writings of Ronald Reagan that Reveal His Revolutionary Vision for America* (New York: Simon & Schuster, 2001), xiv–xv.

12. Clippings included reports from California newspapers, including the *National Observer, Los Angeles Times, Beverly Hills Reporter, San Diego Union, San Francisco Examiner,* and *Sacramento Union.* British newspaper clippings were from the *Sun,* the *Daily Mirror,* the *Daily Mail,* the *Daily Sketch,* and the *Guardian.* The clippings can be found in Research File, Foreign Travel (RR), Europe 10/28–11/69 (2/2), Molly Sturges Tuthill, Ronald Reagan Governor's Papers, Ronald Reagan Presidential Library (hereafter Reagan Library); Research File, Foreign Travel (RR), Europe 10/28–11/69 (2/2), Molly Sturges Tuthill, Ronald Reagan Governor's Papers, Reagan Library.

13. For Reagan's career as governor of California, see Cannon, *Governor Reagan.*

14. Letter, Sir Derek Pritchard to Ronald Reagan, June 18, 1969, Research File, Foreign Travel (RR), Europe 10/28–11/69 (1/2), Molly Sturges Tuthill, Ronald Reagan Governor's Papers, Reagan Library.

15. Ibid.

16. "Reagan Backs US Policy: Nixon's Vietnam Tack Called Course to Peace," *Evening Tribune,* November 3, 1969; "Speaking of People," *National Observer,* November 10, 1969; both extracts from Research File, Foreign Travel (RR)—Europe—10/28–11/69 (2/2), Molly Sturgis Tuthill, Ronald Reagan: Gubernatorial Papers 1966–1975, Governor's Office Files, GO 178, Reagan Library.

17. "How to Star in the Governor Ronald Reagan Cliché Show," *Daily Mirror,* November 4, 1969, Research File, Foreign Travel (RR), Europe 10/28–11/69 (2/2), Molly Sturges Tuthill, Ronald Reagan Governor's Papers, Reagan Library.

18. Cannon, *Governor Reagan,* 291–93.

19. "How to Star," *Daily Mirror.*

20. Ibid.

21. Dermot Purgavie, "Enter Reagan, with His Best Good-Guy Smile," *Daily Sketch,* November 4, 1969, Research File, Foreign Travel (RR), Europe 10/28–11/69 (2/2), Molly Sturges Tuthill, Ronald Reagan Governor's Papers, Reagan Library.

22. Geoffrey Moorhouse, "Sunny Ronnie," *Guardian,* November 4, 1969, Research File, Foreign Travel (RR), Europe 10/28–11/69 (2/2), Molly Sturges Tuthill, Ronald Reagan Governor's Papers, Reagan Library.

23. John Dodd, "The Fastest Tongue in the West Rides into Town," *Sun,* November 4, 1969.

24. Moorhouse, "Sunny Ronnie."

25. "Speaking of People," *National Observer,* November 10, 1969; Martin Linton, "Reagan Warns of '1,000 Years of Darkness,'" *Daily Mail,* November 4, 1969; UPI, "Reagan in London, Praises Nixon Courage," *International Herald Tribune,*

November 4, 1969; all in Research File, Foreign Travel (RR), Europe 10/28–11/69 (2/2), Molly Sturges Tuthill, Ronald Reagan Governor's Papers, Reagan Library.

26. Governor Ronald Reagan, "The New Noblesse Oblige" (Speech to the Institute of Directors, November 6, 1969), Research File, Foreign Travel (RR), Europe 10/28–11/69 (1/2), Molly Sturges Tuthill, Ronald Reagan Governor's Papers, Reagan Library.

27. Ibid.

28. "Industry Urged to Lend Government's Best Men," *Daily Telegraph,* November 7, 1969.

29. Peter Hillmore, "Reagan Looks to Big Shots," *Guardian,* November 7, 1969.

30. John Campbell, *Margaret Thatcher Volume One: The Grocer's Daughter* (London: Jonathan Cape, 2000), 357.

31. Margaret Thatcher, *The Autobiography* (London: HarperPress, 2013), 213.

32. Barbara Castle, *The Castle Diaries 1964–1970* (London: Weidenfeld and Nicolson, 1984), 726; photograph of Reagan sitting next to Castle, *Daily Telegraph,* November 7, 1969. (According to the caption, Reagan was photographed laughing at Castle's joke after she told the IOD that "as a sign of her emancipation, she intended to treat the delegates as equals.")

33. Castle, *Diaries*, 725.

34. Excerpts of remarks, Governor Ronald Reagan, British National Export Council, November 10, 1969, London, England, Research File, Foreign Travel (RR), Europe 10/28–11/69 (1/2), Molly Sturgess Tuthill, Ronald Reagan Governor's Papers, Reagan Library.

35. Ibid.

36. UPI, "Reagan in London, Praises Nixon Courage," *International Herald Tribune,* November 4, 1969, Research File, Foreign Travel (RR), Europe 10/28–11/69 (2/2), Molly Sturges Tuthill, Ronald Reagan Governor's Papers, Reagan Library; Paris (Reuters), "Reagan in Paris for Three-Day Visit With Top French Officials," *Los Angeles Times,* November 6, 1969, Research File, Foreign Travel (RR), Europe 10/28–11/69 (2/2), Molly Sturges Tuthill, Ronald Reagan Governor's Papers, Reagan Library.

37. See Anne Edwards, *Early Reagan: The Rise of an American Hero* (London: Hodder & Stoughton, 1987); Cannon, *President Reagan,* 73–84.

38. Cannon, *President Reagan,* 461–62.

39. Note, Research File, Foreign Travel (RR), Europe/NATO, 7/3–22/72 (1/2), Ronald Reagan Governor's Papers, Reagan Library.

40. Text of Press Briefing by Jerry Warren, Deputy Press Secretary to President Nixon (To White House Newsmen, June 14, 1972), Research File, Foreign Travel (RR), Europe/NATO, 7/3–22/72 (1/2), Ronald Reagan Governor's Papers, Reagan Library.

41. Dobson, *Anglo-American Relations,*139–41.

42. See Catherine Hynes, *The Year That Never Was: Heath, the Nixon Administration and the Year of Europe, 1970–1974* (Dublin, 2009); Robb, *Strained Partnership,* 73–90.

43. Douglas Brinkley and Luke A. Nichter, *The Nixon Tapes* (Boston: Houghton Mifflin High Court, 2014), 495.

44. The National Archives: PREM 15/1267: Visit of US Governor Ronald Reagan and Mrs. Reagan to UK, Prime Minister Gave Luncheon July 17, 1972. Biography of Governor Reagan attached to a letter from Patrick Grattin (at the Foreign and Commonwealth Office) to AJC Simcock (at 10 Downing Street) on July 5, 1972, (UK National Archives, hereafter TNA).

45. TNA: PREM 15/1267. A Short Briefing for Governor Reagan's Luncheon at 10 Downing Street, attached to a letter from Patrick Grattin to Lord Bridges (at 10 Downing Street) on July 12, 1972.

46. Ibid.

47. Robb, *Strained Partnership*, 38–39, 75–76.

48. TNA: PREM 15/1267. Guest List for a Lunch to Be Held in Honour of Governor and Mrs. Reagan, Monday, July 17, 1972.

49. See Margaret Thatcher Foundation, http://www.margaretthatcher.org/archive/us-reagan.asp, accessed November 25, 2015.

50. TNA: PREM 15/1267. Letter from UK Prime Minister, Edward Heath, to the Governor of California, Ronald Reagan, July 24, 1972.

51. TNA: PREM 15/1267. Letter from US President, Richard Nixon, to UK Prime Minister, Edward Heath, August 8, 1972.

52. TNA: PREM 15/1267. A Short Briefing for Governor Reagan's Luncheon at 10 Downing Street, attached to a letter from Patrick Grattin to Lord Bridges (at 10 Downing Street), July 12, 1972.

53. Robb, *Strained Partnership*, 29–30.

54. Photograph and caption, *Guardian*, July 18, 1972.

55. "Mr. Reagan's Tour of Europe Begins," *The Times*, July 4, 1972.

56. "Mr. Reagan's London Talks," *The Times*, July 18, 1972.

57. Ronald Reagan Schedule, United Kingdom, April 2–9, 1975, Research File, Foreign Travel (RR), Switzerland, England 4/3–9/75, Governor's Office, Molly Sturges Tuthill, Ronald Reagan Governor's Papers, Reagan Library.

58. Geoffrey Smith, *Reagan and Thatcher* (London: Bodley Head, 1990), 5.

59. Ronald Reagan, *An American Life* (London: Hutchinson, 1990), 204.

60. Margaret Thatcher interviewed by Geoffrey Smith about Ronald Reagan for his *Reagan and Thatcher*, January 8, 1990, www.margaretthatcher.org/document/109324.

61. Diplomatic Correspondent, "Warning that Europe is Main Soviet Prize," *The Times*, April 8, 1975. For the Portuguese revolution, see Ronald H. Chilcote, *The Portuguese Revolution: State and Class in the Transition to Democracy* (Plymouth, UK: Rowman & Littlefield, 2010).

62. Ibid.

63. "Ronald Reagan Letter to Margaret Thatcher (Fall of Saigon)," April 30, 1975, www.margaretthatcher.org/document/110357.

64. Ibid.

65. AP wire photo, *Pasadena Star-News,* April 9, 1975, Research File, Foreign Travel (RR), Switzerland, England 4/3–9/75, Governor's Office, Molly Sturges Tuthill, Reagan Library.

66. Ronald Reagan, "On My Christmas List . . . ," from King Features Syndicate, 235 East 45th St., New York, N.Y. For release Friday, December 23, 1977, Research File, Foreign Travel (RR), Switzerland, England 4/3–9/75, Governor's Office, Molly Sturges Tuthill, Reagan Library.

67. Ronald Reagan, "Peace," *Reagan in His Own Hand,* 4.

68. Hugo Young, *One of Us: A Biography of Margaret Thatcher* (London: Macmillan, 1989), 100.

69. This is widely discussed in the historiography. For Thatcher's use of One Nation Conservatism "to domesticate" American New Right economic policies, see Stephen Evans, "The Not So Odd Couple: Margaret Thatcher and One Nation Conservatism," *Contemporary British History* 23 (2009): 101–21. For Thatcherism as a "hegemonic project" in the Conservative Party, see E. H. H. Green, *Thatcher* (London: Hodder Arnold, 2006), 53–54.

70. Young, *One of Us,* 100: Young argued that Thatcher was judged "a mistake that should never have happened."

71. Thatcher's North American tours were discussed in Young, *One of Us,* 120–21; John Campbell, *Margaret Thatcher Volume One: Grocer's Daughter* (London: Pimlico, 2000), 345–47, 356–67.

72. Campbell, *Grocer's Daughter,* 345.

73. Brian Brivati, *Hugh Gaitskell* (London: Richard Cohen, 1996), 100–102, 109–10, 129, 286, 314.

74. David J. Gill, *Britain and the Bomb: Nuclear Diplomacy, 1964–70* (Stanford, CA: Stanford University Press, 2014), 65–68.

75. Memorandum; Henry A. Kissinger to the President re Your Breakfast Meeting with Harold Wilson (April 30 at 8:00 a.m.); April 29, 1971; folder National Security Council Files, Country Files Europe, United Kingdom vol. 6, April 31–August 1971 [2 of 4]; box 728; National Security Council (NSC) files, Country Files—Europe; Richard Nixon Library.

76. Ibid.

77. John Campbell, *Edward Heath: A Biography* (London: Pimlico, 1994), 642.

78. See Smith, *Reagan and Thatcher,* 228; Anthony Seldon, *Blair* (London: Free Press, 2005), 366–71; Alex Spillius, "David Cameron to Meet George W. Bush in US," *Daily Telegraph,* November 30, 2007, http://www.telegraph.co.uk/news/politics/conservative/1570881/David-Cameron-to-meet-George-W-Bush-in-US.html.

79. State Department note on Margaret Thatcher's defeat of Heath, February 4, 1975, Ford Library (White House Central File C0160, box 56), http://www.margaretthatcher.org/document/110507.

80. State Department note on Margaret Thatcher's victory over Whitelaw, February 11, 1975, Ford Library (NSC Country File box 15), http://www.margaretthatcher.org/document/110508.

81. Tony Allen-Mills, "US Dismissed Margaret Thatcher as Suburban Matron Who Would Never Win Power," *Sunday Times,* October 28, 2007 (State Department files), http://www.margaretthatcher.org/document/111070.

82. Ibid.

83. Green, *Thatcher,*161.

84. Giles Scott-Smith, "'Her Rather Ambitious Washington Program': Margaret Thatcher's International Visitor Program Visit to the United States in 1967," *Contemporary British History* 17, no. 4 (2003): 65–86.

85. Alan Clark, *Diaries* (London: Phoenix, 1993), 219.

86. Lewis Baston, *Reggie: The Life of Reginald Maudling* (Stroud: Sutton, 2004), 469.

87. Campbell, *Grocer's Daughter,* 338–39; Stuart Ball, *The Conservative Party since 1945* (Manchester: Manchester University Press, 1998), 142–62.

88. Margaret Thatcher, "Speech to Chelsea Conservative Association," July 26, 1975, http://www.margaretthatcher.org/document/102750.

89. Campbell, *Grocer's Daughter,* 340.

90. Ibid, 344.

91. Ibid, 345.

92. Ibid, 344.

93. Alan Greenspan note for President Ford ("Britain as a Warning to the United States"), April 23, 1975, Ford Library (C0160 box 56), http://www.margaretthatcher.org/document/110509.

94. Henry Kissinger conversation with President Ford ("Britain is a Tragedy"), January 8, 1975, Ford Library (NSC NSA Memcons box 8), http://www.margaretthatcher.org/document/110510.

95. Stephen Barber, "America Looks to Mrs. Thatcher for Reassurance," *Daily Telegraph,* September 13, 1975.

96. Ibid.

97. TNA: FC082/490 (Part C): Visit to North America by the Leader of the Opposition, Mrs. Thatcher MP. Briefing on the US Political Scene.

98. Ibid.

99. Campbell, *Grocer's Daughter,* 345.

100. TNA: FC082/488: Summary of Meeting in Mrs. Thatcher's Office Regarding her Visit to New York, July 7, 1977, written by Derek Thomas (North America Department, FCO).

101. TNA: FCO 82/489 (Part B), File no. AM3/548/7: Visit to North America by the Leader of the Opposition, Mrs. Thatcher MP. Letter from G. N. Smith (North America Department, FCO) to D. Howe (c/o Mrs. Thatcher's office), July 21, 1975.

102. Letter from Derek Howe to Margaret Thatcher, July 24, 1975, THCR 6/4/1/6, Margaret Thatcher Papers, Churchill Archives Centre, Cambridge, UK (hereafter THCR).

103. Ellen Warren, "Tory Mrs. Thatcher to Visit Here," *Chicago Daily News,* July 23, 1975, THCR 6/4/1/1.

104. Daniel J. Edelman, "British Party Leader to Speak in New York," September 3, 1975, press release for the Institute for Socioeconomic Studies, THCR 6/4/1/6.

105. Ibid.

106. Letter from Derek Howe to Margaret Thatcher, August 14, 1975, THCR 6/4/1/6.

107. Letter from Arthur L. Gavshon (Diplomatic and Political Editor, Associated Press) to Derek Howe, September 8, 1975, THCR 6/4/1/6.

108. Letter from Derek Howe to Margaret Thatcher, September 8, 1975, THCR 6/4/1/6.

109. Letter from Derek Howe to Margaret Thatcher, September 11, 1975, THCR 6/4/1/6.

110. "Tory Leader on Cause of 'English Sickness,'" *The Times,* September 16, 1975.

111. Editorial, "Mrs. Thatcher's New York Speech," *The Times,* September 17, 1975.

112. Editorial, *Daily Telegraph,* September 16, 1974.

113. Peter Kihss, *New York Times,* September 16, 1975.

114. "The Fashionable Mrs. T. Wows New York," *Daily Express,* September 17, 1975.

115. Ibid.

116. TNA: FCO 82/491 (Part D), File no. AM/3/348/7: Visit to North America by the Leader of the Opposition, Mrs. Thatcher MP. Remarks made by the Rt. Hon. Margaret Thatcher, MP, to the Pilgrims of the United States, New York, September 16, 1975.

117. Ibid.

118. TNA: FCO 82/491 (Part D), File no. AM/3/348/7. Transcript of interview with Margaret Thatcher on NBC *Today* program, September 16, 1975.

119. Ibid.

120. Ian Ball, "Britain Is at the 11th Hour," *Daily Telegraph,* September 17, 1975.

121. Simon Winchester, "Thatcher Dropped from TV Show," *Guardian,* September 19, 1975.

122. TNA: FCO 82/491 (Part D), File no. AM/3/348/7. Record of Mrs. Thatcher's meeting with members of the Senate Foreign Relations Committee, Capitol Hill, September 18, 1975.

123. Ibid.

124. TNA: FCO 82/491 (Part D), File no. AM/3/348/7. Meeting between Margaret Thatcher and House International Relations Committee, September 18, 1975.

125. Ibid.

126. "Enter Mrs. Thatcher, Flower among Thorns," *Daily Mail,* September 19, 1975.

127. Kissinger briefing for Ford meeting with Margaret Thatcher, September 16, 1975, Ford Library (NSC Country File box 15), http://www.margaretthatcher.org/document/110527.

128. TNA: FCO 82/490 (Part C), File no. 3/548/7. P. E. Ramsbotham, "Conversation between President Ford and Mrs. Thatcher, September 18, 1975," September 19, 1975.

129. Margaret Thatcher letter to President Ford, September 21, 1975, Ford Library (White House Central File C0160 box 56), www.margaretthatcher.org/document/110546.

130. Fred Emery, "Mrs. Thatcher Charms US Politician Out of Cynicism on Britain," *The Times,* September 22, 1975.

131. Richard Beeston, "No Foul, Says Mrs. Thatcher," *Daily Telegraph,* September 19, 1975.

132. Fred Emery, "Mrs. Thatcher Feels She Has Won International Acceptance," *The Times,* September 26, 1975.

133. "Enter Mrs. Thatcher, Flower among Thorns," *Daily Mail,* September 19, 1975.

134. Winchester, "Thatcher Dropped."

135. Philip Fin, "I Think Your Politicians are Wonderful! Washington Cop's Verdict on Maggie," *Daily Mail,* September 22, 1975.

136. Editorial, "Into the Trap?," *Daily Express,* September 17, 1975.

137. David Cross, "Britain's Twin Evils—by Margaret Thatcher," *Daily Mail,* September 16, 1975.

138. "Callaghan Attack on Tory Leader's View of Britain," *The Times,* September 26, 1975.

139. Margaret Thatcher, *The Path to Power* (New York: Harper Collins, 1995) 359.

140. Ibid, 360.

141. TNA: FCO 82/491 (Part D): Letter from James Callaghan to Margaret Thatcher, October 17, 1975; Patrick Cosgrove, "Mrs. Thatcher and the Impudent Politicians of the FO," *Spectator,* October 18, 1975.

142. TNA: FCO 82/491 (Part D): Letter from Derek Thomas (North America Department, FCO) to RM Russell (British Embassy, Washington, DC), September 30, 1975.

143. Ibid.

144. For an account of Reagan's 1976 presidential campaign, see Craig Shirley, *Reagan's Revolution: The Untold Story of the Campaign that Started It All* (Nashville: Thomas Nelson, 2010).

145. John O'Sullivan, *The President, the Pope, and the Prime Minister* (Washington, DC: Regnery, 2006), 30.

146. Ronald Reagan, "Wanted: A New Dream for America; Why I Am a Candidate for the Presidency,"*Daily Telegraph,* November 20, 1975.

147. Ibid.

148. Ibid.

149. Norman Moss, "The American Election Circus Comes to Britain," *The Times,* July 7, 1976.

150. Stephen Barber, "Reagan Promises Gentlemanly Fight against Ford," *Daily Telegraph,* November 21, 1975.

151. Jonathan Steele, "California Split," *Guardian,* November 21, 1975.

152. "Reagan in Gun Scare," *Guardian,* November 21, 1975.

153. Jane Gaskell, "America," *Daily Mail,* November 21, 1975.

154. Editorial, "The Republican Choice," *The Times,* August 20, 1976.

155. "Early Start in Race for Presidency," *The Times,* August 4, 1978.

156. Brian Vine, "Reagan Rides off into the Sunset . . . the End," *Daily Express,* August 20, 1976.

157. Jonathan Steele, "Ford Picks a No. 2 with Aggression," *Guardian,* August 20, 1976.

158. Briefing material for President Carter, March 21, 1977, Carter Library (NLC-1–1-3–28–26), available from www.margaretthatcher.org/document/110875.

159. *New York Times,* May 9, 1977, 14.

160. TNA: FCO 82/774 (Part B): Telegram from Peter Jay (British Ambassador to Washington, DC) to the FCO, July 28, 1977.

161. TNA: FCO 82/774 (Part B): Telegram from Peter Jay to the FCO, August 1, 1977; Telegram from Peter Jay to the FCO, August 8, 1977; Letter from Miss M. E. Hunt (FCO) to Mrs. R. J. Meadway (No. 10 Downing Street), August 8, 1977; Telegram from Peter Jay to the FCO, August 9, 1977.

162. Dobson, *Anglo-American Relations,* 144.

163. "Post-Socialist Era near Says Mrs. Thatcher," *Daily Telegraph,* September 9, 1977.

164. Ross Mark, "What a Swell Party It Was!" *Daily Express,* September 13, 1977. Thatcher was first subject to Soviet condemnation as an inflexible "Iron Lady" by the *Red Star,* a Soviet Army newspaper, on January 24, 1976. This was in response to her speech at Kensington Town Hall ("Britain Awake") on January 19, 1976; see http://www.margaretthatcher.org/document/102939.

165. Ross Mark, "Just Like a Woman: Maggie Tells How the Feminine Touch Would Work at No. 10," *Daily Express,* September 15, 1977.

166. Ibid.

167. "It's Super Nanny, the Leader with Some Medicine," *Daily Mail,* September 14, 1977.

168. TNA: FCO 82/774 (Part B): Letter from Ramsay Melhuish (North America Department FCO) to Mr. Graham (PS/PUS, British Embassy), September 13, 1977.

169. TNA: FCO 82/774, (Part B): Letter from R. M. Russell (British Embassy, Washington, DC) to M. R. Melhuish Esq. (North America Department, FCO), September 26, 1977.

170. Arguably, Hayek proved to be more significant in the United Kingdom than Friedman. For instance, Thatcher's monetarist policies were more in line with Hayek's views than the gradualist approach advocated by Friedman. See James Cooper, *Margaret Thatcher and Ronald Reagan: A Very Political Special Relationship* (London: Palgrave Macmillan, 2012), 49–51.

171. PRO FCO 82/774, (Part B): Visit to the United States of Margaret Thatcher, September 6–14, briefings enclosed with letter from Ramsay Melhuish (North America Department, FCO) to the Hon. Adm. Butler, MP, August 25, 1977.

172. *New York Times,* September 14, 1977.

173. Ross Mark, "Get Me to the President on Time!" *Daily Express,* September 14, 1977.

174. Ibid.

175. Margaret Thatcher letter to President Carter September 15, 1977, Carter Library (White House Central File: C0167), available from www.margaretthatcher.org/document/110486.

176. TNA: FC082/774, (Part B): Letter from Ramsay Melhuish (North America Department, FCO) to Mr. Hall and Mr. Graham (British Embassy in Washington, DC), September 30, 1977.

177. TNA: FCO 82/774, (Part B): Letter from the Rt. Hon. Mrs. Margaret Thatcher, MP, to Ramsay Melhuish Esq., September 21, 1977.

178. TNA: FCO 82/774, (Part B): Letter from R. M. Russell (British Embassy, Washington, DC) to M. R. Melhuish Esq. (North America Department, FCO), September 26, 1977. (In this instance, P.U.S.S is an abbreviation for parliamentary undersecretary of state.)

179. Ibid.

180. Brzezinski memo for Carter ("Thatcher No Longer 'The Dogmatic Lady' Who Visited in 1977"), May 12, 1979, Carter Library (Brzezinski Donated Papers, box 42), available from www.margaretthatcher.org/document/110467.

181. Author unknown, handwritten note, Research File, Foreign Travel (RR), Europe 11/25–12/3/78, Governor's Office, Molly Sturges Tuthill, Reagan Library.

182. Ronald Reagan schedule, Europe, November 25–December 3, 1978, Research File, Foreign Travel (RR), Europe 11/25–12/3/78, Governor's Office, Molly Sturges Tuthill, Reagan Library.

183. Ibid.

184. Smith, *Reagan and Thatcher,* 7.

185. Ibid.

186. Ronald Reagan, "Miscellaneous II," *Reagan in His Own Hand,* 47.

187. Smith, *Reagan and Thatcher,* 11.

188. Ibid, 23.

189. Ibid, 19.

190. Ibid, 22.

191. Arthur Laffer, "Margaret Thatcher's Tax Increase," *Wall Street Journal,* August 20, 1979.

192. David Cross, "Mr. Reagan Offers Same Old Recipes," *The Times,* November 15, 1979.

193. Warren Weaver Jr., "Anderson Traveling Overseas Tomorrow," *New York Times,* July 6, 1980.

194. Richard Nixon, Letter to the Editor, "The Foreign Travels of Ronald Reagan," *New York Times,* July 17, 1980.

195. Cannon, *President Reagan,* 461–62.

196. Peter Jay, "Adjusting to the President Reagan Era," *The Times,* November 6, 1980.

197. Ibid.

198. Editorial, "Democracy but Scarcely Justice," *Guardian,* November 6, 1980.

199. Margaret Thatcher, *The Downing Street Years* (London: HarperCollins, 1993), 156.

200. See "Margaret Thatcher—Personal Attributes," *Ipsos MORI,* https://www.slideshare.net/IpsosMORI/margaret-thatcher-poll-rating-trends, accessed December 15, 2017.

201. "No. 10 Telephone Conversation, Margaret Thatcher and Ronald Reagan," January 21, 1981, http://www.margaretthatcher.org/document/114254. "PR" is President Reagan, "PM" is Prime Minister Thatcher.

202. FCO 82/1110: Steering Brief, Brief by Foreign and Commonwealth Office, February 19, 1981, Prime Minister's Visit to the United States, February 25–28, File no. AMU 026/7 Part B, Prime Minister's Visit to the US: Briefing, TNA.

203. Ronald Reagan, "Remarks at the Welcoming Ceremony for Prime Minister Margaret Thatcher of the United Kingdom," February 26, 1981, http://www.reagan.utexas.edu/archives/speeches/1981/22681b.htm.

2. A Political "Special Relationship," 1981

1. John Campbell, *Margaret Thatcher, Volume Two: The Iron Lady* (London: Vintage, 2008), 6.

2. Eric J. Evans, *Thatcher and Thatcherism: The Making of the Contemporary World,* 2nd ed. (London: Routledge, 2004), 21.

3. "No. 10 Telephone Conversation, Margaret Thatcher and Ronald Reagan," January 21, 1981, http://www.margaretthatcher.org/document/114254, ("PR" is President Reagan, "PM" is Prime Minister Thatcher).

4. Editorial, *Daily Telegraph,* December 17, 1979.

5. Margaret Thatcher, Speech at White House Arrival Ceremony, December 17, 1979, margaretthatcher.org/document/104194.

6. Nicholas Henderson, *Mandarin: The Diaries of Nicholas Henderson* (London: Weidenfeld and Nicolson, 1994), 316–17.

7. Ibid, 319.

8. Brian Vine, "A Call to Arms—Maggie's 'Danger Decade' Warning," *Daily Express,* December 19, 1979.

9. Stephen Baker, "Thatcher Backs Iran Trade Ban; Carter Planning Sanctions Move," *Daily Telegraph,* December 18, 1979.

10. William Rees-Mogg, "How America Sees Europe, Best of Friends with Britain Again," *The Times,* May 6, 1980.

11. Thomas Robb, *Jimmy Carter and the Anglo-American "Special Relationship"* (Edinburgh: Edinburgh University Press, 2016), 137–41.

12. For an introductory to the "Troubles," see Richard English, *Armed Struggle: A History of the IRA* (Oxford: Oxford University Press, 2003); David McKittrick, *Making Sense of the Troubles* (Belfast: Blackstaff, 2000); Jack Holland, *Hope Against History: The Ulster Conflict* (London: Coronet Books, 1999); Sabine Wichert, *Northern Ireland since 1945* (London: Longman, 1999). For "Irish-America" and Northern Ireland, see Seán Cronin, *Washington's Irish Policy, 1916–1986* (Dublin: Anvil Books, 1987); Andrew J. Wilson, *Irish America and the Ulster Conflict 1968–1995* (Belfast: Blackstaff, 1995); Ray O'Hanlon, *The New Irish Americans* (Niwot, CO: Roberts Rinehart, 1998); Joseph E. Thompson, *American Policy and Northern Ireland: A Saga of Peacebuilding* (London: Praeger, 2001).

13. "Cabinet Office Briefing for Margaret Thatcher, Washington Visit, UK Objectives," November 28, 1979, http://www.margaretthatcher.org/document/112131.

14. Ibid.

15. Thompson, *American Policy,* 86–87. For a detailed account of this issue, see Andrew Sanders, "The Role of Northern Ireland in Modern Anglo-American Relations: the US Department of State and the Royal Ulster Constabulary, 1979," *Journal of Transatlantic Studies* 12, no. 2 (2014): 163–81.

16. Wilson, *Irish America,* 159–60. For O'Neill and Northern Ireland, see, for instance, James Cooper, "'A Log-Rolling, Irish-American Politician, Out to Raise Votes in the United States': Tip O'Neill and the Irish Dimension of Anglo-American Relations, 1977–1985," *Congress and the Presidency,* 42 (2015): 1–27.

17. "Margaret Thatcher Plenary Meeting with President Jimmy Carter," December 17, 1979, http://www.margaretthatcher.org/document/112136.

18. Ibid.

19. "Record of a Meeting between the Prime Minister and Members of the US Congress at the US Senate, Washington, DC, on Monday, December 17 at 1600 hours," [Prepared by] British Embassy, Washington, December 19, 1979, http://www.margaretthatcher.org/document/112139.

20. Ibid.

21. See, for instance, Andrew Denham, *Think-Tanks of the New Right* (Dartmouth: Routledge, 1996).

22. "Alfred Sherman Paper for Margaret Thatcher," February 8, 1981, http://www.margaretthatcher.org/document/114255.

23. The National Archives (UK National Archives, hereafter TNA): FC082/1110: Steering Brief, Brief by Foreign and Commonwealth Office, February 19, 1981, Prime Minister's Visit to the United States, February 25–28, 1981.

24. TNA: FC082/1110: Exchanges about United States and United Kingdom Economic Policy, Brief by HM Treasury, February 20, 1981.

25. Ibid.

26. TNA: FC082/1110: Brief by Foreign and Commonwealth Office, United States Internal Political and Economic Scene, February 19, 1981.

27. Ibid.

28. TNA: FC082/1110: Steering Brief, Brief by Foreign and Commonwealth Office, February 19, 1981, Prime Minister's Visit to the United States, February 25–28.

29. Ibid.

30. Ibid.

31. TNA: FC082/1110: Brief by Foreign and Commonwealth Office, United States Internal Political and Economic Scene, February 19, 1981, Prime Minister's Visit to the United States, February 25–28. Both Reagan and Thatcher were particularly interested in the future of Belize amid Guatemalan claims on the country. London saw an independent Belize as a means to reduce its financial commitment to a former colony while also gaining a new country's commitment to the British Commonwealth. Washington, DC, saw Belizean independence as a bulwark against leftish expansion in the region. For a fuller discussion on US involvement in the Anglo-Guatemalan dispute, see Sally Ann Treharne, *Reagan and Thatcher's Special Relationship: Latin America and Anglo-American Relations* (Edinburgh: Edinburgh University Press, 2015), 145–95.

32. TNA: FCO 82/1110: Northern Ireland (If Raised), Brief by the Northern Ireland Office, February 19, 1981.

33. Ibid.

34. Memorandum, Alexander Haig to Ronald Reagan, "Visit of Prime Minister Thatcher," Briefing Book re visit of British Prime Minister Thatcher, February 25–28, 1981, (binder 1/2) box 91434 (RAC 1), Executive Secretariat, NSC: VIP Visits, Ronald Reagan Library (hereafter Ronald Reagan Library).

35. Ibid.

36. See "No. 10 Record of Conversation (MT-US Senate Members) (*Reagan Administration, defence, nuclear weapons, Soviet Union, Poland, economy, socialism, NATO*)," February 26, 1981, http://www.margaretthatcher.org/document/127292; "No. 10 Note of Conversation (Reagan-Thatcher meeting) (*plenary session*)," February 26, 1981, http://www.margaretthatcher.org/document/113943.

37. "Martin Anderson Note to Senior White House Staff, ('Reaganism and Thatcherism')" February 26, 1981, http://www.margaretthatcher.org/document/111729.

38. Ibid.

39. Memorandum, Alexander Haig to Ronald Reagan, "Visit of Prime Minister Thatcher," Briefing Book re visit of British Prime Minister Thatcher, February 25–28, 1981, binder 1/2, box 91434 (RAC 1), Executive Secretariat, NSC: VIP Visits, Ronald Reagan Library.

40. Ibid.

41. Ibid.

42. Department of State, Briefing Paper, UK Domestic Economic Policy, February 17, 1981, Briefing Book re visit of British Prime Minister Thatcher, February 25–28, 1981, binder 1/2, box 91434 (RAC 1), Executive Secretariat, NSC: VIP Visits, Ronald Reagan Library.

43. Memorandum, Alexander Haig to Ronald Reagan, "Visit of Prime Minister Thatcher."

44. Memorandum, Chuck Tyson to Jim Rentschler, Thatcher Visit and Related Thoughts, Official Working Visit of Prime Minister Thatcher of UK, 2/26/81, box 4, Charles Tyson Files, Ronald Reagan Library.

45. Ibid.

46. Ibid.

47. Philip Geyelin, "In Thatcher's Tracks," *Washington Post,* February 24, 1981.

48. Ibid.

49. Ross Mark, "Britain 'On the Slippery Slope,'" *Daily Express,* February 26, 1981.

50. Henderson diary, *Mandarin,* February 18, 1981, http://www.margaretthatcher.org/archive/displaydocument.asp?docid=110521.

51. Ibid.

52. John Warden, "Red Carpet for Winner Maggie," *Daily Express,* February 26, 1981.

53. Ronald Reagan, "Remarks at the Welcoming Ceremony for Prime Minister Margaret Thatcher of the United Kingdom," February 26, 1981, http://www.reagan.utexas.edu/archives/speeches/1981/22681b.htm.

54. Margaret Thatcher, "Remarks Arriving at the White House," February 26, 1981, http://www.margaretthatcher.org/document/104576.

55. "No. 10 Note of Conversation, Reagan-Thatcher Meeting (plenary session)," February 26, 1981, http://www.margaretthatcher.org/document/113943.

56. Ronald Reagan, *The Reagan Diaries,* ed. Douglas Brinkley (New York: HarperCollins, 2007), 5.

57. Ronald Reagan, "Remarks of the President and Prime Minister Thatcher of the United Kingdom Following Their Meetings," February 26, 1981, http://www.reagan.utexas.edu/archives/speeches/1981/22681c.htm.

58. Margaret Thatcher, "Remarks Leaving the White House," February 26, 1981, http://www.margaretthatcher.org/document/104577; see John Warden, "Maggie: Don't Rush to Russia," *Daily Express,* February 28, 1981; Ian Aitken, "Salvador Dominates Thatcher Talks in US," *Guardian,* February 27, 1981.

59. Anthony Holden, "The Sweet Smell of Summitry Goes Sour," *Observer,* March 1, 1981.

60. Reagan, *Reagan Diaries,* 5.

61. Holden, "Sweet Smell of Summitry," 13.

62. Donald Regan's Criticism of Mrs. Thatcher's Economic Policy, Transcript from BBC Radio 4, *Today,* February 27, 1981, attached to letter from Sir Kenneth Couzens KCB, Overseas Finance, HM Treasury, to Mr. Beryl Sprinkel, Under Secretary Designate, Monetary Affairs, US Treasury, March 3, 1981, http://www.margaretthatcher.org/document/114256.

63. Ibid.

64. David S. Broder, "Thatcher Meets Reagan; Sharing 'Shock' Therapy," *Washington Post,* February 25, 1981.

65. Peter Simmonds, "In Step with Reagan—but not without a Stumble," *Sunday Telegraph,* March 1, 1981.

66. See http://www.margaretthatcher.org/document/111729, accessed August 26, 2015; Holden, "Sweet Smell of Summitry," 13.

67. Letter, Sir Kenneth Couzens KCB, Overseas Finance, HM Treasury, to Mrs. Beryl Sprinkel.

68. Ibid.

69. Ibid.

70. See Thatcher's speech in New York City accepting the Donovan Award ("The Defence of Freedom"), February 28, 1981, http://www.margaretthatcher.org/document/104584. This speech was naturally favorably reported as delighting the American audience in the *Sunday Telegraph,* March 1, 1981.

71. Margaret Thatcher, "Press Conference for Washington Press Club," February 26, 1981, http://www.margaretthatcher.org/document/104578.

72. Ibid.

73. Ibid.

74. Ibid.

75. Ibid.

76. Ibid.

77. Margaret Thatcher, "TV Interview for CBS Morning News," February 27, 1981, http://www.margaretthatcher.org/document/104473.

78. Ibid.

79. Ibid.

80. Margaret Thatcher, "Speech at Georgetown University," February 27, 1981, http://www.margaretthatcher.org/document/104580.

81. Ibid.

82. Ibid.

83. Ian Aitken, "Thatcher Lectures US on Health of Dollar," *Guardian,* February 28, 1981.

84. Margaret Thatcher, Radio Interview for IRN, February 28, 1981, http://www.margaretthatcher.org/document/104583.

85. Ibid.

86. The "wets" were judged to be ineffective in implementing Thatcherite policies. The "wet/dry" labels among members of the Thatcher government were also a social division: "wets" being traditional Conservative Party grandees and "dries" typically self-made men. See Richard Vinen, *Thatcher's Britain: The Politics and Social Upheaval of the 1980s* (London: Pocket Books, 2009), 117–18. In the American case, the Republicans controlled the Senate and there was scope for Reagan to work with the Democrat-controlled House of Representatives. See, for instance, Karl Gerard Brandt, *Ronald Reagan and the House Democrats: Gridlock, Partisanship, and the Fiscal Crisis* (Columbia: University of Missouri, 2009).

87. Ronald Reagan, "Toasts of the President and Prime Minister Margaret Thatcher of the United Kingdom at the Dinner Honoring the President," February 27, 1981, http://www.reagan.utexas.edu/archives/speeches/1981/22781c.htm.

88. Simmonds, "In Step with Reagan."

89. Margaret Thatcher, "House of Commons Statement (Prime Minister, American Visit)," March 2, 1981, http://www.margaretthatcher.org/document/104585.

90. Ibid.

91. Ibid.

92. Letter, Margaret Thatcher to Sir Nicholas Henderson, March 5, 1981, http://www.margaretthatcher.org/document/114259.

93. Ibid.

94. "Cabinet: Minutes of Full Cabinet—CC(81) 9th," March 5, 1981, http://www.margaretthatcher.org/document/127196.

95. Ibid

96. Ibid.

97. Memorandum, Richard V. Allen to President Reagan, "Britain Drifts," July 31, 1981, http://www.margaretthatcher.org/archive/displaydocument.asp?docid=110522.

98. Ibid. [The Labour Party opposed much of the Reagan administration's foreign and domestic policies. Similarly, the Reagan administration viewed the Labour Party's policy of unilateral nuclear disarmament as potentially disastrous for the Western Alliance.]

99. Memorandum, Richard V. Allen to President Reagan, "Your Meeting with US Ambassador to the United Kingdom," November 9, 1981, http://www.margaretthatcher.org/archive/displaydocument.asp?docid=110524.

100. Memorandum, Richard V. Allen to President Reagan, "Your Meeting with John Louis: A Few Key Points for the Record," November 9, 1981, http://www.margaretthatcher.org/archive/displaydocument.asp?docid=110524.

101. Allan H. Meltzer, "Economic Scene: Policy in the USA and Britain," *New York Times,* August 7, 1981.

102. Don Oberdorfer, "Anglo Accord; US-British Accord Proclaimed 'On All Major Strategic Issues,'" *Washington Post,* March, 1 1981.

103. Richard Aldous, *Reagan & Thatcher: The Difficult Relationship* (London: Hutchinson, 2012), 41–42.

104. Opinion, "Face to Face, Eye to Eye," *Daily Express,* February 26, 1981.

105. Aitken, "Thatcher Lectures US on Health of Dollar."

106. Oberdorfer, "Anglo Accord."

107. Campbell, *Iron Lady,* 124–25.

108. For an examination of Reagan and Thatcher's monetarist policies and taxation reforms, see James Cooper, *Margaret Thatcher and Ronald Reagan: A Very Political Special Relationship* (London: Palgrave Macmillan, 2012), 31–117. For American and British economic circumstances in the context of the 1981 Ottawa Summit, see Aldous, *Reagan and Thatcher,* 45–54.

109. Steven Rattner, "Reagan and Thatcher Differ Over Economics," *New York Times,* July 19, 1981.

110. Ibid.

111. Aldous, *Reagan and Thatcher,* 47–48.

112. See, for instance, John Best, "Politics Loom Large at Economic Summit," *The Times,* July 18, 1981.

113. Ronald Reagan, *An American Life: The Autobiography* (New York: Simon & Schuster, 1990), 350.

114. Ibid.

115. David Blake and Nicholas Ashford, "US Interest Rates Keep the Summit Simmering," *The Times,* July 21, 1981.

116. Henry Giniger, "Reagan Joins Six World Leaders for Economic and Political Talks," *New York Times.*

117. Aldous, *Reagan and Thatcher,* 49.

118. TNA: FCO 82/1093: Bilateral Talks between President Reagan and PM Thatcher, July 20, 1981.

119. Ibid.

120. Ibid.

121. TNA: FCO 82/1093: Chancellor's Meeting with the Secretary of the US Treasury, July 20, 1981 at 0800.

122. Ibid.

123. Wilson, *Irish America,* 194.

124. "Reagan Still Steers Clear of Jail Fast," *Belfast News Letter,* July 21, 1981, TNA: CJ 4/2914, Security Issues in Northern Ireland. For the breakfast meeting, see PRO, FCO 82/1093: Memorandum of Conversation, July 20, 1981, "Bilateral Meeting with President Reagan," Bilateral talks between Ronald Reagan, US President, and Margaret Thatcher, UK Prime Minister, Chateau Montebello, Ottawa, July 20, 1981.

125. Lou Cannon, "Reagan Describes Summit Meeting as 'Worth Its Weight in Gold,'" *Washington Post,* July 23, 1981.

126. Reagan, *Reagan Diaries,* 31.

127. Ibid, 32.

128. Margaret Thatcher, *The Autobiography* (London: Harper Press, 2013).

129. Leonard Silk, "German Urges US to Battle Inflation with Fiscal Policy," *New York Times,* July 22, 1981.

"Declaration of the Ottawa Summit," July 21, 1981,

130. http://www.g8.utoronto.ca/summit/1981ottawa/communique/economy.html.

3. Conflicts at Home and Abroad, 1982

1. Richard Aldous, *Reagan and Thatcher: The Difficult Relationship* (London: Hutchinson, 2012), 61–62.

2. Margaret Thatcher, *The Autobiography* (London: HarperPress, 2013), 387. (For an excellent account of this saga and how it is indicative of the Reagan-Thatcher relationship, see Aldous, *Reagan and Thatcher,* 61–68.

3. For Reagan's response, see H. W. Brands, *Reagan: The Life* (New York: Doubleday, 2015), 382–89.

4. Bert Chapman, *Export Controls: A Contemporary History* (Lanham, MD: University Press of America, 2013), 4.

5. Ibid, 11.

6. Ibid, 17.

7. The National Archives: PREM 19/942 (UK National Archives, hereafter TNA): Possible visit by President Reagan to UK, Telegram, Washington, DC, (Nicholas Henderson, hereafter Washington) to Foreign and Commonwealth Office (hereafter FCO), "President Reagan's Visit," February 12, 1982.

8. Ibid.

9. TNA: PREM 19/942: Memorandum, A. J. Coles to Margaret Thatcher, February 12, 1983.

10. Ibid.

11. Jorgen Rasmussen and James M. McCormick, "British Mass Perceptions of the Anglo-American Special Relationship," *Political Science Quarterly* 108, no. 3 (Autumn 1993): 515–41, 526.

12. TNA: PREM 19/942: Cabinet Office Memorandum, D. J. Wright to R. A. Burns and John Coles, "Visit to Britain by President Reagan," February 15, 1982.

13. Ibid.

14. TNA: PREM 19/942: Telegram, Washington to FCO, March 7, 1982.

15. President Reagan (Address to Parliament), HC Deb March 8, 1982 vol. 19 cc605–6, hansard.millbanksystems.com/commons/1982/mar/08/president-reagan-address-to-parliament.

16. TNA: PREM 19/942: Telegram, Washington to FCO, March 8, 1982.

17. Ibid.

18. TNA: PREM 19/942: Letter [Record of Conversation], Clive Whitmore (Principal Private Secretary, 10 Downing Street) to Brian Fall (FCO), "Visit by President Reagan," March 8, 1982.

19. Ibid.

20. TNA: PREM 19/942: Letter, Margaret Thatcher to David Owen, March 9, 1982.

21. Ibid.

22. TNA: PREM 19/942: Letter, Margaret Thatcher to David Steel, March 9, 1982.

23. TNA: PREM 19/942: Letter, Margaret Thatcher to Michael Foot, March 9, 1982.

24. TNA: PREM 19/942: Telegram, Washington to FCO, "President Reagan's Visit," March 9, 1982.

25. Ibid.

26. TNA: PREM 19/942: CC (82) 10th, March 11, 1982, item 2.

27. Ibid.

28. TNA: PREM 19/942: Letter, Michael Foot to Margaret Thatcher, March 11, 1982.

29. Ibid.

30. TNA: PREM 19/942: Cable, Ronald Reagan to Margaret Thatcher, March 13, 1982.

31. PREM 19/942: Letter, Clive Whitmore (Principal Private Secretary, 10 Downing Street) to John Halliday (Home Office), March 18, 1982.

32. Ibid.

33. Ibid.

34. TNA: PREM 19/942: Telegram, Washington to FCO, "President's Visit," March 21, 1982.

35. Ibid.

36. TNA: PREM 19/942: Telegram, Washington to FCO, March 23, 1982.

37. Ibid.

38. TNA: PREM 19/942: Memorandum, Bernard Ingham to Margaret Thatcher, "President Reagan's Visit—Media," March 23, 1982.

See Margaret Thatcher, "TV Interview for NBC," June 9, 1982, http://www.margaretthatcher.org/document/104794; Margaret Thatcher, "TV Interview for ABC," June 9, 1982.

39. http://www.margaretthatcher.org/document/104795; Margaret Thatcher, "TV Interview for CBS," June 9, 1982, http://www.margaretthatcher.org/document/104960.

40. Richard Vinen, *Thatcher's Britain: The Politics and Social Upheaval of the Thatcher Era* (London: Simon & Schuster, 2009), 134–38.

41. Ibid, 139.

42. For a history of the Falklands War, see Lawrence Freedman, *The Official History of the Falklands Campaign* (London: Routledge 2005); Stephen Badsey, Rob Havers, Mark Grove, eds., *The Falklands Conflict Twenty Years On: Lessons for the Future* (New York: Frank Cass, 2005).

43. Don Oberdorfer, "A Diplomatic Dilemma: US Has Pacts with Feuding Nations Feuding Nations Have Treaties with the US," *Washington Post,* April 4, 1982.

44. Ronald Reagan, *The Reagan Diaries,* ed. Douglas Brinkley (New York: HarperCollins, 2007), 78.

45. Richard Vinen, *Thatcher's Britain*, 142.

46. Nicholas Henderson, *Mandarin: The Diaries of Nicholas Henderson* (London: Weidenfeld and Nicolson, 1994), 467–68.

47. "Margaret Thatcher Message to Ronald Reagan," April 16, 1982, http://www.margaretthatcher.org/document/122860.

48. National Security Council Meeting Minutes, Archive (Reagan Library), April 30, 1982, http://www.margaretthatcher.org/document/114329.

49. Ibid.

Ronald Reagan, *An American Life: The Autobiography* (New York: Simon & Schuster, 1990),

50. 359–60.

51. Telegram from Secretary of State Haig to the Department of State, London, April 9, 1982m 0131Z; Alexander R. Wieland and Adam M. Howard, ed., *Foreign*

Relations of the United States, 1981–1988, vol. 13, Conflict in the South Atlantic, 1981–1984, (Washington, DC: United States Government Publishing Office, 2015), Document 82.

52. Ibid.

53. Barry Sussman, "President's Rate of Approval Declines, Continuing Slump," *Washington Post,* June 4, 1982.

54. "No. 10 Record of Conversation (Margaret Thatcher, Geoffrey Howe, 'Versailles Summit')," May 26, 1982, http://www.margaretthatcher.org/document/137515.

55. Ibid.

56. TNA: PREM 19/943: Visit by President Reagan, June 1982: Meetings with Prime Minister; part 2, Alan Walters, "Briefing Note for the Prime Minister on the United States Deficit Interest Rates and Taxes," June 1, 1982.

57. Ibid.

58. TNA: PREM 19/943: Alan Walters, "Background Note Deficit and Interest Rates," June 1, 1982.

59. Ibid.

60. TNA: PREM 19/943: Letter, Geoffrey Howe to Margret Thatcher, "President Reagan and the US Budget Debate," June 3, 1982.

61. Ibid.

62. TNA: PREM 19/943: Letter, F. N. Richards (FCO, Private Secretary) to A. J. Coles (Private Secretary, 10 Downing Street), "Existing Contracts (John Brown)," June 8, 1982.

63. Ibid.

64. TNA: PREM 19/943: Steering Brief, President Reagan's Visit to London June 7–9, 1982, Talks with the Prime Minister, 9 am Wednesday June 9, Brief by the FCO, June 4, 1982.

65. Ibid.

66. TNA: PREM 19/943: Letter, D. B. Omand (Ministry of Defense) to A. J. Coles (10 Downing Street), "President Reagan's Visit—US Assistance in the Falklands Context," June 4, 1982. (According to Omand, the United States had provided extensive material assistance and logistical support. Material assistance included antimissile defenses; antiaircraft defenses; communications; mines; ground weapons and ammunition; anti-radar missiles; personnel protection; night vision; engineering spares and equipment. Logistical support revolved around Ascension Island; airfield matting; sea transport capacity; air-to-air refuelling; and intelligence.)

67. Leonard Downie Jr., "Reagan Flies to Britain, Plans Talks With Thatcher on Falklands," *Washington Post,* June 8, 1982.

68. *Foreign Relations of the United States,* Document 322, Memorandum from Secretary of State Haig to President Reagan, "Paris," undated.

69. Ibid.

70. *Foreign Relations of the United States,* Document 326, Memorandum from Secretary of State Haig to President Reagan, "London," undated, "Your Meeting with UK Prime Minister Margaret Thatcher, June 9, 1982."

71. Ibid.

72. John Coles (10 Downing Street) to Brian Fall (FCO), June 9, 2016, "No. 10 Record of Conversation (Margaret Thatcher and Ronald Reagan)," June 4, 1982, http://www.margaretthatcher.org/document/122121.

73. Ibid.

74. "No. 10 Record of Conversation (Conversation between Heads of Delegation on the Evening of Friday)," 4 June 1982, http://www.margaretthatcher.org/document/137561.

75. Leonard Silk, "A Gloomy View from Versailles: Europe Fears the Decade ahead Will Mean More Joblessness and Perhaps a New Outburst of Inflation," *New York Times,* June 6, 1982.

76. "G7: Cabinet Office Record of Conversation (Versailles Economic Summit: First Plenary Session)," June 5, 1982, http://www.margaretthatcher.org/document/137725.

77. Ibid.

78. Reagan, *Reagan Diaries,* 87.

79. Thatcher, *Autobiography,* 389.

80. Ibid.

81. "Candy Caper: Jelly Beans, 1 Reagan, 0," *Washington Post,* June 7, 1982.

82. Reagan, *Reagan Diaries,* 88.

83. Reagan, *American Life,* 555. For full transcripts of these two speeches, see "Address to Members of the British Parliament, June 8, 1982," The Public Papers of President Ronald W. Reagan, Ronald Reagan Presidential Library, https://www.reaganlibrary.gov/archives/speech/address-members-british-parliament; and "Address before the Bundestag in Bonn, Federal Republic of Germany, June 9, 1982," The Public Papers of President Ronald W. Reagan, Ronald Reagan Presidential Library, https://www.reaganlibrary.gov/archives/speech/address-bundestag-bonn-federal-republic-germany.

84. Ronald Reagan, "Address to Members of the British Parliament, Palace of Westminster, June 8, 1982"; Ronald Reagan, *Speaking My Mind: Selected Speeches* (Simon & Schuster: London, 1989), 107.

85. Margaret Thatcher, *The Downing Street Years,* (London: HarperCollins, 1993), 258.

86. Ibid.

87. Ibid. Regarding Autocue, it allows someone to read the text of a speech projected to a large piece of glass, enabling the illusion of the speaker presenting to the audience without the aid of notes or a script.

88. William Borders, "Reagan at Westminster: Red Carpet All the Way," *New York Times,* June 9, 1982.

89. Reagan, "Address to Members of the British Parliament, Palace of Westminster, June 8, 1982," 116.

90. Ibid.

91. Ibid.

92. Ibid, 120.

93. Ronald Reagan, "Address to Members of the British Parliament, Palace of Westminster, June 8, 1982," 114–15.

94. Ian Atkin, "Thatcher Stands Firm with New Reagan Support," *Guardian,* June 9, 1982.

95. Robert Porter, "We Support You," *Daily Mail,* June 9, 1982.

96. Opinion, "Reagan's Rhetoric," *Daily Express,* June 9, 1982.

97. "The President's Beliefs," *Daily Telegraph,* June 9, 1982.

98. Andrew Alexander, "So Charming Mr. Reagan, but I Must Refuse Your Invitation to a Crusade," *Daily Mail,* June 9, 1982.

99. Editorial, "Mr Reagan Calls for a Crusade," *The Times,* June 9, 1982.

100. "American Sweet and Sour," *Guardian,* June 9, 1987.

101. Opinion, "Reagan's Rhetoric," *Daily Express,* June 9, 1987.

102. R. W. Apple Jr., "President Urges Global Crusade for Democracy," *New York Times,* June 9, 1982.

103. Lou Cannon, "President Calls for 'Crusade': Reagan Proposes Plan to Counter Soviet Challenge," *Washington Post,* June 9, 1982.

104. Donnie Radcliffe, "Center Stage at the Castle: At the Banquet at Windsor, Exchanging Toasts & Mixing China," *Washington Post,* June 9, 1982.

105. Ibid.

106. Ibid.

107. "Conservative Party Election Broadcast," June 7, 1983, https://www.margaretthatcher.org/document/105382.

108. TNA: PREM 19/943: Visit by President Reagan, June 1982: Meetings with Prime Minister; part 2: Record of a Meeting between the Prime Minister and the President of the United States of America on Wednesday 9 June 1982 at 10 Downing Street at 0945.

109. Ibid. (For British views on nuclear arms control, see Thomas K. Robb, *Jimmy Carter and the Anglo-American "Special Relationship"* [Edinburgh: Edinburgh University Press, 2018], 41–44, 148.)

110. Margaret Thatcher, "Speech at Lunch for US President (Ronald Reagan)," June 8, 1982, http://www.margaretthatcher.org/document/104957.

111. Ibid.

112. Ibid.

113. Margaret Thatcher, "Remarks Following Talks with President Reagan," June 9, 1982, http://www.margaretthatcher.org/document/104961.

114. Ibid.

115. See William Borders, "Reagan at Westminster: Red Carpet All the Way," *New York Times,* June 9, 1982; Steven Rattner, "Britons Reassured by Reagan's Visit," *New York Times,* June 10, 1982.

116. *Foreign Relations of the United States,* Document 343, Telegram from the Embassy in the United Kingdom to the Department of States, London, June 15, 1982, 1314Z.

117. Ibid.

118. *Foreign Relations of the United States,* Document 352, Message from President Reagan to British Prime Minister Thatcher, Washington, DC, June 18, 1982, 1520Z.

119. *Foreign Relations of the United States,* Document 356, Memorandum from Secretary Haig to President Reagan, Washington, DC, June 19, 1982, "Falklands Crisis."

120. Ibid.

121. "State Department Brief for President Reagan (meeting Margaret Thatcher)," June 22, 1982, http://www.margaretthatcher.org/document/110518.

122. Ibid.

123. *Foreign Relations of the United States,* Document 361, Memorandum of Conversation, Washington, DC, June 23, 1982, "President's Meeting with UK Prime Minister Thatcher."

124. Ibid.

125. "White House Record of Conversation ('President's Meeting with UK PM Margaret Thatcher'—Bush, Haig, Clark also)," June 23, 1982, http://www.margaretthatcher.org/document/136353.

126. Ibid.

127. John Coles (10 Downing Street) to Brian Fall (FCO), "No. 10 Record of Conversation (Margaret Thatcher, Ronald Reagan, George H. Bush, Alexander Haig, Nicholas Henderson, William P. Clark)," June 23, 1982, http://www.margaretthatcher.org/document/145054.

128. Ibid. (There is, of course, an established historiography about Anglo-American economic competition, despite close security and strategic cooperation. See, for instance, Alan Dobson, *Anglo-American Relations in the Twentieth Century: Of Friendship, Conflict and the Rise and Decline of Superpowers* [London: Routledge, 1995], 29–31, 81–90.)

129. Reagan, *Reagan Diaries*, 90.

130. Thatcher, *Autobiography.*

131. Nicholas Ashford, "Confident Thatcher Woos US on Falklands," *The Times,* June 24, 1982.

132. Lou Cannon, "Thatcher Meets with President, Reasserts Falklands Sovereignty: Thatcher Reasserts Falklands Sovereignty after Addressing UN, Meeting President," *Washington Post,* June 24, 1982.

133. "Cold War: Weinberger Note of a Meeting with Margaret Thatcher," September 8, 1982, https://www.margaretthatcher.org/document/110636.

134. Ibid.

135. Aldous, *Reagan and Thatcher,* 123–24.

4. Reelections, 1983–1984

1. Geoffrey Smith, *Reagan and Thatcher* (London: Bodley Head, 1990), 141–44, 165.

2. The National Archives (UK National Archives, hereafter TNA): Prem 19/1008: Williamsburg Economic Summit, May 28–30 1983: Record of a Conver-

sation between the Prime Minister and Mr. Edwin Meese, Counsellor to President Reagan, May 4, 1983, at 10 Downing Street.

3. Ibid.

4. Hendrick Smith, "For Reagan, Twin Goals: He Seeks Vindication as Well as Solidarity," *New York Times*, May 29, 1983.

5. TNA: PREM 19/1009: Williamsburg, Economic Summit, May 28–30, 1983, Letter, May 30, 1983, Mr. Coles (Private Secretary, 10 Downing Street) to Brian Falls (Foreign and Commonwealth Office), Prime Minister's Discussion with President Reagan.

6. Ibid.

7. TNA: PREM 19/1009: Record of Discussion between the Chancellor and Secretary Regan on May 28, 1983, in Williamsburg.

8. Ibid.

9. Ibid.

10. TNA: PREM 19/1009: Notes taken at a Plenary Session of the Economic Summit Conference at the Williamsburg Inn, Williamsburg, May 29, 1983.

11. Ibid.

12. No. 10 Record of Telephone Conversation, June 10, 1983, http://margaretthatcher.org/document/140750.

13. Letter, Ronald Reagan to Margaret Thatcher, June 15, 1983, http://margaretthatcher.org/document/109273.

14. Ibid.

15. For a full account of this case, see http://supreme.justia.com/us/463/159/case.html, accessed August 14, 2017.

16. Ibid.

17. Jane Seaberry, "Reagan Decides for States on Taxes," *Washington Post*, September 24, 1983.

18. Letter, Sir Oliver Wright to Mr. Edwin Meese III, September 20, 1983, 324228, C0167, WHORM: Subject file, Ronald Reagan Library.

19. Memorandum, Peter R. Sommer to William P. Clark, "Presidential Reply to Mrs. Thatcher: Unitary Tax," September 22, 1983, 30859, box 35, Executive Secretariat, National Security Council (NSC): Head of State file, United Kingdom: Prime Minister Thatcher (830569–8306168), Ronald Reagan Library.

20. Memorandum (briefing materials), Charles Hill to William P. Clark, September 23, 1983, 22452, United Kingdom, Prime Minister Thatcher, Working Visit, September 29, 1983, box 91437, RAC, Executive Secretariat: NSC VIP Visits, Ronald Reagan Library.

21. Letter, Ronald Reagan to Margaret Thatcher, September 23, 1983, United Kingdom Prime Minister Thatcher (8305659–8306168), box 35, Executive Secretariat, NSC: Head of State file: Records, Ronald Reagan Library.

22. Ibid.

23. TNA: PREM 19/1153, Prime Minister's Visit to Washington: Telegram, Washington to FCO, September 21, 1983.

24. Ibid.

25. TNA: PREM 19/1153, Prime Minister's Visit to Washington, September 1983: Robert Armstrong, to Mr. Coles, September 23, 1983, Prime Minister's Visit to Canada and the United States: September 25–30, 1983, Game Plan: Washington (September 29).

26. Ibid.

27. "US Ambassador (London) to Secretary of State (British hopes for Thatcher US visit)," September 15, 1983, http://www.margaretthatcher.org/document/109408.

28. "Cold War: NSC Briefing for President Reagan," September 19, 1983, http://www.margaretthatcher.org/document/110602.

29. "Cold War: Shultz Briefing for President Reagan (Thatcher meeting)," September 20, 1983, http://www.margaretthatcher.org/document/109389.

30. Ibid.

31. TNA: PREM 19/1153, Prime Minister's Visit to Washington, September 1983: Prime Minister's Visit to Washington: Note on the Ambassador's Dinner for the Prime Minister and American Industrialists, September 28.

32. Ibid.

33. TNA: PREM 19/1153, Prime Minister's Visit to Washington, September 1983: Prime Minister's Visit to Washington: Summary Record of Breakfast Meeting with Senate Foreign Relations Committee on September 29.

34. Ibid.

35. TNA: PREM 19/1153: Record of a Meeting between the Prime Minister and Mr. Paul Volcker, Chairman of the Board of Governors of the Federal Reserve System at the Federal Reserve Building, Washington, on September 29, 1983.

36. Ibid.

37. TNA: PREM 19/1153: Record of a Meeting between the Prime Minister and Treasury Secretary Regan on September 29, at the Department of the Treasury, Washington.

38. Ibid. (For more on the Container Corporation case, see US Reports: Container Corp. v. Franchise Tax Bd., 463 US 159, 1983, https://www.loc.gov/item/usrep463159/.)

39. TNA: PREM 19/1153: Record of a Conversation between the Prime Minister and the President of the United States at the White House on September 29, 1983.

40. TNA: PREM 19/1153: Record of a Conversation at a Working Lunch Given by the President of the United States for the Prime Minister at the White House on September 29, 1983.

41. Ibid.

42. White House Record of Conversation (Thatcher-Reagan) on September 29, 1983, http://www.margaretthatcher.org/document/133913.

43. TNA: PREM 19/1153: Record of a Conversation at a Working Lunch Given by the President of the United States for the Prime Minister at the White House on September 29, 1983.

44. Ibid.

45. White House Record of Conversation (Thatcher-Reagan) September 29, 1983, http://www.margaretthatcher.org/document/133913.

46. Ibid.

47. "US: UKE Washington to FCO, (Prime Minister's Visit to Washington, September 28–30)," http://www.margaretthatcher.org/document/131316.

48. Ibid.

49. Ibid.

50. Donnie Radcliffe, "Margaret Thatcher, in Her Prime; at the Embassy, An Award & Churchillian Praise," *Washington Post,* September 30, 1983.

51. "Remarks of the President and Prime Minister Margaret Thatcher of the United Kingdom Following Their Meetings, September 29, 1983," The Public Papers of President Ronald W. Reagan, Ronald Reagan Presidential Library (hereafter Public Papers), https://www.reaganlibrary.archives.gov/archives/speeches/1983/92983c.htm.

52. Ibid.

53. Ibid.

54. Ibid.

55. Margaret Thatcher, "Press Conference after Meeting President Reagan," September 29, 1983, http://www.margaretthatcher.org/document/105447.

56. Ibid.

57. Ibid.

58. Ibid.

59. See Steven R. Weisman, "US Deficit Worries Mrs. Thatcher," *New York Times,* September 30, 1983.

60. "Cabinet: Minutes of Full Cabinet—CC(83) (Foreign Affairs, EC Affairs)," October 6, 1983, http://www.margaretthatcher.org/document/128269.

61. Richard Aldous, *Reagan & Thatcher: The Difficult Relationship* (London: Hutchinson, 2012), 144; John Campbell, *Margaret Thatcher Volume Two: The Iron Lady* (London: Vintage, 2008), 273.

62. Aldous, *Reagan & Thatcher,* 145.

63. Ibid, 146–48.

64. Ronald Reagan, *The Reagan Diaries,* ed. Douglas Brinkley (New York: HarperCollins, 2007), 190.

65. Aldous, *Reagan & Thatcher,* 151–53. For the full transcript, see "Reagan Phone Call to Thatcher," October 26, 1983, http://www.margaretthatcher.org/document/109426.

66. George Shultz, *Turmoil & Triumph: My Years as Secretary of State* (New York: Charles Scribner's Sons, 1993), 340.

67. Aldous, *Reagan & Thatcher,* 154.

68. "House of Commons PQs," October 27, 1983, http://www.margaretthatcher.org/document/105459.

69. Aldous, *Reagan & Thatcher,* 145. (Thatcher made this statement during a phone-in program on the BBC World Service, October 30, 1983. See http://www.margaretthatcher.org/document/110628.)

70. See Barnaby J. Feder, "US Was Warned by Mrs. Thatcher: She Urged Caution on Reagan," *New York Times,* October 26, 1983; Peter Osnos, "Thatcher Says She Attempted to Dissuade Reagan: Labor Party Leader Claims US Action Represents a 'Humiliation' for Government," *Washington Post,* October 26, 1983.

71. H. W. Brands, *Reagan: The Life* (Doubleday: London, 2015), 400. See also Brands's account of the 1982 conflict between Israel and Lebanon, 382–95.

72. TNA: PREM 19/1151: Visit of Kenneth Dam, US Deputy Secretary of State on November 7, 1983, Record of a Conversation between the Prime Minister and Mr. Dam of the US State Department on Monday November 7, 1983.

73. Ibid.

74. Ibid.

75. Ibid.

76. Ibid.

77. Letter, Ronald Reagan to Margaret Thatcher, May 14, 1984, United Kingdom: Prime Minister Thatcher (8400187–8404387), box 35, Executive Secretariat, NSC: Head of State file: Records, Ronald Reagan Library.

78. Ibid.

79. The Final Report of the Worldwide Unitary Taxation Working Group, Chairman's Report and Supplemental Views, August 1984, Office of the Secretary, Department of the Treasury, http://www.archive.org/stream/finalreportofwor00unit/finalreportofwor00unit_djvu.txt,.

80. Letter, Ronald Reagan to Margaret Thatcher, May 14, 1984, United Kingdom: Prime Minister Thatcher (8400187–8404387), box 35, Executive Secretariat, NSC: Head of State file: Records, Ronald Reagan Library.

81. E. D. Dover, *Images, Issues, and Attacks: Television Advertising by Incumbents and Challengers in Presidential Elections* (Plymouth, DE: Lexington Books, 2006), 28–29.

82. Reagan job approval rating for June 29, 1984, to July 2, 1984, data adapted from the Gallup poll and compiled by Gerhard Peters, Gerhard Peters, and John T. Woolley, eds., *The American Presidency Project,* http://www.presidency.ucsb.edu/data/popularity.php?pres=40&sort=pop&direct=DESC&Submit=DISPLAY, accessed April 23, 2018.

83. "Cabinet: Minutes of Full Cabinet—CC(84) 21st," June 7, 1984, http://margaretthatcher.org/document/133180.

84. Memorandum for the President from Robert C. McFarlane, Subject: Your European Trip: Bilateral Aspects, the President's Trip to Europe: Ireland, UK, and Normandy (1 of 6), June 1 to June 6, 1984, box 20, Coordination, NSC, Office of Records, Reagan Library.

85. Ibid.

86. Memorandum for the President, from George P. Shultz, Subject: Your Trip to the United Kingdom: Setting and Issues, May 14, 1984, The President's Trip to

Europe: Ireland, UK and Normandy (1 of 6), June 1 to June 6, 1984, box 20, Coordination, NSC, Office of Records, Reagan Library.

87. Ibid.

88. Hobart Rowen, "Doubters Await Reagan at Summit: Reagan's Economic Outlook Likely to Be Challenged at Summit," June 4, 1984.

89. PREM 19/1210: UKE Embassy to FCO, London Economic Summit, Telegram June 1, 1984, "Economic Summit: American Expectations."

90. Ibid.

91. "London Economic Summit Conference Declaration, June 9, 1984," (Public Papers), https://www.reaganlibrary.archives.gov/archives/speeches/1984/60984a.htm.

92. Margaret Thatcher, "Press Conference at London G7 Summit," June 9, 1984, http://www.margaretthatcher.org/document/105700.

93. "Remarks and a Question-and-Answer Session with Reporters on the London Economic Summit Conference, June 10, 1984," (Public Papers), https://www.reaganlibrary.archives.gov/archives/speeches/1984/61084a.htm.

94. Ibid.

95. "Cabinet: Minutes of Full Cabinet—CC(84) 22nd," June 14, 1984, http://margaretthatcher.org/document/133181.

96. Reagan, *Reagan Diaries,* 246.

97. Miller Center, Kathleen Osborne Oral History, Personal Assistant to Reagan, April 26, 2003, https://millercenter.org/the-presidency/presidential-oral-histories/kathleen-osborne-oral-history-personal-assistant-reagan. "G7: UKE Washington Telegram to FCO ('US Public Reactions to the Summit')"

98. June 11, 1984, http://margaretthatcher.org/document/145784.

99. Ibid.

100. Editorial, "A Long Way from Normandy," *Washington Post,* June 10, 1984.

101. "G7: US Ambassador Charles Price Letter to MT," June 14, 1984, http://margaretthatcher.org/document/136370.

102. "G7: UKE Washington Telegram to FCO ('Reagan on Summits')," June 15, 1984, http://www.margaretthatcher.org/document/145785.

103. "US: MT Note to Ronald Reagan," November 6, 1984, http://margaretthatcher.org/document/137669.

104. "US: MT Telegram to Ronald Reagan," November 7, 1984, http://margaretthatcher.org/document/136657.

105. "Cabinet: Minutes of Full Cabinet—CC(84) 36th," November 8, 1984, http://margaretthatcher.org/document/133195.

106. "US: No. 10 Record of Conversation (MT, US Ambassador)," November 8, 1984, http://www.margaretthatcher.org/document/149861.

107. Smith, *Reagan and Thatcher,* 141.

108. Ibid.

109. Ibid.

110. Ibid, 142.

111. Cable, Margaret Thatcher to Ronald Reagan, March 29, 1983, United Kingdom: Prime Minister Thatcher, 6420, box 35, Executive Secretariat, NSC, Head of State file: Records, Ronald Reagan Library.

112. Ibid.

113. Ibid.

114. Memorandum for the President, William P. Clark to Ronald Reagan, Subject: Reply to Mrs. Thatcher's Letter on Airline Antitrust Investigation," April 6, 1983, United Kingdom: Prime Minister Thatcher, 2176, box 35, Executive Secretariat, NSC, Head of State file: Records, Ronald Reagan Library.

115. Cable, Ronald Reagan to Margaret Thatcher, April 6, 1983, United Kingdom: Prime Minister Thatcher, 2176, box 35, Executive Secretariat, NSC, Head of State file: Records, Ronald Reagan Library.

116. Ibid.

117. "US: No. 10 Record of Conversation (MT, US Ambassador)," November 8, 1984, http://www.margaretthatcher.org/document/149861.

118. "US: No. 10 Briefing for MT, ('Call by American Ambassador'), November 8, 1984, http://www.margaretthatcher.org/document/149860.

119. Ibid.

120. Ibid.

121. Meeting between the Prime Minister and Secretary Shultz at the British High Commissioner's Residence in New Delhi November 3, 1984, http://www.margaretthatcher.org/document/149849.

122. Ibid.

123. Smith, *Reagan and Thatcher,* 144.

124. Reagan, *Reagan Diaries*, 278.

125. See Alex Brummer and Michael Smith, "Reagan Lifts US Laker Threat to BA," *Guardian,* November 20, 1984; Stephen Aris and Peter Stothard, "Why Reagan Let B.A. Fly away Free," *The Times,* November 21, 1984; "Crash Landing for Free Enterprise," *New York Times,* November 23, 1984.

126. Letter, Senator Howard M. Metzenbaum (D-OH) to Ronald Reagan, November 20, 1984, "Thatcher Visit December 1984 (4)," 277510, box 90920, European and Soviet Affairs Directorate, Ronald Reagan Library.

127. Ibid.

128. See Ian Aitken, "Thatcher to Take Firm Line on Star Wars," *Guardian,* December 21, 1984; "Thatcher Expected to Tell Reagan of 'Star Wars' Fears," *Washington Post,* December 22, 1984.

129. Philip Geyelin, "Thatcher and Reagan," *Washington Post,* December 21, 1984.

130. Reagan, *Reagan Diaries*, 289.

131. Margaret Thatcher, *The Downing Street Years* (London: HarperCollins, 1993), 466.

132. Ibid.

133. Ronald Reagan, *An American Life: The Autobiography* (New York: Simon & Schuster, 1990), 258.

134. Michael Schaller, *Reckoning with Reagan* (Oxford: Oxford University Press, 1992), 130–32.

135. See James Cooper, "From Reykjavik to Fulton: Reagan, Thatcher, and the Ending of the Cold War," *Journal of Transatlantic Studies* 14, no. 4 (2016): 383–400.

136. For the "Four Horsemen" and the extent of presidential in Northern Ireland in this period, see James Cooper, *The Politics of Diplomacy: US Presidents and the Northern Ireland Conflict, 1967–98* (Edinburgh: Edinburgh University Press, 2017), 73–194.

137. For Reagan and Northern Ireland, see James Cooper, "'The Situation over There Really Bothers Me': Ronald Reagan and the Northern Ireland Conflict," *Irish Historical Studies* 41, no. 159 (May 2017). For the relationship between Reagan and O'Neill generally, see Chris Matthews, *Tip and the Gipper: When Politics Worked* (New York: Simon & Schuster, 2013).

138. James Cooper, "'A Log-Rolling, Irish-American Politicians, out to Raise Votes in the United States': Tip O'Neill and the Irish Dimension of Anglo-American Relations, 1977–86," *Congress & the Presidency* 42, no. 1 (2015): 17.

139. Richard Burt to George Shultz, Briefing Memorandum, Visit of Prime Minister Thatcher to Washington, DC, December 22, 1984, [dated December 19, 1984], http://margaretthatcher.org/document/109393.

140. Ibid. (For more on the Clayton Act, including its opposition to unfair business practice and expansion on the 1890 Sherman Law, see William E. Leuchtenburg, *The American President: from Teddy Roosevelt to Bill Clinton* [Oxford University Press: Oxford, 2015], 77–78.)

141. "Cold War: President Reagan's Briefing Cards for Camp David Meeting," December 19, 1984, http://margaretthatcher.org/document/109405.

142. "Cold War: US Treasury Briefing for President Reagan (Thatcher visit)," December 19, 1984, http://margaretthatcher.org/document/109409.

143. Ibid.

144. "Memorandum, George Shultz to President Reagan, December 20, 1984, Subject: Your Meeting with Margaret Thatcher, Prime Minister of the United Kingdom," December 22, 1984, http://margaretthatcher.org/document/10922.

145. Ibid.

146. Ibid. (For the politics of Anglo-American aviation diplomacy, see Alan P. Dobson, "Aspects of Anglo-American Aviation Diplomacy 1976–1993," *Diplomacy and Statecraft* 4, no. 2, [1993]: 235–57; Alan P. Dobson and Joseph A. McKinney, "Sovereignty, Politics and US International Airline Policy," *Journal of Air Law and Commerce* 74 no. 3, [2009]: 527–52.)

147. NSC Briefing, from Robert C. McFarlane to President Reagan, December 21, 1984, http://margaretthatcher.org/document/109223.

148. "US: Ronald Reagan Letter to MT," December 21, 1984, http://margaretthatcher.org/document/136659.

149. Ibid.

150. “Cold War: Record of a Meeting between the Prime Minister and President Reagan at Camp David on December 22, 1984”, http://margaretthatcher.org/document/136436.

151. Ibid.

152. See Alan P. Dobson, *Flying in the Face of Competition: The Policies and Diplomacy of Airline Regulatory Reform in Britain, the USA and the European Community 1968–94* (Aldershot, England: Ashgate, 1995), 147–78.

153. See Dobson, *Face of Competition,* 119–45; Alan P. Dobson, *Peaceful Air Warfare: The United States, Britain, and the Politics of International Aviation* (Oxford: Clarendon Press, 1991), 246–86.

154. Dobson, *Face of Competition,* 4.

155. Ibid, 140.

156. “Cold War: Record of a Meeting between the Prime Minister and President Reagan at Camp David on December 22, 1984,” http://margaretthatcher.org/document/149847.

157. Ibid.

158. Ibid.

159. Leuchtenburg, *American President,* 198.

160. “Cold War: Record of a Meeting between the Prime Minister and President Reagan at Camp David on December 22, 1984,” http://margaretthatcher.org/document/109185.

161. Garret FitzGerald, *All in a Life: An Autobiography* (London: Gill and Macmillan, 1991), 527.

162. Memorandum of Conversation, Subject: Meeting with British Prime Minister Margaret Thatcher, December 22, 1984, http://margaretthatcher.org/document/109185.

163. Ibid.

164. “Press Conference after Camp David Talks,” December 22, 1984, http://margaretthatcher.org/document/109392.

165. Ibid.

166. Thatcher, *Downing Street Years,* 467.

167. See “Wedge-Driving Just Isn’t On,” *Washington Post,* December 25, 1984; Ian Aitken, “Thatcher Back amid Camp David Euphoria,” *Guardian,* December 24, 1984.

168. Memorandum of Conversation, Subject: Private Meeting with Prime Minister Margaret Thatcher of Great Britain, Participants: the President, Jack F. Matlock (NSC), Prime Minister Thatcher, Robin Butler (principal private secretary), February 20, 1985, NSC: Records, box 90902, folder: Mrs. Thatcher Visit February 1985 (2), Ronald Reagan Library.

169. Ibid.

170. Smith, *Reagan and Thatcher,* 165.

171. Thatcher, *Downing Street Years.*

172. Cooper, *Politics of Diplomacy,* 165–73.

Conclusion

1. Lord Curzon, Speech at the London Conservative and Unionist Association, November 8, 1922, quoted in G. H. Bennett, *British Foreign Policy during the Curzon Period, 1919–24* (London: Palgrave Macmillan, 1995), 187.

2. Miller Center, "Richard Allen Oral History," Assistant to the President for National Security Affairs, May 28, 2002, https://millercenter.org/the-presidency/presidential-oral-histories/richard-allen-oral-history-assistant-president-national.

3. Miller Center, "William P. Clark Oral History," Assistant to the President for National Security Affairs; Secretary of the Interior, August 17, 2003, https://millercenter.org/the-presidency/presidential-oral-histories/william-p-clark-oral-history-assistant-president.

4. Miller Center, "Caspar Weinberger Oral History," Secretary of Defense, November 19, 2002, https://millercenter.org/the-presidency/presidential-oral-histories/caspar-weinberger-oral-history-secretary-defense.

5. Interview with Lord Lawson of Blaby, House of Lords, February 27, 2007.

6. Interview with Lord Powell, 24 Queen Anne's Gate, London, June 15, 2007.

7. Interview with Lord Heseltine, Haymarket Publishing, Hammersmith, London, February 28, 2007.

8. Ibid.

9. Interview with Sir Colin Budd, Café Churchill, Westminster, London, February 27, 2007.

10. Classical realism refers to the importance of self-interest and power and international relations. For a discussion about realism, see Barry Buzan, "The Timeless Wisdom of Realism," in *International Theory: Positivism and Beyond*, ed. Steve Smith, Ken Booth, and Marysia Zalewski (Cambridge: Cambridge University Press, 1996), 47–65.

11. Interview with Sir Bernard Ingham, Institute of Directors, Pall Mall, London, February 27, 2007.

12. Ibid.

13. For an excellent summary of Thatcher's relationship with Reagan in foreign affairs and the criticism that she received, see John Campbell, *Iron Lady: Margaret Thatcher, from Grocer's Daughter to Prime Minister* (New York: Penguin, 2009), 253–300.

14. Jorgen Rasmussen and James M. McCormick, "British Mass Perceptions of the Anglo-American Special Relationship," *Political Science Quarterly* 108, no. 3 (1993): 526.

15. Ibid, 528.

16. Frank Newport, Jeffrey M. Jones, and Lydia Saad, "Ronald Reagan from the People's Perspective: A Gallup Poll Review," June 7, 2004, http://www.gallup.com/poll/11887/ronald-reagan-from-peoples-perspective-gallup-poll-review.aspx.

17. See Margaret Thatcher, "Reagan's Leadership, America's Recovery," *National Review,* December 30, 1988, 22–24; Ronald Reagan, "Margaret Thatcher and the Revival of the West," *National Review,* May 19, 1989, 21–22.

18. "Speeches at White House Arrival Ceremony (Margaret Thatcher and Ronald Reagan)," November 16, 1988, http://www.margaretthatcher.org/document/107381.

19. Ibid.

20. Margaret Thatcher, "Eulogy for President Reagan," June 11, 2004, http://www.margaretthatcher.org/document/110360.

21. See statistics at "The UK Deficit since World War II," http://www.ukpublicspending.co.uk/uk_national_deficit_analysis, accessed August 21, 2017; "Thatcher's Britain: The State of Britain under Margaret Thatcher," *The Economist,* April 9, 2013, https://www.economist.com/blogs/graphicdetail/2013/04/daily-chart-5.

Selected Bibliography

Diaries and Memoirs

Castle, Barbara. *The Castle Diaries 1964–70*. London: Weidenfeld and Nicolson, 1984.

Clark, Sir Alan. *Diaries*. London: Phoenix, 1993.

Henderson, Nicholas. *Mandarin: The Diaries of Nicholas Henderson*. London: Weidenfeld and Nicolson, 1994.

Howe, Geoffrey. *Conflict of Loyalty*. London: Macmillan, 1994.

Reagan, Ronald. *An American Life: The Autobiography*. New York: Simon & Schuster, 1990.

Reagan, Ronald. *The Reagan Diaries*. Edited by Douglas Brinkley. New York: HarperCollins, 2007.

Thatcher, Margaret. *The Autobiography*. London: HarperPress, 2013.

Thatcher, Margaret. *The Downing Street Years*. London: HarperCollins, 1993.

Oral Histories with the Author

Interview with Sir Colin Budd, Café Churchill, Westminster, London, February 27, 2007.

Interview with Lord Heseltine, Haymarket Publishing, Hammersmith, London, February 28, 2007.

Interview with Sir Bernard Ingham, Institute of Directors, Pall Mall, London, February 27, 2007.

Interview with Lord Lawson of Blaby, House of Lords, February 27, 2007.

Interview with Lord Powell, 24 Queen Anne's Gate, London, June 15, 2007.

Archives

National Archives of the United Kingdom

Ronald Reagan Presidential Library

Websites

The American Presidency Project (http://www.presidency.ucsb.edu/)

The Foreign Relations of the United States (https://history.state.gov/historical documents)

The Margret Thatcher Foundation (www.margaretthatcher.org)

Miller Center (https://millercenter.org/)

The Public Papers of President Ronald W. Reagan. Ronald Reagan Presidential Library (http://www.reagan.utexas.edu/archives/speeches/ and https://reaganlibrary.archives.gov/archives/speeches/)

Index

Allen, Richard, 40, 62
Alphand, Herve, 17
Anderson, Martin, 51, 52, 56
Annenberg, Walter H., 14, 19
Armstrong, Robert, 47, 74, 113
Atkins, Humphrey, 38
aviation, 132–33, 136–39, 140, 143

Baker, James, 3
Berkeley, University of California, 14, 15
Biaggi, Mario, 47, 135
Blair, Tony, 24
Bridges, Lord, 19
British Airways, 6, 9, 27, 106, 107, 132, 133, 136, 138, 140, 141, 143, 145, 146, 150
Brock, William E., 40
Brown, Clarence, 31
Brzezinski, Zbigniew, 37–38
Budd, Colin, 149
Burt, Richard, 136
Bush, George H. W., 128

Callaghan, James, 12, 32, 39
Cameron, David, 24
Carey, Hugh, 68, 135
Carrington, Peter, 19, 66, 75, 76, 97
Carter, Jimmy, 1, 9, 12, 22, 35, 36, 37, 38, 40, 45, 46, 47, 48, 51, 53, 67, 72, 101, 135, 139, 140
Castle, Barbara, 16, 17
Caterpillar, 72, 101
Central Office of Information, 28
China, 18, 20
Churchill, Winston S., 1, 2, 13, 22, 61, 63, 119
Clark, William P., 73, 79, 101, 102, 113, 148
Congress, US, 4, 6, 13, 23, 24, 47, 48, 50, 56, 59, 60, 62, 64, 71, 72, 85, 90, 91, 93, 97, 108, 110, 112, 114, 115, 122, 124, 127, 133, 135, 136, 138, 139, 141, 142, 143, 144, 146
Conservative Party, 9, 11, 13, 16, 20, 22, 23, 24, 25, 26, 27, 28, 29, 31, 34, 38, 39, 40, 42, 46, 49, 51, 58, 60, 96, 147
Coordinating Committee for Multilateral Export Controls (CoCom), 72
Couzens, Kenneth, 56, 57

Dam, Kenneth, 121–27
Deaver, Michael, 73, 74, 76, 77, 78, 79
détente, 18, 25, 29, 30, 61, 72, 93
Dole, Robert, 35
Douglas-Home, Alec, 19

El Salvador, 50, 51, 55, 57, 61
European Economic Community (EEC), 3, 18–19
Export Administration Act, 72, 106, 109, 113, 120
Export-Import Bank of the United States (EXIM), 107, 145
extraterritoriality, 106, 107, 109, 110, 113, 114, 121, 128

Falklands, 3, 5, 9, 10, 71, 79, 80–82, 86–91, 94–101, 103–5, 107, 113, 115, 123–25, 150

FitzGerald, Garret, 68, 142, 144
Foot, Michael, 61, 62, 75, 76–79
Ford, Gerald R., 9, 13, 24, 26, 30, 31, 33–35, 37, 40, 45
Friedman, Milton, 6, 37, 83

G7 Summits: London Summit 1984, 127–31; Ottawa Summit 1981, 64–69; Versailles Summit 1982, 89–93; Williamsburg Summit 1983, 107–12
General Electric, 13, 72, 100, 101
Gorbachev, Mikhail, 9, 135, 140, 144
Greenspan, Alan, 26
Grenada, 3, 9, 121–26, 128, 146

Haig, Alexander, 51, 52, 53, 66, 74, 75, 80, 81, 88, 89, 97, 99, 101, 102, 103, 111
Heath, Edward (Ted), 16, 18, 19, 20, 22, 24, 30, 60
Henderson, Nicholas, 46, 54, 61, 73, 74, 75, 78, 79, 80, 102, 103
Heseltine, Michael, 148
Howe, Geoffrey, 2, 20, 64, 67, 68, 82, 85, 86, 107, 109, 110, 111, 118, 122, 124, 125, 131, 149

Ingham, Bernard, 79, 149
International Monetary Fund, 36, 44, 84
Iranian Hostage Crisis, 1, 46
Irish Republican Army (IRA), 47, 48, 51, 68, 87, 135, 143, 144

Jay, Peter, 35, 41
John Brown Engineering, 72, 86, 88, 96, 100, 101, 102, 103, 105, 150
Johnson, Lyndon B., 23, 92
Joseph, Keith, 20, 49

Kennedy, Edward (Ted), 68, 135
Kennedy, John F., 63
Kinnock, Neil, 24, 29, 123
Kirkpatrick, Jeane, 80, 119
Kissinger, Henry, 19, 26, 31

Laffer, Arthur, 4, 5, 40, 41
Laker Airways, 9, 26, 106, 107, 113, 132, 133, 134, 136, 138, 140, 141
Lawson, Nigel, 127, 148
Louis, John, 62, 98, 99, 113

Macmillan, Harold, 46, 63
Maudling, Reginald, 20, 25
McFarlane, Bud, 137, 139
Meese, Edwin, 66, 67, 97, 107, 108, 128
Meir, Golda, 27
Middle East, 51, 53, 57, 62, 89, 96, 97, 101, 113, 124, 126, 128
Mitterrand, François, 35, 36, 65, 92, 130
Mondale, Walter, 127, 131
Moynihan, Daniel P., 68, 135

Nicaragua, 3, 116, 124, 126, 146
Nixon, Richard M., 12, 13, 14, 15, 17, 18, 19, 20, 23, 26, 41, 42
North Atlantic Treaty Organization (NATO), 18, 50, 52, 53, 72, 82, 87, 89, 98, 119
Northern Ireland, 10, 18, 23, 27, 50, 53, 67, 69, 89, 106, 115, 136, 137, 139, 142, 145, 146; the Troubles, 47, 48, 51, 68, 80, 87, 135, 143, 144

Obama, Barack H., 13
O'Neill, Thomas P. "Tip," 47, 48, 51, 68, 106, 135, 136, 139, 142, 143, 146
Osborne, Kathleen, 130
Owen, David, 38, 76

Price, Charles, 131, 132, 133, 136, 138, 141, 145

Ramsbotham, Peter, 27, 31
Reagan, Nancy, 45, 63
Reaganism, 4, 6, 9, 44, 52, 54, 56, 57, 59, 61, 63, 64, 69, 71, 85, 119, 147, 150, 151, 152
Reaganomics, 4, 9, 57, 59, 63, 65, 83, 114, 128, 129, 151, 152
Reece, Gordon, 26
Regan, Donald T., 56, 67, 68, 85, 93, 109, 110, 111, 115, 116, 117, 119, 121, 128, 131
Republican Party, 10, 11, 13, 26, 31, 33, 34, 35, 39, 40, 41, 49, 127
Rockefeller, Nelson, 26

Romney, Mitt, 13
Roosevelt, Franklin D., 2, 13, 63
Royal Ulster Constabulary (RUC), 47, 48, 51

Shultz, George, 111, 113, 114, 119, 122, 123, 128, 134, 136, 137, 138, 139, 143
Siberian gas pipeline, 72–73, 86, 105, 133
Steel, David, 76, 78
Stockman, David, 49, 56
Strategic Defense Initiative (SDI or "Star Wars"), 134, 135, 140, 145

Thatcher, Denis, 16, 21, 63
Thatcherism, 4, 5, 6, 9, 44, 45, 49, 52, 54, 56, 57, 59, 61, 63, 64, 69, 71, 85, 119, 147, 150, 151, 152
Trudeau, Pierre, 65, 91, 130

unitary taxation, 9, 106, 107, 112, 113, 114, 115, 116, 117, 119, 120, 121, 126–27, 128, 137, 146
United Nations (UN), 24, 50, 67, 80, 94, 98, 105, 119

Vietnam War, 12, 15, 18, 19, 40, 61, 81, 92, 123
Volcker, Paul, 5, 85, 115, 119, 142

Walters, Alan, 83–85
Watergate scandal, 12, 17, 26, 40, 41
Weinberger, Caspar, 80, 88, 103, 104, 122, 128, 148
Whitelaw, William (Willie), 24, 78
Wilson, Harold, 23, 32, 39
Wright, Oliver, 113

Studies in Conflict, Diplomacy, and Peace

Series Editors: George C. Herring, Andrew L. Johns, and Kathryn C. Statler

This series focuses on key moments of conflict, diplomacy, and peace from the eighteenth century to the present to explore their wider significance in the development of U.S. foreign relations. The series editors welcome new research in the form of original monographs, interpretive studies, biographies, and anthologies from historians, political scientists, journalists, and policymakers. A primary goal of the series is to examine the United States' engagement with the world, its evolving role in the international arena, and the ways in which the state, nonstate actors, individuals, and ideas have shaped and continue to influence history, both at home and abroad.

Advisory Board Members

Books in the Series

Truman, Congress, and Korea: The Politics of America's First Undeclared War
Larry Blomstedt

The Legacy of J. William Fulbright: Policy, Power, and Ideology
Edited by Alessandro Brogi, Giles Scott-Smith, and David J. Snyder

The Gulf: The Bush Presidencies and the Middle East
Michael F. Cairo

Reagan and the World: Leadership and National Security, 1981–1989
Edited by Bradley Lynn Coleman and Kyle Longley

A Diplomatic Meeting: Reagan, Thatcher, and the Art of Summitry
James Cooper

American Justice in Taiwan: The 1957 Riots and Cold War Foreign Policy
Stephen G. Craft

Soccer Diplomacy: International Relations and Football since 1914
Edited by Heather L. Dichter

Diplomatic Games: Sport, Statecraft, and International Relations since 1945
Edited by Heather L. Dichter and Andrew L. Johns

Nothing Less Than War: A New History of America's Entry into World War I
Justus D. Doenecke

Aid under Fire: Nation Building and the Vietnam War
Jessica Elkind

Enemies to Allies: Cold War Germany and American Memory
Brian C. Etheridge

Grounded: The Case for Abolishing the United States Air Force
Robert M. Farley

Foreign Friends: Syngman Rhee, American Exceptionalism, and the Division of Korea
David P. Fields

The Myth of Triumphalism: Rethinking President Reagan's Cold War Legacy
Beth A. Fischer

The American South and the Vietnam War: Belligerence, Protest, and Agony in Dixie
Joseph A. Fry

Lincoln, Seward, and US Foreign Relations in the Civil War Era
Joseph A. Fry

The Turkish Arms Embargo: Drugs, Ethnic Lobbies, and US Domestic Politics
James F. Goode

Obama at War: Congress and the Imperial Presidency
Ryan C. Hendrickson

Fourteen Points for the Twenty-First Century: A Renewed Appeal for Cooperative Internationalism
Edited by Richard H. Immerman and Jeffrey A. Engel

The Cold War at Home and Abroad: Domestic Politics and US Foreign Policy since 1945
Edited by Andrew L. Johns and Mitchell B. Lerner

US Presidential Elections and Foreign Policy: Candidates, Campaigns, and Global Politics from FDR to Bill Clinton
Edited by Andrew Johnstone and Andrew Priest

Paving the Way for Reagan: The Influence of Conservative Media on US Foreign Policy
Laurence R. Jurdem

The Conversion of Senator Arthur H. Vandenberg: From Isolation to International Engagement
Lawrence S. Kaplan

Harold Stassen: Eisenhower, the Cold War, and the Pursuit of Nuclear Disarmament
Lawrence S. Kaplan

JFK and de Gaulle: How America and France Failed in Vietnam, 1961–1963
Sean J. McLaughlin

Nixon's Back Channel to Moscow: Confidential Diplomacy and Détente
Richard A. Moss

Breaking Protocol: America's First Female Ambassadors, 1933–1964
Philip Nash

Peacemakers: American Leadership and the End of Genocide in the Balkans
James W. Pardew

The Currents of War: A New History of American-Japanese Relations, 1899–1941
Sidney Pash

Eisenhower and Cambodia: Diplomacy, Covert Action, and the Origins of the Second Indochina War
William J. Rust

So Much to Lose: John F. Kennedy and American Policy in Laos
William J. Rust

The Sailor: Franklin D. Roosevelt and the Transformation of American Foreign Policy
David F. Schmitz

Foreign Policy at the Periphery: The Shifting Margins of US International Relations since World War II
Edited by Bevan Sewell and Maria Ryan

Lincoln Gordon: Architect of Cold War Foreign Policy
Bruce L. R. Smith

Thomas C. Mann: President Johnson, the Cold War, and the Restructuring of Latin American Foreign Policy
Thomas Tunstall Allcock